THERE'S ONLY ONE
NEIL REDFEARN

The ups . . .

THERE'S ONLY ONE
NEIL REDFEARN

. . . and downs of my footballing life

Neil Redfearn
with Andrew Collomosse

headline

First published in 2006
by HEADLINE BOOK PUBLISHING

1

A CIP catalogue record for this title is available from the British Library

ISBN 0 7553 1376 3

Typeset by Palimpsest Book Production Limited,
Polmont, Stirlingshire

Printed and bound in Great Britain by
Clays Ltd, St Ives plc

Headline's policy is to use papers that are natural, renewable and recyclable products and
made from wood grown in sustainable forests. The logging and manufacturing processes
are expected to conform to the environmental regulations of the country of origin.

HEADLINE BOOK PUBLISHING
A division of Hodder Headline
338 Euston Road
London NW1 3BH

www.headline.co.uk
www.hodderheadline.com

Jacket photographs:
Front, top – Barnsley win promotion to the Premier League, April 1997;
bottom – sent off as Halifax crash out of the Football League, April 2002
Back, top – the penalty for Oldham that secured the Second Division title, May 1991;
centre – jousting with Gazza in Bradford's first Premiership game, at Middlesbrough,
August 1999; bottom – goal! Charlton win 5–0 at home to Southampton in August 1998

To Sue, Aimee and Lois, whose support has never wavered

CONTENTS

ACKNOWLEDGEMENTS

A lot of people have given me their time and assistance and I'd like to thank them all. I'm particularly grateful to Andrew Lodge at the *Barnsley Chronicle*, Robert Gledhill at the *Yorkshire Post* and Dave Fletcher at the *Halifax Courier* for their expert knowledge – and to Andrew Collomosse for pulling the whole thing together. It's been a lot of fun. This is also my chance to say thanks to all the fans who have backed me over the years, people I've never really been able to thank before.

THE WARM-UP

Name: Neil David Redfearn

Date of birth: 20 June 1965

Occupation: Professional footballer

Debut: 19 February 1983, for Bolton Wanderers at Rotherham United, Division Two

Senior appearances for league clubs: 917

Goals scored: 181

Senior appearances for all professional clubs: 981

Goals scored: 198

Clubs: Nottingham Forest (apprentice), Bolton Wanderers, Lincoln City, Doncaster Rovers, Crystal Palace, Watford, Oldham Athletic, Barnsley, Charlton Athletic, Bradford City, Wigan Athletic, Halifax Town, Boston United, Rochdale, Scarborough

Managers: Brian Clough, George Mulhall, John McGovern, Colin Murphy, John Pickering, George Kerr, Dave Cusack, Steve Coppell, Steve Harrison, Joe Royle, Mel Machin, Viv Anderson, Danny Wilson, Alan Curbishley, Paul Jewell, John Benson, Bruce Rioch, Paul Bracewell, Alan Little, Neil Thompson, Steve Parkin, Nick Henry – not to mention Neil Redfearn

Highs: Promotion to the top flight with Oldham and Barnsley, reaching the play-offs with Watford and Wigan, playing in an FA Cup semi-final with Oldham and a quarter-final with Barnsley

Lows: Relegation from the Premiership with Barnsley and Charlton, relegation from the Football League with Halifax Town, finishing bottom of the Conference with Scarborough

Worst game: When we've lost and I've played badly – it hasn't happened often!

Best game: The next one

David Beckham was seven years old when I made my first league appearance. Wayne Rooney wasn't even born, Bobby Robson was the new England manager and England's cricketers had just said farewell to the Ashes for 22 years. The Premiership didn't exist, nor did Sky Television.

Swansea, Notts County and Brighton, who would be FA Cup finalists against Manchester United three months later, were in the First Division, now the Premiership. Chelsea, Newcastle, Bolton and Blackburn were in the Second Division and just a handful of foreign players graced the English game. The Metro was the UK's best-selling car, Shergar, the 1981 Derby winner, had just gone missing, and Kajagoogoo were top of the UK charts with 'Too Shy'.

Since that first match for Bolton at Rotherham in February 1983, I have seen football reel under the curse of hooliganism and shared the grief of all those involved in the tragedies at

Hillsborough, Heysel and, at first hand, Valley Parade. My first decade as a professional was an era when gates slumped and some people began to express serious concerns about football's future. Now, thanks to the non-stop success story of the Premiership, the game has never been so popular. Peers, pop stars, politicians and 'celebs' can't jump on the bandwagon fast enough. The last 23 years have been an incredible journey for football – and for me.

My life has revolved around the game for over 30 years. It grabbed me when I was seven years old and has never loosened its grip. Football governs the way I eat, drink, sleep and relax. When I'm alone in the car, I think of nothing else. I hardly ever switch off. Sometimes, on a Saturday night, when my wife, Sue, and I are at home watching the telly, she'll look across at me and say, 'Come on, Neil, put the ball away. The match ended five hours ago.' Not for me it didn't. I'm still kicking every ball, making every tackle, analysing what went right or wrong, jotting down mental notes for the next game.

An obsession? Yes. A matter of life and death, as the legendary Liverpool manager Bill Shankly maintained? No. I was playing for Lincoln City against Bradford City on 11 May 1985, the day 56 people lost their lives in the Valley Parade fire. They were all either from Bradford, where I was brought up, or Lincoln, where I was living at the time. My dad and some of his mates were in the stand. So were Sue's father and sister. They all survived but since that day I've been able to appreciate the real importance of football better than most. Even so, I understand Shanks's sentiments.

I've always said that I'll never give up football – football will have to give up on me. Sometimes I wish I could step back a bit and take a more laid-back approach but I know I can't. Nothing's going to change. I've already gained my UEFA coaching certificate and B Licence and started the A Licence course, which will qualify me to manage a Premiership club, if and when the opportunity arises.

I've been involved in the professional game since joining Nottingham Forest as an apprentice in 1981 and I've been through a lot. I've learned that no two managers are the same and no two clubs are the same. My career certainly hasn't all been a bed of roses and I've made mistakes. So have the people around me and maybe my story will show young hopefuls the kind of pitfalls that may await them and how, or how not, to deal with them.

The two constant themes of my career have been my ambition and my will to win. Those traits have got me into trouble at times but while my attitude has never changed, my approach has. I've learned to be a bit cute, when to speak and when to keep my mouth shut. I still want to be the best but I've learned how to approach chairmen, managers, coaches, players, media and supporters and make my point without rocking the boat. It's been an important lesson to learn.

I've also worked out how to deal with other people's expectations. Once a player achieves a certain level of success, he is expected to keep performing to that level and above. When he doesn't, he is criticised. From early in my career, I regularly scored goals from midfield and it soon reached the stage when I was expected to do so. Nobody seemed to look at other aspects of my game. They just noted whether or not I was scoring goals. If I wasn't, they assumed I wasn't performing well. Sometimes that wasn't easy to handle and it was always an added pressure that I had to come to terms with.

I started the 2005–06 season, my 24th as a professional, aged 40 and with 959 senior appearances to my name for 14 clubs, including 39 games for Scarborough in the Conference. I didn't know I was approaching 900 until a journalist gave me the nod towards the end of 2003 but since then, the target of 1,000 games in all competitions has been at the back of my mind. A lot of factors are involved, though, not least my fitness. Over the years, I've been very lucky with injuries and I hope to stay that way, but it's significant that four of the five English players to make over 1,000 senior appearances for Football League clubs – Peter Shilton, Ray Clemence, Pat Jennings and David Seaman – have been goalkeepers.

The fifth was Tony Ford, like me a journeyman pro. He played for eight clubs over 26 seasons before retiring in 2001 at the age of 42 with 1,072 appearances to his name. That's incredible. I forfeited any realistic chance of reaching 1,000 appearances at league level when I moved into the Conference in 2004, and my appointment as manager of Scarborough in November 2005 placed another possible restriction on the number of games I may play in the future. I still see 1,000 professional appearances as a huge achievement however, and if passion and enthusiasm count for anything, I won't be far away when I finally call time on my playing career.

It was that passion and enthusiasm that prompted me to jump at the chance to join Boston United in the summer of 2002. At the time, some people might not have even heard of Boston, promoted from the Conference at the end of the previous season, and no one would pretend that Lincolnshire is a hotbed of football. I knew that playing for Boston would mean a daily battle through morning rush-hour traffic from my home near Holmfirth, a few miles south of Huddersfield – a 100-mile journey of around two hours, road works permitting, with a return trip during the evening rush hour at the other end of the day. I didn't think twice. Signing for Boston as player and coach meant I could continue with my daily fix on the training ground and my 90 minutes at the sharp end on a Saturday afternoon. Yes, the travelling was a pain but a small price to pay for what was waiting for me at the end of the journeys. At Boston, there was the training ground, the dressing-room banter and the camaraderie; at home were Sue, my daughters, Aimee and Lois, and the knowledge that I'd be putting my head on my own pillow at bedtime. My family and my football – nothing else has ever really mattered.

Since I joined Nottingham Forest as an apprentice in 1981, there have been loads of highs and a few lows. I've made a lot of friends along the way and no doubt collected some enemies, too. That's life. I was once described by no less an authority than Arsenal manager Arsene Wenger as the dirtiest player in the Premiership so I suspect that he isn't a member of the Neil Redfearn Appreciation Society. I can handle that and, as it happens, he was wrong but everyone is entitled to an opinion. And perhaps Mr Wenger won't be surprised to learn that I have a few of my own . . .

1 LEARNING THE GAME

WHEN I WAS A KID, I WAS THE PROUD OWNER OF TWO FOOT-
balls, one white, one brown. I'd be about eight at the time and a
gang of us used to play on the school playing field across the road
from our house. The white ball was our pride and joy. It was
nearly new and not a million miles away from the balls we used
to see on the telly when we watched Leeds United, Manchester
United, Arsenal and the rest on 'Match of the Day' and 'Soccer
Sunday'. The brown one was a bit of a collector's item. No, it
didn't have a bladder and a lace – I'm not *that* old! Let's just say
it was well past its sell-by date when my cousin Stephen passed
it on to me. It used to rattle. We reckoned there was a dried bean
inside but I suppose it was a bit of hard, old leather that had
worked loose from the inside of the casing, or maybe part of the
adapter that we used to blow it up had broken off.

We always played well into the evenings and when it started
to get really dark and we couldn't see the white ball any more,
we'd switch balls. We couldn't see the brown one either but we'd
know when it was coming because we could hear it rattling a mile
off. If you were playing up front, you had to work out from the
sound of the ball which side of the field was in use and how far
you were from the action. As the volume increased, you'd move
into the danger zone, wait for the cross and then it was a case of

potluck when it came to judging the height and speed of the ball. We'd launch ourselves into headers when the ball was only a foot above the ground, or aim a spectacular volley as the ball flew past at head height. We had some real laughs with that old ball.

In the school holidays, we'd be up at seven, grab a bite of breakfast and be out playing by eight. We'd use our jumpers as goalposts. Sometimes there'd be 40 or 50 of us and it ended up around 20-a-side. We'd play all morning, go home for some dinner and then be straight back out – same routine at teatime. Sometimes one or two of the lads would get a bit fed up and we'd play hide and seek instead, or go off on our bikes, but basically it was football, football and more football. These days we have organised soccer academies for the best young players from the age of seven upwards but I believe I attended the best academy of them all on that school field in Birkenshaw on the outskirts of Bradford. Without knowing it, I was finding my own way, honing my skills, working on my game morning and afternoon. Nowadays, if we're not careful, we try to manufacture skills in youngsters rather than letting them develop on their own and, in my view, academies can be élitist. There was no élitism on our playing field. We were all pals, all encouraging one another and having a great time into the bargain. It was fun – isn't that the point of football at that age?

Funnily enough, I wasn't interested in the game when I was very young, even though I grew up in a football household. My dad, Brian, had been a professional but was forced to retire because of an ankle injury a year or so before I was born. When I was little, he used to take me to visit my grandma every Sunday after-noon. She lived at the top of a high-rise block in the Holme Wood area of Bradford. It was a pretty tough area – still is. She was a big woman and wouldn't stand any nonsense from anyone. My granddad had died a few years before and they'd never had much money, but she gave me a lot of affection. She had one of those big old iron kettles that used to whistle when it boiled and it would be on the hob when we arrived. She always had a half-pound bag of nut toffee and would give me a piece when I walked through the door. It tasted horrible and stuck in my teeth. I used to think, 'Why the hell does she buy that stuff?'

Before long, Dad would sit down in front of the old black and white telly to watch 'Soccer Sunday' on Yorkshire TV. I think Keith Macklin was the commentator. I used to think, 'Oh no, not football again. I hate football,' and I'd look around for some way to pass the time until the programme ended. Grandma would take me down to the local shopping arcade. There was a pub, a baker's, a launderette – I'll always remember the smell of the clothes in the hot-air driers – and a big newsagent's that stayed open all day and seemed to sell everything. She'd give me a few pence and I'd head straight for the toy section and root through the shelf of Corgi cars before making my choice. In the end, I had drawers and drawers of them. They'd be worth quite a bit now but I threw them away years ago. Every week I'd buy a new one and go back and play with the whole collection until the football was over. Those cars were far more interesting than football. I couldn't work out what Dad saw in it.

I caught the bug big-style when I was seven. We lived in a three-bedroomed semi on an estate in Birkenshaw. It was a brand new house when my mum, Joyce, and dad moved in from Liversedge, a small town nearby. I think my dad paid about £3,500 for the house. I was three at the time, and because my sister Tina was five years older than me, she had the bigger bedroom. The house stood opposite the local secondary school, and there were a lot of kids of my age on the estate who were all keen on football, so I suppose it was a case of 'if you can't beat 'em, join 'em' and I started playing, too. In the evenings and at weekends, we used to sneak on to the playing field at the back of the school. There were no goalposts but the surface was like Wembley – beautiful. Of course, we weren't allowed on there and every now and then the coppers would roll up and clear us off. Ten minutes later we'd be back.

Sometimes, if the police refused to take no for an answer, we'd take ourselves off to an area called Low Moor, about five minutes' walk away through a snicket. There was some spare ground up there, although it was as rough as a bear's arse and we'd take ages trying to sort out a flat pitch among all the potholes and craters. It wasn't easy, and trying to make a cricket pitch in the summer was even harder. One year we found a rusty old lawnmower that someone had abandoned and used that to cut back all the weeds. We tried to prepare a proper wicket, without much success.

Dad had been involved with the professional game for 16 years after starting as an apprentice at Bradford Park Avenue, who were still in the Football League in those days. He moved on to Blackburn, Darlington, Halifax Town and Bradford City. Then he had a season playing semi-pro for Buxton in Derbyshire. He combined that with a part-time job at Firth's Carpets in Brighouse and when he gave up football, he worked full-time at the carpet factory. He was made redundant in his mid-fifties and went to work in Bradford Library, retiring after five years. I never saw him play but a lot of people have said to me, 'You're just like your dad – but not as physical.' He played centre-forward or left-wing. He was bigger than me, 6ft 1in whereas I'm 5ft 10in, and he weighed in at 13 ½ stone, compared with my 12 ½. Apparently, he was good with his head and very dangerous coming in at the back stick to meet a cross. One of his team-mates at Halifax was Eric Harrison, who later became youth-team coach at Manchester United and was responsible for the development of young players including David Beckham, Ryan Giggs, Paul Scholes, the Neville brothers and Nicky Butt.

Dad never made a lot of money as a pro. After five seasons with Park Avenue, he was transferred to Blackburn for £11,000, a decent sum in those days. He was due a testimonial of £500 because he'd been at Bradford for five years, but when he asked Avenue for the money, they said no. So he told them the deal was dead. He wasn't going to sign for Blackburn until Bradford paid up. They still refused and, in the end, Blackburn added £500 to the transfer fee, which was then handed over to my dad. He used to say, 'That's football loyalty for you. I hadn't even signed for Blackburn and they were prepared to give me the £500. I'd played around 150 games for Avenue but they wouldn't give me what I was owed. In football, there's no such thing as loyalty.' That's a lesson I've never forgotten and something I've been reminded of many times down the years.

I didn't make a big thing about Dad being an ex-pro – or, for that matter, about him being a hell of a good cricketer, an all-rounder, who might easily have turned professional at either sport. I can remember watching him play cricket for East Bierley, Yeadon and Hartshead Moor in the Bradford League, which was a very high standard. A few years later, I played one or two games in the same team as Dad in a minor league. He was still playing as a club pro in his mid-forties but, in the end, the football injury ended his cricket career, too. He encouraged me to play both games and I had quite a lot of ability at cricket but I was always more interested in football. I sometimes think I'll go back to cricket when I finish football – if I ever finish.

As soon as I began to show a real interest, Dad started taking me along to Elland Road to watch Leeds United. That was the start of my football education. In the early seventies, Don Revie's side were the best team in the country and in his 13 years at the club, they won just about everything. Allan Clarke was my idol. He did the two things I dreamed about doing myself – he wore the white Leeds United strip and he scored goals. I stuck pictures of the Leeds team all over my bedroom walls and I had both the home and away replica strips. I was given the all-white strip one Christmas. I put it on straight away and dashed out of the house before breakfast to practise finishing like Clarke. It was absolutely freezing but I didn't care. The shirt had a blue number 8 on the back and I insisted that it was washed brilliant white. I used to drive my mum mad.

We'd go to Leeds United on a Saturday and then watch rugby league at Bradford Northern on a Sunday. I sometimes used to think it was a bit strange watching Leeds when we lived in Bradford, because there's no love lost among the supporters and Dad was a Bradford Park Avenue man at heart. But he wanted me to learn from watching the best and that Leeds team had a massive influence on me. Clarke, Billy Bremner, Johnny Giles,

Peter Lorimer, Eddie Gray, Paul Madeley and the rest were real top players and Dad used to talk me through games, pointing out little things that most fans never even noticed. He was always talking about a player's first touch. He'd say, 'Did you see that first touch? That pass looked so simple, so straightforward, but it wasn't. It only looked easy because the first touch was right.' What better football education could I have had? I was watching the best team in the land and being taught by a former professional who knew all the ins and outs of the game, a man who was keen for me to do well. He was also my dad and he loved me as a son.

We used to go out and practise together and he always insisted on me working on my weaker left foot. I'd spend hours concentrating on my 'wrong' foot and, eventually, I was equally at home with either foot. I've always used my right for penalties or corners but if I had to use the left, it wouldn't be a problem. I've scored some pretty decent goals from set-pieces using my left foot. To this day, Dad and I sometimes pop out on the park to practise shooting. We take three or four balls and he has me shooting with both feet from all heights and angles. I've been so lucky to have him around.

I'm sure that, deep down, he always wanted me to be a pro but he let me find my own way. He wanted me to have every possible chance of making it but if I hadn't been good enough, he would have been happy for me to step back and play at a lower level, even for a pub team on the park on a Sunday morning. I think he knew there was something there, though – not least determination and doggedness. There were a lot of better players around, lads we expected to go all the way, but by the time I was a professional, most of them had fallen by the wayside. Pro football isn't just about ability, it involves hard work and determination and, in some cases, sheer bloody-mindedness.

My first taste of organised football came when I was 11 and started playing for the Under-13s at Birkenshaw Middle School in Bradford. I already had my first boots, a pair of Puma Hat Tricks. Allan Clarke used to wear them for Leeds and I remember thinking, 'If they're good enough for him, they're good enough for me.' They were black with a yellow stripe down the side. Fantastic! Best boots I ever had. The yellow stripe made them different. These days, boots come in all the colours of the rainbow but as far as I can recall, Puma Hat Tricks were the first to feature anything but black and white.

Our PE teacher at Birkenshaw, Wayne Nicholson, was really keen on football. We had a good side and Dad used to come to watch every game. At first, Wayne played me at left-back and I remember Dad pulling him to one side one day.

'Listen, Wayne, if you want to win anything, put Neil up front because he can finish,' Dad told him.

'We see him more as a defensive player. He can tackle,' Wayne replied, but Dad wasn't having that.

'He's wasted at full-back, put him up front,' he insisted.

So Wayne moved me up front and I finished the season with 27 goals in 19 matches. We won the league and the cup. That was the first time Dad really had a say in where I was going.

Around that time, I also started playing on Sundays for Hunsworth Juniors, a local side run by my dad. Richard Blakey, who went on to play cricket for Yorkshire and England, played for Hunsworth, too. I have always thought he was our goalkeeper, probably because he went on to be Yorkshire's wicketkeeper for so many years, but I'm assured from the horse's mouth that Dick was the man who knocked in the goals at the other end. Another Yorkshire cricketer who played for us was Simon Kellett. He was a good player, not too mobile perhaps but he had a good touch and might easily have made it as a pro. He chose cricket instead and is still playing in the leagues.

Ian Ormondroyd, the 6ft 5in striker who went on to play for Bradford City, Aston Villa, Derby, Leicester, Oldham and Scunthorpe, was in the same Hunsworth side and we had a lad called Nicky Beaumont who went to Arsenal but was released. Steve Parrish, our goalkeeper, ended up playing rugby for Bradford Northern and his brother, Mick, played for Wakefield Trinity. Our best player was Steve Watson, a midfield man. He was a big lad with great ability. He never needed to use his physical attributes because he could open a can of peas with his left foot. We all thought he would go right to the top but he just fizzled out. He wasn't the only one, not by a long way.

I also represented Spen Valley Boys, the area team. Spen Valley is the region between Bradford and Huddersfield and the team included kids from places such as Halifax, Cleckheaton and Heckmondwike. The area was always regarded as more of a rugby league community and, to be honest, we didn't have the strongest of teams. Every year, we played in the English Schools competition but never made much progress. In my time, we struggled against the stronger, more physical sides, such as Rotherham and Barnsley, but there were highlights. One year we beat Cleveland Boys 2–1 at The Shay, Halifax Town's ground, which earned us a trip to Oakwell to play Barnsley in the second round. We lost 3–0. Oakwell and The Shay! Little did I know that a few years down the line, I'd be leading Barnsley out at Oakwell in the Premiership and then flogging my guts out at The Shay to keep Halifax in the Football League.

I was a useful player but I was quite small for my age, as I discovered when I was called up for the Yorkshire Boys trials. Hundreds of kids were there and they all seemed to play for Leeds City Boys or some other representative side. Just about everyone was bigger than I was and at the end of the session, the guy in charge took me to one side and said, 'You've got a lot of ability, son, but you're too small.' I was devastated. When I got home and told my dad, he just laughed. 'You're only twelve,' he said. 'You won't finish growing 'til you're seventeen or eighteen, so how can anyone say you're going to be too small?'

I've bumped into one or two of the successful triallists down the years and none of them seem to be involved in football any more, certainly not at a professional level. They were being pushed ahead of smaller kids who had more ability just because they were bigger. Steve Taylor, who played regularly for Yorkshire Boys, was 14 and built like a grown man. He had big powerful thighs, blistering pace and used to score 30 or 40 goals a season. At 14 and 15 he looked a world beater. Manchester United were chasing him, Leeds were desperate to sign him, but he never made it. Why? Because all the lads who were much smaller at 14 grew up, and all of a sudden Steve didn't look quite so big and fast any more. He was a prime example of what I saw as a condemnation of schoolboy football. To some extent the same thing still applies today. Teachers, schoolboy coaches and other people who should know better make decisions based on a player's physical attributes without looking at skill levels first.

When I was 14, I started playing for Stansfield Rangers, a local Saturday side who played at Apperley Bridge, a village between Bradford and Leeds. Our pitch was next door to Bradford City's training ground – another place where I would spend a lot of time as a Premiership player a few years down the line. The manager at Stansfield was Tony Fawthrop. He later had a spell as youth-development officer and chief scout under Eddie Gray at Leeds United and he was also involved with Bristol City. By a happy coincidence, Tony had a fish and chip shop in Cleckheaton, just down the road from Whitcliffe Mount, my secondary school, and I spent more time in the chip shop nattering about football with Tony than I did at school. I wasn't exactly the model pupil, to put it mildly. I did everything I shouldn't have done and not a lot of what I should have been doing.

My schooling suffered terribly. I was involved with a group who didn't go in for lessons. It was easier to be a rebel than a student, and not much street cred was attached to kids who did their homework. Needless to say, I'm a different man when it comes to my own kids' schooling. Aimee, my elder daughter, was born in November 1987 while I was playing for Crystal Palace. She's done really well at school and sixth-form college – she must be like her mum – and wants to be an equine vet, which will mean university and a lot of hard work along the way. While she's inherited her mother's attitude to education, she's also got my determination and she's totally committed. It's fascinating to see how much she's learning about so many different things and I can't help saying to myself, 'You've missed out here, lad.' Lois, my younger daughter, was born just before Christmas 1993 when I was at Barnsley. She takes after her sister at school, and she's not a bad little footballer, either. She scores a lot of goals, just like her dad.

I wasn't stupid and I could do the work if I really had to, but the only thing that mattered to me was football. I was going to be a professional footballer and the sooner the better – to hell with schoolwork. I see now that not taking my education seriously was the worst thing I could have done. If I hadn't been signed, I've no idea what I would have done – manual labour, I suppose, with a bit of part-time football at weekends. I was taking a huge chance and, in this respect, I'm no sort of example for young kids to follow. I always encourage them to make sure they complete their schooling before committing themselves to football. They should go for everything – be bright, intelligent, get an education and be a footballer as well.

I was good at geography, mathematics, when I put my mind to it, and technical drawing, because I liked it. I enjoyed PE but hated cross country. I did everything I could to avoid it, without much success, but cross country taught me an important lesson about myself. The school was situated alongside the M62 and the route took us over a motorway road bridge, round some playing fields and then on into the back of beyond. When race day came around in my last year, the weather was appalling – snowing heavily, blowing a blizzard and freezing cold.

I positioned myself near the back of the field as usual but before long, I started thinking to myself, 'Bloody hell, I'm going to have run hard here just to keep warm.' So I selected second gear and soon started to pass people. 'Hey up,' I thought. 'I'm not bad at this, after all.' So I moved up another gear, passed a few more and soon I was among the leading bunch. By this time, I had gone through top gear and into overdrive and, after a strong finish, I ended up in second place. I even passed a couple of lads who ran for Yorkshire Schools. Until then I'd had a bit of a phobia about long-distance running. I couldn't see how it would help my foot-ball, it was too much like hard work for my liking and I'd convinced myself that I would never be any good at it. That race broke down an important mental barrier. For probably the first time, I realised that if I really put my mind to something, I could do it as well as the next person.

I got away with my lack of interest in school work. Tony Fawthrop's sides played good football and, even though I never played representative football for Yorkshire in any of the age groups, one or two people were starting to take notice of me. Tony had a contact at Nottingham Forest and I used to go down there and train during school holidays. Ronnie Fenton, who was Brian Clough's assistant at Forest and a contemporary of my dad's, was in charge of those sessions. Ray Minshull, the former Liverpool and Southport goalkeeper, who had played with Dad at Bradford Park Avenue, was involved with Everton and desperate for me to sign schoolboy forms, but Dad advised me to keep my options open for a while longer. Leeds showed a passing interest and Bradford City were also keen but I was drawn more and more towards Forest.

They were a big club. Brian Clough, arguably the biggest name in football, was their manager and they'd just won the European Cup twice in a row. When they offered me a two-year apprenticeship in the spring of 1981, I jumped at the chance. I left school straight away, just before my 16th birthday, without even taking my GCSEs. A month before the start of pre-season training, the club held an open day for all the apprentices. Clough was there but Fenton did all the talking, telling the mums and dads, 'Your boys are my responsibility. We'll look after them and see they are given an education as well as a football apprenticeship. We'll make sure they eat properly and learn to use their money wisely. So at the end of the two years, if they aren't good enough and we release them, at least they'll have something to fall back on.'

At that point, my dad stood up. 'Whoa, whoa, hang on a minute,' he said. 'You say you'll release them if they're not good enough. What you should really be saying is that you'll release them if, in your opinion, they're not good enough.' Cloughie started to sit up and take notice. My dad went on, 'Football is a game of opinions.

Nottingham Forest may think a player isn't good enough but that doesn't mean every other club will agree with them. These lads won't be finished with football just because Nottingham Forest don't sign them on.'

I was sitting beside him, cringing and thinking to myself, 'Shut up, Dad,' but now I understand what he was getting at and he was right. He was speaking with the benefit of his own experience in the game and I could see all the parents who had been prepared to accept Fenton's line were starting to think again. Nearly 20 years later, when I was caretaker-manager at Halifax Town, I had to tell three young lads that I was going to release them. It was an awful job because, like so many kids, they had grown up dreaming of the day when they would become a professional footballer and now Neil Redfearn was pulling the ladder away. I remembered my dad's words and told them, 'Look, I can't do anything for you here but that doesn't mean you can't go out there and find another club. This doesn't have to be the end of the line. I might not be right, so go out and prove me wrong.'

In some ways, that's what I've been doing for most of my career. I've played for 15 clubs, including my apprentice days at Forest, and just about everywhere I've been, the manager has told me I can't do this or I can't do that. I've been told I can't run, I can't pass the ball, I'm no good in the air — even that I can't tackle. Now if there's one thing I have always been able to do it's tackle, but not according to one or two of the 22 managers I've played for. If I'd accepted all the criticism, I would hardly have kicked a ball as a professional, never mind played nearly a thousand games.

2 LOST IN THE FOREST

FAST FORWARD THREE MONTHS TO AUGUST 1981. I'M IN THE BOOT room at the City Ground, Nottingham, working away at Peter Shilton's boots. Shilton is a goalkeeping great, on his way to 125 England caps and a British record of 1,387 appearances in all competitions. He's one of the main men around the place. He's also a stickler where his boots are concerned, so I'm giving them a good polish after scraping all the dirt off when I nick my little fingernail on one of the studs. It splits the nail across the top and, after inspecting the damage, I try to bite off the loose piece.

'Stop biting your nails,' booms a voice from behind me. I think it's one of the lads messing about, mutter, 'Bollocks to you, pal,' under my breath and start to bite the nail again. 'Young man, I told you to stop biting your nails,' shouts the voice again. 'It's a disgusting habit.'

This time I turn round – and there, standing a few feet away in his trademark baggy green sweatshirt and tracksuit bottoms, is Brian Clough. I drop the boot and the brush, bend down to pick them up, drop the brush again and mumble an apology. I promise never to bite my nails again. Cloughie just nods, gives me a knowing stare, turns on his heels and walks out of the room. Ten minutes later, I haven't stopped shaking and Shilton's boots are still waiting for their final polish.

Clough had that effect on the apprentices. Come to think of it, he probably had the same effect on everybody at the City Ground. If Cloughie was around, you stopped messing about and made a big show of getting on with whatever job you were supposed to be doing at the time. He was the Big Man and we all knew it. He frightened us to death. Looking back, I can't quite work out why because he wasn't a bit of bother, really. I suppose it was the sheer weight of his personality and his presence around the club. Apart from giving me that rollicking for biting my nails, he hardly ever spoke to me and I can't recall another cross word. I think most of the apprentices would say the same thing.

He used to watch almost every game we played but he didn't interfere with the tactics or the coaches. He would stand on the touchline or sit in the stand and say something only now and again, but we all knew he was there. We had a left-back called Nigel Thrower, inevitably nicknamed Percy after the TV gardening expert, Percy Thrower, and in one game, he knocked the ball up to a team-mate in the middle of the park. It was a straightforward pass, the lad had a bit of space and as he hit the ball, Percy called, 'Hold it!' Unfortunately, the ball took an horrendous bobble, hit the lad on the knee and then caught him a glancing blow on the side of the head as it flew out of play. Straight away, an unmistakable voice cried out from the touchline, 'Hold it? Hold it? What do you think he is, a bloody sea lion?'

Once my dad came to watch one of our games with our next-door neighbour, Geoff Kelly. It took place at the Nottingham Co-op ground, where we played most of our home games, and as we were warming up before kick-off I couldn't spot either of them on the touchline. Cloughie wasn't around either and it was only after we'd been playing for a few minutes that I noticed all three of them, together with Ron Fenton, in a huddle around Geoff's car. I did my best not to let it distract me but it wasn't easy and I was glad when the quartet finally arrived on the touchline midway through the first half.

It turned out that Geoff had locked his keys in the car and while he and Dad were trying to work out what to do, Cloughie and Ron had arrived on the scene armed with a coat hanger. Eventually, amid much laughter and a fair bit of banter from the Forest contingent, they managed to prise the window down far enough for the coat hanger to go through, lever up the door handle and open the door. Normal service was then resumed on the touch-line. Cloughie hadn't met my dad, apart from at the apprentices' meeting, or Geoff but he was more than happy to help out. That was a measure of the man and I always had a tremendous amount of respect for him.

He was one of the main factors behind my decision to join Forest. I had to obtain a special dispensation from the Football League to sign on at 15 and also permission from the school to leave early without taking my exams – I don't suppose I would have passed that many anyway – and I reported for duty with seven more young hopefuls at the end of May. As first-year apprentices, we received £40 a week. We paid £20 for our board at the club hostel and another £10 into a savings account – another of Cloughie's rules – so there wasn't a lot left over. In the second year, the wage went up to £45 and after that, the club decided whether or not to offer professional terms.

The hostel was a big terraced house that backed on to the City Ground, between the stadium and Trent Bridge cricket ground. Tom and Olive ran the place. They were Geordies and did their best to treat us as their own. Olive was small and dumpy and she seemed to spend most of her time in the kitchen, churning out meals. Tom was roughly the same shape and did the waiter's job. Trouble was, he had problems with his breathing and we could hear him wheezing in the corridor as he brought in the trays of food. It was a bit off-putting at first but we got used to it.

The portions were massive. It was like having Sunday lunch every teatime. Tom would arrive with plates stacked high with wholesome English food such as meat and potato pie or beef stew plus piles of spuds and a mountain of cabbage, peas or carrots, sometimes all three. A farmer's field of vegetables was loaded on every plate, and covered in bags of gravy. We did our best but we'd no chance of finishing it all and there was always a bit of bother when we didn't eat up. Tom would tell us, 'You'll never be a player if you don't eat all your carrots.'

The idea was to build us up, which was in line with the thinking about diet at the time. Olive's food mountains, washed down with mugs of sweet tea, were par for the course for developing young-sters. We even had our own tub of biscuits. Every week we had a whip round and one of us trotted off to the supermarket to replenish the stocks. Sometimes, if we couldn't be bothered to go to the shops, we raided Olive's biscuit supply. She had a few cupboards of her own, which were strictly out of bounds, but one of the lads would break in and nick a few chocolate digestives or custard creams. She always found out and there'd be all hell to pay for a couple of days.

After tea, Tom and Olive went off to their own quarters, while we headed for the common room with its telly, pool table and dartboard. Every now and again we'd catch the bus into town and strut around pretending to be superstar professional footballers. The trouble was we didn't have enough cash to scratch our back-sides with, so there wasn't much chance of painting the town red. I shared a bedroom with Neil Cowan, a defender, and Dave Longhurst, a striker. In 1990, Dave tragically collapsed and died while he was playing for York City against Lincoln. Neil Thompson, later a team-mate at Barnsley and my manager at Boston, was a second-year apprentice at the time and he was in the hostel, too.

On our first morning we reported at the City Ground to be kitted out. We were each given a full set of training gear and a pair of adidas boots. They must have been the worst pair of boots adidas ever designed. They felt like flippers. I had always worn Puma boots so I saved up as much as I could out of my first three weeks' wages and went into town to buy myself a pair of decent boots. The senior players couldn't have done that so openly because Forest were sponsored by adidas at the time and they had to wear their boots in first-team matches. Players always have a prefer-ence, though, even at the top of the range, and where there's a will, there's a way. There was a big tub of thick, white paint in the boot room – in fact, it was more like glue than paint – and the players who preferred another brand of boot got the apprentices to black out the rival logo and paint on three adidas stripes instead. That paint was real high-octane stuff and smelt awful. If we weren't careful, we'd have been as high as kites by the time we'd finished painting the three stripes on to each boot.

We were obliged to offer a decent 'repair' service, too, because if a player had a favourite pair of boots he was always reluctant to sling them away. We had to polish them up, cut away all the loose bits that were hanging off the edges, cover over the tears – and then paint on the stripes again. You wouldn't believe the number of Forest players who went off to play European and international football in clapped-out boots that looked as good as new on the television screen for the benefit of the sponsors.

The pros weren't due back from their summer break for about a month, so we had to help the groundsman cut the grass, sweep the terraces, give parts of the stadium a coat of paint, check that all the balls and tackle were up to scratch and generally prepare for the start of pre-season training. When the pros finally returned, we soon discovered that our football education came second. The first team took priority. They arrived for training at 10 a.m., an hour after the apprentices, who had already laid out their kit, made sure the boots were clean and that the dressing room was spick and span. Cloughie always insisted on the pros having a glass of milk after training and had a dispenser installed in the corner of the dressing room. It held about 20 pints and we had to fill it every morning.

As soon as we'd finished all those jobs, we rushed into the away team dressing room, got changed and started to take the tackle down to the training ground. Balls, bibs, cones and markers all had to be ready when the first-team squad arrived. When they did, we trotted off to the other side of the training ground for our own session. At the end of training, we had to collect all the gear together and take it back to the City Ground before starting our sweeping and cleaning duties. I was responsible for the referee's room, where Cloughie and the coaches changed, and the physio's room, which obviously had to be spotless to cut down the risk of infection. That was a hard job and plenty of times I was told to give it a second going-over with the mop.

Basically, we were just dogsbodies who worked from nine to five, doing a lot of pretty menial jobs, with a bit of football training slotted in during the morning. These days it's frowned upon if YTS kids are expected to do that kind of work but without wanting to sound like an old fuddy-duddy, I don't think it did me any harm. I desperately wanted to be a professional footballer and I was prepared to put it up with a bit of hard labour on the way.

On match days, after we'd laid out the kit for the first team we weren't allowed into the dressing rooms again until all the players had left after the match. We used to hang around in the boot room until we were given a signal by one of the coaching staff that it was all clear to go in. The place was always an absolute tip – kit strewn all over the floor along with towels, tie-ups, shin-pads, bandages and empty teacups. The contents of the cups would usually be swilling around on the floor along with chunks of grass and lumps of mud. Four of us took the home dressing room, another quartet got stuck into the away dressing room and nothing less than a complete make-over would do. Both rooms had to be spotless – and then it was time to start on the ref's room, the boot room and the physio's room. It would be a couple of hours after the match before we'd finished – and bearing in mind that we'd played our own intermediate match in the morning, we were knackered by the time we got back to the hostel.

I had to look after four senior pros' boots – Shilton, Viv Anderson, Trevor Francis and John Robertson. Viv, Trevor and Peter were established England players, while John was a Scottish international, widely regarded as one of the best left-sided players in Europe and a crucial part of the Forest system. He was brilliant with me. When he went off on Scotland trips he would bring something back for me, such as a pair of shorts, a jersey or a tee shirt. He was always asking me how I was getting on. Unlike most of the senior players, he treated me as an equal – even when it came to asking for my opinion on his written transfer request.

One day I was sweeping out the drying room, where we used to hang up the players' kit after it had been in the laundry, when I noticed a plume of smoke swirling around in the far corner of the room. I couldn't see properly because of all the kit hanging around but I thought straight away that one of the dryers had overheated and caught fire. I rushed across to investigate, ready to raise the alarm, and there, sitting on a bench in the corner, was Robertson. He was holding a cigarette in one hand and a pen in the other, and on his knee was a sheet of paper. It was a transfer request.

'Come here and sit down,' he said, and read out the letter he was proposing to hand in to Cloughie. 'What do you think?' he asked. I didn't have a clue. I was 16, John was an established international and here he was asking for my opinion on a transfer request.

'It's all right, I suppose,' I said, made my excuses and left. Cloughie can't have been too impressed because John stayed put.

Robertson probably liked me because we had similar personalities. I was fiery and a bit of a rebel. I had opinions – apprentices weren't supposed to have those – and I wasn't afraid to say what I thought. All the apprentices loved him because he went out of his way to involve us. John was a real character and would think nothing of having a chat with us during a game. We used to sit on little plastic seats alongside a wall by the dug-out and when the ball was on its way out to him, he'd turn and say, 'Watch this, fellas.' Then he'd flick the ball past his marker, set off down the wing and fire in another of those trademark crosses. On his way back to the halfway line, he'd call out, 'What did you think of that, then?' Different class!

Apart from Robertson, I didn't have much to do with the first-team squad. As well as John, Shilton, Anderson and Francis, the senior players included Larry Lloyd, Kenny Burns, Frank Gray, Martin O'Neill, John McGovern and Garry Birtles. I expected them to be a bit distant and aloof because they were senior professionals and I was just one of the next batch of kids who may or may not make it one day. Most of them treated us with respect but not a lot more. Shilton and Francis never made a big deal about the way I cleaned their boots, so long as I did it properly, and Anderson was the same. Just over ten years later, he was my boss at Barnsley.

O'Neill has become one of the game's top managers, usually with Robertson as his number two. I'm sometimes asked what O'Neill was like and whether he had obvious management potential, but since I hardly had anything to do with him I never formed a lasting impression at the time. I rated him as a player and always felt that if Martin was on his game, Forest performed well, too. That was just a personal view. The closest I got to finding out what made any of the senior pros tick, apart from Robertson, was when we watched them playing five-a-sides and tuned in to the banter. What impressed me most was their confidence, even in friendly five-a-sides. They had ability and they knew it. They genuinely believed they were good enough to beat anyone.

Somewhere along the line the apprentices played a bit of football. The youth coach was Frank Clark, the former Newcastle and Forest player who later managed Orient, Forest and Manchester City. He was a brilliant coach and especially good with the kids. He always had loads of time for us. Liam O'Kane was the reserve-team coach and Ronnie Fenton was also involved with the apprentices. Those two believed in a much tougher regime than Frank did. Sometimes they made us go into the first-team dressing room and squat down with our backs to the wall – like sitting down without the seat. It was murder. Our legs would be shaking like leaves after about a minute but it worked wonders for muscle strengthening. Then we'd have to stand against the wall and tense our stomach muscles. One of the coaches would come and punch us in the stomach to test the muscle strength. Sometimes they'd 'accidentally' aim the blow a bit high and catch us on the chin, just to see how we'd respond if someone got nasty on the pitch. It couldn't happen today, of course – they might end up in court for that kind of thing. In those days it was all part of the toughening-up process.

Young players who had just come through the two years'

apprenticeship included Stuart Gray, Colin Walsh, Chris Fairclough and Bryn Gunn. They all had decent careers. So did Neil Thompson, who played for Scarborough, Ipswich, Barnsley and York, while Steve Hodge was one of the second-year apprentices. He went on to play for England. Steve Sutton, who succeeded Shilton as Forest's goalkeeper, was in his second year, too. The fall-out rate was high and of the lads who joined in my first year, only Dave Longhurst, Ronnie Sinclair, our goalkeeper, and I came through. Ronnie never made it at Forest but had a decent career with five clubs, including Leeds and Stoke City. I don't recall any others from my intake making the grade. Jim McKechnie arrived from Scotland with a massive reputation and certainly looked the part but, for some reason, he never quite made it and returned north. I think he played for a few seasons but eventually drifted away from the professional game.

There was also a kid by the name of Nigel Clough, the manager's son. Nigel started playing for the intermediate team when he was 16 or 17, although he wasn't an apprentice. He just came in from nowhere and began playing in the side. We all knew who was behind it and no one argued, although when he walked into the dressing room, the place went quiet. None of us wanted to say too much in case it got back to the manager. I felt a bit sorry for Nigel. He never made a big deal of being the manager's son. He kept himself to himself and just got on with his game, although at the time I wasn't convinced he was much of a player.

He was one-paced and his first touch was clumsy. On the face of it, he didn't have a tremendous amount going for him. It looked as though he would be a useful player, but no more than that. We used to reckon that he probably wouldn't be in our strongest side and he certainly didn't look like a man who would go on to play over 300 games for Forest, move to Liverpool for more than £2 million and collect 14 England caps. So why, despite his limitations, did he develop into a hugely effective player for Forest? I believe it was because Cloughie designed the system around Nigel and played to his strengths, side-stepping his weaknesses. It worked perfectly for Forest but Nigel was nothing like as effective when he moved on to Liverpool after Forest had been relegated in 1997.

I soon made my debut for the reserves, aged 16, and played a handful of games for them. It was almost unheard of at the time for a first-year apprentice to make the reserve team. I played in central defence alongside Fairclough, who joined Leeds a few years later. My first game was against my boyhood idols, Leeds United, whose side included Alex Sabella, an Argentinian who had cost them £250,000 from Sheffield United. I must admit I was a bit worried about him. I remember thinking, 'I'm going to get a right chasing here,' but Sabella wasn't really up for it. I fancy he thought he was a bit above playing for the reserves, so I was able to get on with my game without worrying too much about him. Allan Clarke was the manager and put himself down as a sub. It was quite a step-up from Stansfield Rovers but I wasn't overawed, even though my hero was on the touchline. I still have the teamsheet today.

I also played in the FA Youth Cup side, which consisted mainly of second-year apprentices. We had a decent run before going out against Villa. We drew two apiece at their place and I got one of the goals, a free kick round the wall. It was a beauty. I did it again in the replay from an identical position, but this time Villa beat us 3–1. Mark Walters, who went on to play for Liverpool and England, was playing up front for them and scored two. He was bigger and stronger than the rest of us and it was obvious he was going to be quite some player. I was playing at left-back against a kid called Tony Hoby, who moved on to Walsall. He was a little guy but he had blistering pace and he tortured me for 90 minutes, going outside, inside, the lot. After the game a couple of the older pros, who had been watching, came over.

'Great free kick, Redders,' said one of them.

'Thanks.'

'Aye,' said the other, 'it was, but you'll not get by on free kicks if you carry on playing like that.' I knew exactly what he meant.

In many ways, those first few months at the City Ground were an exciting time. Forest were among the élite, a bit like Chelsea,

Manchester United, Liverpool and Arsenal today. They had won trophies at home and in Europe and when I signed on, I was captivated by the glamour surrounding the club. With hindsight, if I had looked at my situation more closely, I would have opted for a club nearer home. Before I went to Nottingham, I'd lived in a close, happy and stable family environment. I'd always relied on my mum and dad and they had always been there if I needed help or advice. When I left home, I was thrown in at the deep end. I was 15 and a bit naïve. I didn't realise there would be a downside, but there was – and how!

I was homesick from the very start. I was OK when we were busy and obviously when we were training or playing. That was exciting, new and what I thought being a professional footballer meant. It was when I had finished training, done all my jobs at the ground and returned to the digs that the problems started to kick in. I used to ring home nearly every day and tell my mum and dad I couldn't stand being away. They were sympathetic and tried their best to keep me going but I couldn't come to terms with being separated from my family. I wasn't a mummy's boy and I'd never been soft as a kid but I started to doubt whether I really wanted to be there. All the time I used to think that if I'd gone to Leeds or Bradford, I could have caught the bus to work and been back home with the family every night. I'd have enjoyed the best of both worlds. Instead, I was in a hostel nearly 100 miles away. It seemed more like a million miles.

People at the club saw what was happening and were sympathetic. It was pretty obvious that they wanted me to stay and were prepared to do everything possible to solve my problems. First, they allowed me to pack in the college work we all had to do as part of the apprenticeship. I had opted for a course in groundsmanship and greenkeeping at Loughborough College. Instead, I went to help Ron Alsopp, the groundsman at Trent Bridge cricket ground. I think Cloughie had something to do with it because he was a pal of Ron's. Needless to say, that caused a bit of resentment among the other lads. They had all been told there was no way they could give up their weekly college session and here was

Redfearn being allowed to help Ron instead of making the trek to Loughborough. I could see their point.

Forest even took me with the first-team squad to a tournament in the Italian resort of Rimini. There was no chance of me playing and I was basically there to help with the kit and clean the boots, but it was an indication of how much they wanted me to stay. They also recommended me for trials with the England youth squad at Lilleshall and it looked odds on that I would be selected for the side.

I had meetings with Ronnie Fenton and Liam O'Kane to talk about my homesickness and they said I could have Mondays off to give me more time at home. That only made it worse. I used to arrive home on Saturday night and I'd just settled nicely back into the old routine when it was time to up sticks and get back to Nottingham first thing Tuesday morning. I tried it for two or three weeks but it only showed me what I was missing.

In the end, soon after Christmas, I just packed my bags and walked. I caught a train to Leeds and then a bus back to Birkenshaw. Stepping off that bus was a massive relief. As I walked down the snicket from the bus stop to our house, I could see my dad leaning out of the window – I've no idea what he was doing. When he saw me, he did a quick double take, shut the window, ran downstairs and opened the door.

'What are you doing here?' he asked.

'I've come home. I've had enough. If I'm good enough, I'll get taken on somewhere else nearer home.'

It must have been a hell of a shock for him and he was quiet for a few moments. Then he said, 'You do right, lad. Come in and put t'kettle on.'

3 A HAPPY WANDERER

DID I HAVE ANY REGRETS ABOUT WALKING OUT OF NOTTINGHAM Forest? No. I was always taught that you live your life once so there's no point wasting time with something you don't want to do, whether it's for a day, a week or a year. Life's too short to wonder what might have been and I was certain I'd made the right decision. In many ways, my time at the City Ground had taught me a lesson about the real world and I would know what to expect next time around. It was an important part of my growing-up process.

Even so, I knew I was taking a huge gamble by quitting a secure job at one of Europe's top clubs, where I had made a lot of progress in a short time. Would I find another club? I didn't know. I wrote to Leeds United and Bradford City, asking for a trial. I set out my career so far and why I had left Forest after less than a year. Allan Clarke offered me a trial at Elland Road. He didn't have to ask twice.

I trained with Leeds for a month and played three times for the Intermediates. I thought I was doing OK. In fact, it was more than that. I knew I was doing really well and was convinced they would sign me. It seemed to be a formality. Then one day, out of the blue, Clarke summoned me to his office and said he wouldn't be taking me on. He told me I was too small, that I wasn't good enough in the air and couldn't tackle. I simply couldn't believe what I was hearing. I had discovered since leaving Forest that I would have been selected for the England Youth team if I'd stayed at the City Ground. If I was good enough for England, surely I was good enough for Leeds.

I was certain Clarke was fobbing me off and I sensed there was something or someone else involved. It later turned out that, because I'd walked out on Forest and, in effect, broken my apprenticeship agreement, they had the final say about where I could go next. They agreed to let me have a trial at Leeds but said they would demand compensation if Leeds decided to sign me. Apparently, they thought Leeds had tapped me up while I was at the City Ground. It wasn't true but, whatever the rights and wrongs of the issue, it seemed Leeds weren't prepared to argue the toss about compensation and I was back to square one. Interestingly, Clarke tried to sign me from Doncaster in 1987 during his second spell as Barnsley manager. Perhaps I'd learned to tackle and head the ball by then.

When I left his office, I walked around Elland Road for half an hour or more, trying to come to terms with what had happened. At that moment, I simply didn't want to be involved in football any more. I was ready to try something else, anything else. Fortunately, that sense of despair didn't last long and I got in touch with Bradford City, where Roy McFarland, the former England centre-half, was the manager, with Mick Jones, an experienced coach who later had a spell in charge at Mansfield, as his assistant. Roy had played for Clough at Derby County so perhaps that was why Forest agreed to let me go to Bradford – and maybe Forest would have been given first option if I did well and they decided to cash in. Who knows?

I liked Roy and Mick, it was a professional set-up and they were keen to sign me. I was very tempted but, after leaving Forest, I didn't fancy joining a Fourth Division club until I'd explored every opportunity – including Bolton Wanderers. Their chief scout Frank Pickford had been tracking me for a couple of years so they knew all about me and made contact soon after I was rejected by Leeds. Dad met George Mulhall, the Bolton manager and a former team-mate of Cloughie's at Sunderland, at Cleckheaton Golf Club to thrash out a deal.

Bolton were prepared to offer me a professional contract and agreed to pay me £150 a week. Dad also insisted on £250 appearance money if I played in the first team. It sounded like a fortune to me. As I wasn't yet 17, George said it would be better to pay me a higher basic wage and less appearance money.

'He's only a kid,' he argued.

'I don't care how old he is,' Dad replied. 'I've been to watch your first team and he'll be playing in it next year.'

He was right. I signed a two-and-a-half year contract and was back on track. One of the first people I bumped into after signing was Frank Pickford. He had a real broad Lancashire accent and instead of saying hello, he'd come up and say, 'How's ter doin' then?' He used lots of quaint old Bolton sayings, one of which was 'I'll turn meself round and say this . . .' Sure enough, that first time we met after I signed on, he took me to one side and said, 'I'll turn meself round and say this. Yer should 'ave signed for us in t'first place.' He was probably right.

Bolton had dropped out of the old First Division in 1980 but Burnden Park still had the feel of a big club and there was a lot of support in the town. Some good experienced players were led by Mike Doyle, who had made over 500 appearances for Manchester City and Stoke before joining Bolton, and Paul Jones, who'd played around 500 games for the club. Alan Gowling, who had racked up more than 300 games with Manchester United, Huddersfield and Newcastle and played another 150 plus for Wanderers, was also a senior figure in the dressing room along with former Manchester City midfield man Tony Henry. They formed the core of the first team.

Dad was working at Firth's Carpets in Brighouse by then and was up at half-past five in the morning. He'd wake me at six. Just over half an hour later I'd be waiting for a bus to Bradford Interchange, where I caught the 7.20 train to Manchester Victoria. I can still hear the voice of the announcer calling out all the stops

– Halifax, Sowerby Bridge, Mytholmroyd, Hebden Bridge, Todmorden, Littleborough, Rochdale, Castleton and Moston – either that or he'd be telling us he was sorry for the delay. It took ages. Gary Worthington used to get on the train in Halifax. He was an apprentice at Manchester United and went on to play for Darlington, Wrexham, Wigan and Exeter. He could always be relied on to nick a goal or two but struggled with injuries. He eventually went into coaching and was on the Leeds United Academy staff for a while and later joined the scouting team at Chelsea.

His dad Dave had been a pro and his uncle was the legendary Frank Worthington, who played for nearly as many clubs as I have in what was, to put it mildly, a colourful career. Gary used to relate all sorts of stories about Frank's off-the-field activities and all his conquests, which was riveting stuff. As soon as I got to Burnden Park I'd pass the stories on to the rest of the lads. Frank had played at Bolton a few years earlier and one or two of the players remembered how he would come into the ground some days with a big black bag full of his old clothes, including cowboy shirts, bootlace ties and even the odd Stetson. He'd say, 'Right lads, help yourselves,' and they'd all be scrambling around trying to get a slice of the action.

At Manchester Victoria, I met up with Andy Hodgkinson, one of the apprentices at Bolton, and we'd buy ourselves a mug of tea. Then it was off to another platform to catch the 8.50 to Blackpool, which stopped at Bolton at 9.15. We had to be at the ground for 9.30 and a few more lads would be waiting to clamber aboard the bus down to Burnden Park. They'd arrived from all over the place – Wigan, Preston, Chorley, Blackpool. We could have walked and just about made it on time but that would have meant missing out on a cup of hot soup from the station buffet. The baker's just opposite the ground sold the best pies I've ever tasted. Made on the premises, they were always fresh from the oven. At lunchtime, one of the kids would be sent across with an order from the coaching staff for pies and pasties and it wasn't easy to avoid temptation and order an extra one.

Even though I had signed as a pro, the club wanted me to muck in with the apprentices and I didn't have a problem with that. They were more my age group than the senior players. So it was back to the old Forest routine of washing out the baths and dressing rooms and cleaning the senior players' boots. We always used to mess about in the dressing room and there weren't many days when one of us didn't leave with his face blacked or his hair covered in Vaseline. We helped on the ground, too, and the groundsmen were great. A guy called Alan was in charge of the pitch at Burnden Park and he always had time for a word with the kids. He'd say, 'How's ter doin' lad?' and have a bit of a natter. Sometimes, on cold days, his wife brought a big urn of soup into the dressing room, or she'd make sandwiches for us all. Alan's assistant was a Scot nicknamed, surprise, surprise, Jock. He was in charge of the training ground in Leverhulme Park, which was quite a hike from the main stadium and involved walking across the bridge over St Peter's Way, the main bypass around the town. It was a dual carriageway and the training ground was alongside the southbound lane, surrounded by a high wire fence to prevent balls flying into the traffic.

There were two pitches and Jock tended them with loving care throughout the season. Before we packed in for the summer, we had to dig up all the weeds, fill the holes with soil and then bung in some grass seed. It took an age but Jock wouldn't let us leave until every weed had been removed. Those pitches were his pride and joy and they were immaculate.

The Intermediates used to play their games there against sides ranging from Manchester United's A team to Southport Reserves. Jock was responsible for putting up the nets, which had blue and white stripes and were specially made for the club. They weighed a ton and it took him and his assistants an age to get them fitted. He was well knackered by the time he'd done. Once we played United A – Mark Hughes was in their side – and it was a terrible day. The pitch soon cut up and the ball was bobbling all over the place. The finishing from both sides was dreadful and I was one of the guilty parties. I even managed to clear the wire fence once and threatened to cause a major pile-up on St Peter's Way. Jock was tearing his hair out on the touchline and at the end he came up to me and said, 'Hey, Redfearn. I nearly broke my bloody back putting those nets up. I might as well not have bothered.' I had to go and find the missing ball before I could get changed.

It was a really friendly set-up, all the way down from the great Nat Lofthouse, the club president. He was in charge of the Burnden Park 100 Club, Bolton's first real pre-match hospitality venue. Nat was always around the place and sometimes popped in to say hello to the young lads. He was approaching 60 at the time but he still looked a hard man and I could understand why he'd been one of the most feared centre-forwards of his time. He was an absolute legend at the club and in the town.

Terry Edge was the chairman. He was in his early forties and a nice enough guy but, like quite a few chairmen, he adopted a hands-on approach to the job. The era of the club chairman who was happy to restrict himself to the boardroom and directors' box and leave the manager to get on with the coaching was a thing of the past, and Terry would often have his say about how the kids should be prepared. I suppose someone should really have taken him to one side and pointed out that he ought to leave the coaching to the experts and stick to running the club – but it wouldn't have been easy. He even joined in some of our training sessions.

We'd be working with our coach Charlie Wright, who'd played in goal for Charlton and Wanderers, when the chairman would roll up in his tracksuit and join in. On one occasion, Charlie stopped the session and said, 'Right lads, the chairman wants to make one or two points.'

'The trouble with you modern footballers,' Terry began, either not noticing or ignoring a few groans and sidelong glances, 'is that you don't know how to fall. That's why you all get so many injuries. Here, I'll show you what I mean,' and he set off at top speed for about 10 yards. Then he threw himself face down in the mud, did a perfect forward roll and stood up again, proud as punch. 'There you are,' he shouted. 'That's the way to fall. Now you try it,' and off he went again.

At the end of the day, someone always made sure I didn't miss the train home. I'd just be starting to worry whether I'd make it when Alan or one of his assistants would say, 'Hey up, Redders, what time's your train?'

'Four o'clock.'

'Right lad, you'd better get yourself off then.'

It was always hot on the train home and I'd usually find myself dozing off somewhere between Manchester and Mytholmroyd. Time after time in the early days, I woke up to find myself in Leeds and have to get on the train back to Bradford, but that stopped for ever the day I bumped into Sue at Bradford Interchange. Although we'd gone to infants' school together and then on to middle and secondary schools, I'd never gone out with her. Once I discovered she used to catch the same bus home as me after she'd finished work at WH Smith's, I made a point of being on the bus every night. If I arrived in Bradford early, I used to hang around the Interchange until she appeared at the bus stop. If my train was a bit late, I'd dash down the platform and into the bus station to make sure I caught the same bus. We'd chat about this and that. One day, I'd received the Vaseline treatment on my hair before leaving Bolton. I must have looked a real sight with my hair sticking up all over the place but she just smiled and said, 'Mmm, is that a new hairstyle?' We cracked out laughing and I tried to explain what had been going on. She didn't seem too impressed. We started going out soon afterwards and the rest is history.

Before the start of my second season, I became the proud owner of a little Citroen Visa. I'd started taking driving lessons not long after my 17th birthday and eventually put enough money together to buy my first car. I assumed it would be just a matter of time before I could abandon the train and drive myself over to Bolton. Unfortunately, four driving-test examiners didn't see things the same way and scuppered my plans. After the fourth failure, I decided I wasn't getting enough practice and managed to cajole my mum into sharing the journey across the Pennines once or twice a week. We'd set off first thing and sweep into the main car park at Burnden Park in time for training. Then Mum would spend a few hours in the shops and return to the ground in time for me to chauffeur her back to Bradford in the afternoon. It can't have been much fun for her but it worked – I finally chucked away the L plates at the fifth time of asking.

Fortunately, my football progressed rather more smoothly than my driving and I started playing for the reserves towards the end of my first season. Even though I had always seen myself as a midfield player who could also operate up front, I started out at left-back and played a few games in central defence before I was finally pushed into midfield. I did well straight away and it was obvious that I had found my best position. I felt I was starting to make an impact.

George Mulhall left in the summer and was replaced by John McGovern, who had been captain of Nottingham Forest during my stay at the City Ground. John arrived as player-manager and started the new season in central midfield. He was getting towards the far end as a player and it was pretty obvious he was going to struggle with the two roles. We had an up-and-down start and by New Year we were flirting with the relegation zone, so something had to be done. McGovern opted for youth and brought in three players – Warren Joyce, Steve Thompson and me – for the trip to Rotherham on 19 February 1983. Warren went on to have a successful career with Bolton, Preston, Plymouth, Burnley and Hull, where he was manager for a spell. Steve played over 700 games in all competitions for Bolton, Luton, Leicester, Burnley and Rotherham before ending up at Halifax Town with me in the 2001–02 season.

Apart from the result, a 1–1 draw, two things will always stand out in my mind about the first of my 900-plus senior appearances. First, Rotherham had what we used to call UFO balls. They were white with a red ring all round the middle. I'd never played with one before and seeing it fly through the air was a weird sensation. It was a bit like trying to head the planet Saturn and it took me a while to adjust my timing, which perhaps explains my second vivid memory of Millmoor, 1983 – Gerry Gow.

Like us, Rotherham were struggling at the wrong end of the table, even though they had a couple of useful front men in Ronnie Moore, who later went back to Millmoor as manager in the nineties and led them to two successive promotions, and Tony Towner. They also had Gow directly opposite me in midfield. Now Gow was one of football's most notorious hard men and was approaching the end of his career, spent with Bristol City, Manchester City and now Rotherham. He was a skinny little so-and-so with a mop of grey hair but his CV said he'd tangled with most of the tough guys and usually come out on top. People used to joke that he would have kicked his own mother. Not a lot happened between us as I tried to find the pace in the early stages. In the first 20 minutes I touched the ball three or four times only.

Then a Rotherham defender knocked the ball in towards Gow in central midfield. It was a fifty-fifty ball and I went for it 100 per cent. I really clattered into him with an absolute boneshaker, the sort of tackle Gow was supposed to make on other people. He did three forward somersaults in mid-air and finished up flat out on the turf clutching his leg. The ref signalled for the Rotherham physio and then turned his attentions to me.

'Right, lad,' he said. 'Come over here.'

'Sorry, ref,' I said, putting on my most innocent expression. Tony Henry sprang to my defence straight away.

'Come on, ref,' said Tony, 'he's only a kid. It's his debut. You can't book him for that.' He could – and he did.

By the time the name of Neil Redfearn had gone into the referee's book for the first of many times, Gow was receiving treatment and I bent down to apologise. I never got the chance.

'When I get up, I'm going to break your bloody leg,' he growled. I turned to Tony in a panic.

'Did you hear that? Did you hear what he's going to do?'

'Aw, take no bloody notice,' replied Tony, who had played with Gow at Manchester City. 'He doesn't mean it.' That prompted another growl from the Millmoor mud.

'I bloody well do mean it,' thundered Gow.

He wasn't given an opportunity to put his money where his mouth was because I spent the next 70 minutes making damn sure he never got within ten yards of me. The following week, our skipper Paul Jones wrote in his weekly column in the *Bolton Evening News* that 'young Neil Redfearn has given us some bite in midfield'. I suspect Gerry Gow would have agreed with that sentiment.

I played ten first-team games that first season and even though we were fighting against relegation, I didn't feel any pressure. I was only a kid, happy to be given a chance at first-team level. As a young player, you just enjoy getting paid for doing something you love. What could be better? You have your low moments but most of the time you're living in a dream world. Reality kicks in later when you begin to realise that there's a downside. Football is a job of work and you aren't always going to have it your way. There will be times when you have to uproot yourself and your family and live in an unfamiliar place a long way from home. There will be times when you have no control over your destiny. If a club decides to sell you, you have to move on, even if you don't want to go. You have to be big enough to accept that.

Those stresses and strains might have been a million miles away in those early days at Bolton. When McGovern left me out and decided to opt for more experience in the fight against relegation towards the end of the season, I didn't moan about it. I was 17 and it was good to be back with my mates in the youth team and reserves. If I'd been a couple of years older, it would have been a different story and I'd have been knocking on McGovern's door.

Even so, I reckoned he was wrong. The kids he brought in had turned things round a bit and I have always said we'd have stayed up if he'd kept us in there. Instead, we found ourselves in the old Third Division at the start of the 1983–84 season. McGovern decided to throw the young lads in from the start. Thompson, Joyce, Steve Saunders and I were in midfield, Simon Rudge played up front and Simon Farnworth in goal. We'd all come through together and we did really well in the first half of that season. I scored my first league goal – a free kick against Rotherham at Burnden Park – and we were right up there at Christmas.

Even though Warren and I were young, we had a bit of physical presence in central midfield and could put ourselves about. That was an important ingredient in the team's success. I thought we'd be going back up at the end of the season but we went off the boil a bit in the New Year. That's always going to happen with young players. A manager needs to be ready to tackle it when it does but John didn't seem to have a Plan B. He wasn't decisive enough and seemed to be fiddling around with the team. He let one or two players go out on loan and brought in a few.

Warren and I were among the players who were shunted out of the line-up and McGovern brought in Graham Bell, a little ginger-haired midfield man. He was 28, a former England youth international and he'd played over 300 league matches for Oldham, Preston, Huddersfield (two games) and Carlisle. He wasn't a bad player – but he was only around 5ft 5in and can't have weighed more than about 10 stone sopping wet. Bell simply didn't have the same power and aggression as Warren and I had. The wheels started to come off and our promotion hopes went down the pan.

It went steadily downhill for McGovern and Bolton from there. He hung around for a while but left the club in January 1985, a couple of years before Bolton suffered the indignity of relegation to the old Fourth Division. I wasn't around to bid McGovern farewell, however, because by then I was wearing the red and white stripes of Lincoln City.

4 THE VALLEY OF TEARS

I JOINED LINCOLN ON LOAN IN MARCH 1984, SIGNED FULL-TIME in the summer and had two good seasons at the club. I played regular first-team football for the first time, I was never left out of the side, apart from through injury, and I even had a spell as captain. My career took a significant step forward. After the problems at Forest, I proved to myself and everyone else that I could hack it away from my home environment. I was starting to get to grips with league football.

However, the progress I made as a player in my two seasons at Sincil Bank paled into insignificance alongside what happened in the space of just a few minutes on the afternoon of 11 May 1985, the day of the Bradford City fire. I was in the Lincoln side and we should have been playing our part in one of Bradford City's finest hours. Instead, we were helpless witnesses to one of football's darkest days.

When our team coach rolled into Valley Parade, City had already clinched the championship and, as a Bradford lad, I was really looking forward to coming home and playing in a match that was so important for the people of my home town. I was living in Lincoln but I knew from talking to my folks and Sue's family that it was going to be a carnival day out for everyone. From a personal point of view, I'd be playing in central midfield and marking Stuart McCall, a young lad tipped by many as a star of the future. I wanted to go out there and show the world what I could do, and while City were already making plans for life in a higher division, Lincoln had made sure of avoiding the drop in their penultimate game. So one way or another, it was an afternoon to savour.

The game kicked off late because City were presented with the championship trophy before the match and did a lap of honour before proceedings got under way. We had to hang around in the dressing room until it was over and we could hear all the chants and the cheers as the City players walked round the ground. There was a tremendous atmosphere when we were finally given the green light to leave the dressing room.

The game had an unhappy start when Steve Collins, our left-back, broke his leg early on. He cleared the ball just as John Hawley, the City striker, challenged. They went down in a heap and John fell awkwardly on Steve's leg. It was a complete accident. Steve was carried off and taken to hospital. An hour or so later, he was still in casualty as the first victims of the fire were brought in, suffering from severe burns. I talked to him a few days later and he described the scene in the hospital as 'like a war zone'.

When Steve was injured, I switched to left-back and three minutes before half-time, a ball was knocked in behind me. I tried to shield it out of play for a goal kick and as I was doing so, a few fans started clambering over the wall at the front of the stand and on to the pitch. I couldn't work out what was going on. Why were they invading the pitch on this day of all days? It didn't add up. Then I spotted a few whiffs of smoke towards the back of the stand and straight away the referee blew his whistle to stop the game. He told the players to move into the centre circle. I thought it would be something and nothing, the fire would soon be put out and we would be able to carry on.

Fans were still coming on to the pitch but everything was well organised and there was no panic. Mainly older people and kids were being helped out of the stand and the only real sign of a fire was a bit of smoke. None of us knew that the fire had started below the stand, where years of litter had accumulated, and was rapidly taking hold. The weather was dry and windy, and strong gusts were fanning the flames. All of a sudden, it became apparent from the pitch that those few puffs of smoke at one end had become a serious blaze that was being swept along the length of the stand by the wind, and what had started as an ordered evacuation was degenerating into panic. I could only watch as the flames spread.

Sue had stayed behind in Lincoln but I knew that my dad, Sue's dad and his brother, Sue's sister Catherine and my dad's pal Geoff Kelly were all in there somewhere. I had no idea where they were sitting and I started to run along the side of the pitch in front of the blazing stand, trying to spot them. It was impossible with all the smoke and the hundreds of people who were now falling over themselves to reach the safety of the pitch. Someone from Yorkshire Television asked if I would talk to their reporter John Helm. In a daze, I agreed and went up to the broadcasting box on top of the little stand on the opposite side of the stadium.

From up there, it was an horrendous sight and all too obvious that people would be trapped. I can't remember a word of what I said to John, who also hailed from Bradford, because I realised that if my family and friends were still in there, they would be in real danger. I think I just cut the interview short and rushed back on to the pitch but it was hopeless. Thousands of people were milling around and the police were trying to restore some semblance of order.

I later learned that my dad and the others had been fairly near the front and were able to clamber over the wall to safety. It was a fair drop from the front of the stand on to the track below, probably about six feet, and an old chap sitting nearby hadn't fancied the jump. Dad had realised what was going on and just grabbed hold of him and dropped him on to the track. That probably saved his life.

From the pitch, all I could see were the flames and a mass of people trying to reach the front and jump for safety. I have vivid memories of police, firefighters and stewards going back into the stand, grabbing hold of people and pulling them out. They were fantastic. I saw people on fire, rolling around on the grass in an effort to put out the flames. They were scenes I will never forget. Soon the awful truth dawned that not everyone was going to escape. The fire had taken hold so quickly that it was going to be impossible for all the fans to get out of the stand. We didn't know at the time that the people who had tried to escape via the turnstiles at the back found the doors locked and were trapped.

I can't remember in which order I learned that all my family and friends were safe. I didn't see Dad at the ground but I bumped into Sue's sister and she told me Dad and Sue's dad were OK, but nobody knew whether her uncle David or Geoff Kelly had escaped. Eventually, we learned they were safe.

All the players' gear was in the dressing rooms under the stand and the Lincoln team bus had been burnt out. So some transport had to be found for the journey back to Lincoln. Still wearing our strip, we were taken to a pub on the main road at the top of Valley Parade and asked to wait until something was sorted out. I spotted John Pickering, the Lincoln coach, and confirmed that it was OK for me to slip away home to be with my family. Sue's dad gave me a lift and as soon as we reached my parents' house, I called Sue. None of us had mobile phones in those days so I hadn't been able to contact her with any definite news until then. She had been listening to the radio and knew the players were OK but she'd been desperate to make sure her family were safe. I was able to assure her that they had all survived.

For several weeks, the city of Bradford was the focus of world attention. It was a traumatic time in Lincoln, too. A couple of our fans had died in the blaze and many more were injured. The city was in a state of shock. In the build-up to the match, there had been a lot of talk about how we had succeeded in staying in the division after one or two scares; City were going to celebrate the championship whereas staying up would be a cause for celebration in Lincoln, too. In the aftermath of the fire, both issues seemed totally irrelevant.

Soon afterwards, a memorial service was held at Valley Parade. All the Lincoln players attended and the two teams sat in a single line of chairs in front of what had once been the main stand. All that remained were the metal girders and heaps of black ash. I recall thinking how a short time earlier it had been full to capacity with around 4,000 cheering people, celebrating one of their club's biggest days.

I have never really got over it. If I close my eyes, I can still see the stand on fire, smell the acrid fumes and recall those terrible scenes. My recollection of the game is virtually non-existent. I can remember Collins breaking his leg but if I was asked to say, hand on heart, what was the score at the time the fire broke out, I would say 1–0 to Lincoln. In fact, it was goalless. I can picture McCall and Peter Jackson, City's skipper who later went into management with Huddersfield, playing for Bradford but I can't recall any more of their players and I don't have the slightest recollection of who I was marking after I switched to full-back. It must have been John Hendrie, who played on the right wing for City. Later he and I played at Barnsley for the best part of two seasons, winning promotion and appearing together in the Premiership. We never talked about the fire.

At the time, some speculation arose that the game would have to be replayed at the Odsal Stadium in Bradford, where City played their home matches the following season. How anyone could have even contemplated playing again so soon after the tragedy beggars belief. As no outstanding league issues remained to be settled, the Football League decided to leave the result as it stood, declared the game a goalless draw and each team was awarded a point. I could never have brought myself to play in a rearranged match. I needed a complete break from football after the horrors of Valley Parade and I'm sure all the other players involved felt exactly the same way.

The Lincoln players were offered counselling through the Professional Footballers' Association (PFA) in the immediate aftermath of the tragedy, but I decided against it. I had also opted out of the players' end-of-season break in Mallorca, partly because I wanted to be close to my family and partly because those jaunts have never really been my scene. That trip turned out to be pretty traumatic – the aircraft overran the runway at Leeds-Bradford airport on the return flight and the passengers had to leave the plane via the escape shoots.

I'd initially joined Lincoln on loan just before the transfer deadline the previous year. I was playing reserve-team football at Bolton and Colin Murphy, the Lincoln manager, managed to persuade me that I would be better off in his first team than messing about in the reserves at Burnden Park – and he had a point. So I agreed to go until the end of the season. Compared with Bolton, Lincoln seemed a million miles away – although now, after playing for Boston, I realise it isn't all that far! Deep down, I probably knew it was the end for me at Bolton. I think I realised even then that if a club don't want a player, there's no point in hanging around. I played ten league games on loan and when Murph offered me a two-year deal in the summer, I signed on the dotted line. The fee was £8,250.

Obviously, I couldn't travel to work every day from Bradford any more so Sue and I had to do some thinking. She was only 18 and doing well at WH Smith's but when I signed the loan deal, she said she was prepared to give up her job and take her chance at the Lincoln branch. It must have been an incredibly big step for her because we weren't married and it was her first time away from home. Unlike me at Nottingham, she took it in her stride and it wasn't long before she was offered a job on the management side at Smith's. Come to think of it, she progressed a hell of a lot quicker than I did! My mum and dad and Sue's parents, Cedric and Christine, supported us all the way. They realised it was what we wanted and knew we'd act properly. It wasn't as if we'd caused them a load of bother while we'd been courting. They visited us regularly during our two years in Lincoln. They'd watch the game and then come round for a bite of tea afterwards.

At first we had nowhere to live and during my loan spell we shacked up with one of the lads at Lincoln, John Thomas, and his girlfriend Lesley. John was a decent striker who scored a lot of goals when he was fit but he had big injury problems over the years. He'd played for Bolton, too. They were a smashing couple and did everything they could to make us feel at home. We had our own room and they said we could come and go as we pleased but living in someone else's house is always awkward and even more so as it was the first time Sue and I had been away together.

So after I signed full-time in the summer, we went house-hunting and found a little place on a new estate in Bracebridge Heath, a village not far up the road from the ground. We gave about £17,000 for the two-bedroomed town house, which was as much as we could afford – in fact, it was more than we could afford – and took our first step on the property ladder. For a while, more money seemed to be going out of the house than was coming in and, looking back, I don't know how we managed. The estate soon became a bit of a ghetto for Lincoln City foot-ballers. First, Gary Strodder and his wife Alison moved in, and John McGinlay, a big Geordie striker, and his wife soon followed. If Murph had signed a few more players, we'd have taken over the place.

The estate backed on to RAF Waddington and noise was a problem – not while we were out at work, of course, but it wasn't a lot of fun at weekends. The base was used for Chinook heli-copters and we could here them coming in from about 20 miles away. When they took off again, the noise was incredible. There were Nimrod surveillance planes, too, and they didn't do badly in the decibel stakes. We didn't care. It was our first home and soon we had our first dog, a German Short-Haired Pointer that we christened Souness, in honour of one of my midfield heroes at the time, because it went round biting people's legs and trying to fight all the other dogs. We also adopted a little black and white stray cat, Hoby. Those two went everywhere with us for the next 14 years – seven clubs and loads of different houses. They never batted an eyelid. Poor old Souness died when we were at Charlton. We were all bitterly upset so it wasn't long before we bought a couple of puppies. Same breed. We call them Dexter and Deedee after the cartoon characters and they're lovely dogs. I've always believed in having a dog around the place. A pal who's a copper once told me a dog is the best burglar alarm in the business and I've always felt happier about going off on overnight trips or to long-distance away games knowing there's a dog in the house to keep an eye on the family.

Sue and I were married at Birkenshaw Methodist Chapel in the summer of 1984, soon after I signed for Lincoln. I was just turned 19 and Sue was a year younger. We were just kids and it all seems a long time ago now. Getting married was the best thing I ever did. Once again, I was making my way in an unfamiliar environment but, unlike my time at Nottingham, I had someone to turn to, someone to lean on and someone who was going through the same thing herself. Sue has been brilliant. I couldn't be with a better person. In some ways, she sacrificed her career for mine. She is far more level-headed than I am and she has a great knowledge of the game. I have no qualms about discussing every aspect of football with her because I know I will receive a sensible answer and I trust her opinions.

They were good times, even though it was a struggle financially and money dictated how we spent our time. We had no idea how my career would develop or if I'd progress up the football ladder. Realistically, there was a chance I would stay at that level and then money was going to be tight. We weren't going to blow it all away before I'd really got started, so we looked after the pennies. We'd sometimes pop out for a drink on a Saturday night, either on our own or with one of the other players and his wife, but neither of us was the sort who wanted to go out clubbing or getting blathered every weekend. We preferred the quiet life at home, walking the dogs and enjoying our own company.

A few of the lads grabbed every available opportunity to go out for a drink and it's no secret that quite a drink culture existed in football in those days. A lot of teams used to have a Tuesday Club. Players usually had Wednesday off if they didn't have a game on that day. So Tuesday was the chance to have a skinful, sleep it off and get rid of the hangover on Wednesday before reporting fresh as a daisy on Thursday morning. I suspect some managers actively encouraged it, seeing it as a form of team bonding, although they also had their moles posted around the area. The spies would report back if any of the boys were stepping out of line towards the end of the week. Hefty fines would follow.

I was never really involved with the drinkers. It just never appealed. I'll enjoy a beer or a lager with the next man but I couldn't handle a hangover then and I can't now. I used to get a bit of stick from the lads about being under the thumb but it was nothing to do with Sue. She wouldn't have been too bothered if I'd gone out with the boys. It just didn't fit in with my life as a professional footballer. I wanted to do well in the game, organise myself properly, and nothing was going to get in the way.

Being at a smaller club in a provincial city such as Lincoln helped. Players at any club will always be noticed around town and fans will want to come up to say hello. Sometimes you become vaguely aware that people in a group nearby are nudging one another and pointing. Some shops take the opportunity to offer a bit of discount in the hope that word will get around that players buy their clothes or music there and, inevitably, when you go into those shops, the staff make a bit of a fuss to attract the attention of other customers.

It's easy for players' heads to be turned in those situations but that didn't often happen at Lincoln. The city was a bit of a backwater in football terms, away from the mainstream, a place where fans used to go to watch football on a Saturday afternoon and find other interests for the rest of the week. That atmosphere helped me to keep my feet on the ground. I never felt massively important because, as far as the supporters were concerned, I wasn't. Fair enough.

Colin Murphy was a real character. He was noted for his programme notes. He would often waffle on, putting the world to rights and hardly mentioning football or Lincoln City. Sometimes he would call in one of the kids, sit him down over a cup of tea and ask, 'Now, what have you learned?' It wasn't an easy question to answer but it was Colin's way of introducing a chat about the way the lad was progressing. He once rang me up a couple of years after I'd left Lincoln – I was at Crystal Palace by then – and his first words were, 'Now then, what have you learned?' I was going to ask him if he'd got an hour to spare but instead, I let him have his say. It turned out he was interested in a player I'd worked with and wanted my opinion. Although Colin was a bit of an eccentric, he knew football and his players respected him. He didn't need a big stick to keep us in order and we were always fit and well organised. We didn't score a lot of goals but we didn't give many away either, and we were hard to beat.

Murph knew that, in the old Third Division, teams could get away without having too much ability so long as they worked hard and competed for 90 minutes. The long ball was all the rage and if you weren't prepared to put a foot in and make tackles, you'd be found out. We had some good players at the club, particularly Gordon Mair, a left-winger who had been signed from Notts County. He had a great left foot and loads of ability. He should never have been playing down at that level but, because he couldn't get stuck in, there was no place for him and his career gradually petered out.

Every side we played had one or two hard men and it was a tough school. I soon realised I was going to have to knuckle down and learn to look after myself. I was no longer the little skinny kid who'd been rejected by Yorkshire Schoolboys because I was too small. I'd filled out a lot and, physically, I was a match for more or less anyone. If I tackled someone, he felt it and I soon decided that if the manager wanted a player who would tackle and compete, that's what he was going to get. It was a good lesson for me to learn early in my career and to this day, I'm never intimidated.

I had one or two scrapes, though, notably the day I tangled with Terry Hurlock of Millwall at The Den. He had a fearsome reputation as an enforcer in midfield. He had a fair amount of ability as well but it was the hard man image that loomed large in his legend. We used to laugh that he'd be waiting outside with a shotgun if anyone tried to muscle in on his patch. Guess who did? It was my first appearance at The Den and the first time I'd trotted out on to the pitch under a wire-mesh tunnel to protect me from flying objects thrown by home fans. The atmosphere was unbelievably hostile but I didn't mind that. I've always responded to a bit of intimidation from opposing fans. I was in central midfield, marking Hurlock, and in the opening minutes I caught him late. It was something and nothing really. He helped on a loose, bouncing ball just as I was arriving on the scene with the same plan in mind. Unfortunately, by the time I made contact with him, the ball was on its way towards our penalty box and I took out Hurlock instead. He went down like a sack of potatoes.

There was a deathly hush. I didn't realise 15,000 Millwall fans could be so quiet. It was as if they couldn't believe what they'd just seen. The physio rushed on to treat the stricken Hurlock and once the fans realised it wasn't anything serious, they started chanting, 'Terry's gonna get you, Terry's gonna get you . . .' I thought, 'Bloody hell, I've kicked the wrong man here . . .' Ross Jack, who played alongside me in midfield, thought so, too. He just looked at me as if to say, 'Have you gone mad?' The chants went on for a while but even though Hurlock made it blatantly obvious that he 'was gonna get me', I gave as good as I received and lived to fight another day – and no one was waiting outside with a shotgun afterwards.

However, Millwall fans have long memories, as I discovered two years later when I went back to The Den with Crystal Palace. We won a corner on the left straight from the kick-off and I went across to take it. I used to curl the ball in right-footed, looking for our centre-half, Jim Cannon, who always caused problems in the box – good player, Jim. I was bending down to place the ball when something flew past my left ear. I looked up – and took swift evasive action as a swinging umbrella hurtled towards me, brandished by an old granny. She must have been in her seventies and was wearing a big coat over her Millwall shirt. As she came swinging in for a third time, she yelled, 'You're a dirty bastard, Redfearn!'

'Nay love, give me a chance,' I replied. 'We've only just kicked off.'

I hadn't completely finished with Bolton, either. Relegation meant they were in the same division as Lincoln and sure enough, when we played them at Sincil Bank, I scored one of the goals in our 2–0 victory. It was a good one, too, and I ran across to the Bolton dug-out to make my point.

In the return game, I incurred the wrath of the Burnden Park fans in a big way. Jeff Chandler, their winger, had played at quite a few clubs and had been at Bolton when I was there. He was a good player and could do some damage if you gave him too much room. He had a bit of pace, good feet, nicked a goal or two and crossed a good ball in, but he couldn't tackle a good dinner and definitely didn't like to mix it when the going got tough. I was playing right-back, opposite Chandler. It was a typical Burnden midwinter day – freezing cold – and touch and go whether the game was on or not. The pitch was like a bog. Chandler started really well and turned me inside out a couple of times, so I decided it was time to put some fatherly advice into action. 'Never let anyone make you look stupid,' was how Dad always put it, adding, 'It's worth a booking to stop it happening.' He'd reinforced the message that very morning when we were chatting about the game and the threat Chandler would pose if given a bit of time and space.

The next ball out to Chandler was definitely going to be 60-40 in his favour – until it landed with a splat and stuck in the mud. All of a sudden, the odds were reduced to fifty-fifty and that was enough for me. Chandler was committed but when he saw me coming, he began to look for an escape route. There wasn't one. I slid in at top speed and the lot of us – Chandler, the ball and me – hurtled over the touchline and down the slope on to the gravel track around the pitch in a cloud of spray. We hit the perimeter fence in front of the terraces with a resounding thump. I picked myself up but Chandler stayed down. The physio was called and he took no further part in proceedings. I did, to the accompaniment of non-stop abuse from the natives – 'You dirty bugger, Redfearn, you never were any bloody good!' You know the kind of thing.

It didn't bother me. I'd worked out beforehand that if I just stood up and jockeyed him and allowed him to play, he would give me a tough afternoon. So I had to make my presence felt. It was him or me – simple as that. We drew 0–0 and I wasn't even booked for the challenge. I would have been today, of course, because tackling and physical contact have more or less gone out of the game. Twenty years ago, it was frowned upon if a player went down easily in a tackle. If you dived, you were soft. The referees' approach was different then. You could clatter someone early on and the chances were you'd get away with a quiet word or a warning. Some refs allowed you to make four or five tackles before they got the book out. Now everything is under much closer scrutiny.

Let's get one thing straight – I wasn't trying to injure Chandler seriously. There was absolutely no danger of breaking his leg or causing a big injury with that particular challenge. It was a fifty-fifty ball and he knew I was coming. If the tackle had taken place in the middle of the pitch, I would have flattened him but he would almost certainly have picked himself up and continued, keeping a wary eye out for me from then on. Sliding off the pitch, rolling down the hill and landing face down on the gravel track before hitting the fence was a different matter. I suffered a fair bit of damage, too, but I shrugged it off and got on with the game.

Murph left at the end of my first season, 1984–85, and was succeeded by John Pickering, the first-team coach. He'd already had a spell as manager of Blackburn and later coached at Middlesbrough. One of the good guys was John. Sadly, he died in 2001. I remember him with affection because he always had time for his players, particularly the younger ones. He knew the game inside out and although his training sessions were pretty tough, they were enjoyable. Above all, John always took time out to work with individuals – an early lesson for me in how a coach should operate. Nothing was too much trouble for him.

Soon after he took over, he signed Bob Latchford from Coventry. The former Birmingham, Everton and Swansea centre-forward was a hell of a signing at the time. Bob had been an England player and one of the best goal-scorers in the game. He was a smashing fella and, as a kid, it was great to have him around in the dressing room and on the training ground, although he was a bit back-endish by then. He'd made his name as a big guy who could put himself about and shake things around in the opposition back four – but he'd probably had enough split eyebrows by the time he came to Lincoln, and he wasn't 100 per cent match fit, either. These days older players stay fitter (I would say that, wouldn't I?) but back in the early eighties, they were sometimes a bit less mobile than they might have been. That was the case with Bob – but he still had a fantastic first touch and some of the things he did were way above what a lot of the Lincoln lads were capable of doing.

It didn't really happen for Bob at Lincoln, though, and it didn't happen for John Pickering, who was replaced by George Kerr. He'd had a successful spell at Grimsby but his arrival marked the beginning of the end for me at Sincil Bank. It wasn't anything personal but Kerr, like Pickering and Murph before him, insisted on using me as a utility player. I could accept that approach in my first season when I was still a bit raw but by the time Murphy left, I knew I was ready to play regularly in midfield. Instead, I'd be left-back one week, right-back the next, then on the right wing or filling in as one of the midfield players if we went to 4-3-3. Yet I'd demonstrated often enough that if I played in central midfield, I'd do well and score goals. In two seasons at Lincoln, I scored 12 goals in 86 league starts, and for more than half of those games, I was playing in defence. I've always been convinced that if they'd played me in my proper position, I'd have scored double that figure. The sense of missing an opportunity, for me and for the club, was very frustrating. I was afraid that people were beginning to see me as a Jack of all trades. That was no good to me, and so when I got a whisper that Doncaster were interested, I was more than ready to listen.

Billy Bremner, one of my heroes from Leeds' great days, was Doncaster's manager and he told me that if I joined them when my contract expired in the summer, I would definitely be playing in midfield. Soon afterwards, however, Bremner left to succeed Eddie Gray at Elland Road and I assumed the move had bitten the dust. Then new manager Dave Cusack called, soon after taking over, to say Rovers were still interested. 'In midfield?' I asked. 'In midfield,' was his answer. That was good enough for me. Kerr was still persisting with me at left-back and I was playing so well that Jim Smith wanted to sign me for Oxford United, who were in the top division at the time. I told Smith and Kerr that I wasn't interested in going anywhere as a full-back. I wanted to play in midfield or not at all. Next game, I was picked at left-back. That went on until the end of the season. Early in the summer, Kerr called me in.

'Now then, you're out of contract and I want you to sign for another season,' he said, coming straight to the point. On his desk lay a contract and a Lincoln City shirt with a number eight on the back. 'That's your shirt for next season and you'll be playing in central midfield.'

What he didn't know was that I'd already agreed to join Doncaster – he wasn't best pleased when I told him and nor was John Reames, the chairman. Supporters writing in the local press bandied around words such as traitor but that was way out of order. As far as I was concerned, I was out of contract, I'd received a decent offer and I knew I'd be playing in my best position for Doncaster. Lincoln couldn't complain. They paid just over eight thousand quid for me and collected £17,500 when I moved on.

5 A BRAND NEW ROVER

DONCASTER WERE SO KEEN TO HAVE ME ON BOARD IN THE summer of 1986 that they even offered Sue a job as well. That can't have happened too often. It was an important job – keeping the accounts and balancing the books, which meant we knew exactly what everyone was earning, from the manager down-wards, and who was spending what. Armed with that kind of confidential information, I could have caused mayhem in the dressing room with a few well-chosen words in my team-mates' ears. It was more than Sue's job was worth for me to break those confidences, of course, so we kept all the club's intimate financial details to ourselves. I somehow can't imagine that situation occur-ring anywhere today.

Even without inside information about the club's finances, it was pretty obvious there wasn't a lot of brass around at Belle Vue. We could never be 100 per cent sure our wages would be paid on time and on one occasion, I even had to borrow from the bar takings to buy a pair of boots. My rubbers had reached the stage where they were clearly living on borrowed time.

And when I told Dave Cusack he said, 'No problem. Go and draw a few quid out of petty cash and buy yourself a pair from the sports shop in town. Make sure you break 'em in before Saturday.' So off I went to the office to see Joan Oldale, the secretary.

'The boss says I can take a few quid out of petty cash to buy a pair of boots,' I said.

'We haven't got any petty cash,' she replied.

That was a bit of a conversation stopper. So, what to do next? Anne, her assistant, pointed out that the bar takings from the previous weekend's match still hadn't been paid in at the bank, so perhaps we could use some of that. It seemed a reasonable idea. She went into the back office, unlocked the cupboard and re-appeared, staggering under the weight of a big bag full of cash.

'How much will they cost?' asked Joan. I didn't really have a clue.

'Give us thirty quid,' I said. 'I should be able to find a decent pair for that, and anything I don't spend I'll bring back tomorrow.'

So we tipped out the contents of the sack and counted out £30 in silver. I put the cash into a carrier bag, which weighed a ton, drove into town, found the sports shop, tipped the money out on the counter and said, 'Can I have a pair of rubbers, please?' The shop assistant recognised me and clearly couldn't work out what the hell was going on, but I left with a new pair of boots – and there was a bit of loose change left over. I never did find out how they explained away the drop in bar takings.

It turned out that Doncaster had been keeping an eye on me for two or three years through their chief scout, Dave Blakey, who'd moved to Leeds with Billy Bremner by the time I arrived at Belle Vue. He was a typical old-school scout, who thought nothing of standing on the touchline watching kids or going to a Sunday League game on the park. He'd been coming along on a regular basis to see how I was developing at Bolton and Lincoln but I'd no idea that I was under scrutiny. In fact, it was a side of the game I wasn't aware of at the time. As I've grown older I've seen how the scouting system operates and what a vast network there is. Even small clubs have people out there, watching all sorts of games, filing away details of players they may one day sign or play against. Dave, his successors and others like them have a vast knowledge of the strengths and weaknesses of hundreds, maybe thousands, of players.

As soon as I signed, we put the house in Lincoln up for sale and took our next steps on the property ladder. In the first six years of our marriage, we either owned or rented nine houses all over the country. With the wonderful gift of hindsight, it might not have been a bad idea if we'd hung on to one or two of them because they would be worth a fortune now – easier said than done on Third Division wages, though. One of the Doncaster directors was a builder and he helped us to find a place in Sprotborough, a village on the outskirts of the town. The three-bedroomed detached house set us back about £28,000, which was big money at the time, especially as there still wasn't a lot coming in, even though we were both working. Obviously, we didn't have enough for a deposit until we sold the house in Lincoln, so we had a word with the bank manager and he was happy to help out. He must have been a Rovers fan.

The back of the house overlooked Cusworth Hall, a stately home that was open to the public and these days houses the Museum of South Yorkshire Life. A few farmers' fields separated us and that's where I did my running. I used to take Souness out with me. We'd set off down the side of a railway track that ran alongside the approach to Cusworth Hall, then round the grounds and out on to the fields, where wheat was growing. Souness used to love going into the fields looking for pheasants.

About 100 yards from the house a dirt track led back to the road and I always used to put my foot down on the accelerator for one last burst up the track and into the garden. The first time, Souness was messing about in the field when I started to sprint, and he looked up to see me belting away into the distance. He gave chase but I made it home ahead of him – for the first and last time. From then on, he knew exactly where I would start the final sprint and he was ready for me. We'd set off like the clappers up that last stretch and then collapse in a heap on the lawn. He was a fit dog, all right. If that run was three miles for me, it must have been nine miles for Souness with all his excursions into the fields. He was always up for it and going strong at the end.

I felt at home in the dressing room straight away. The first day of pre-season training was spent pounding round Doncaster race-course, which is just across the road from Belle Vue. It was murder – and it didn't get any easier second and third time around. The St Leger meeting was held a few weeks later and traditionally the club had its own marquee on the course. The players were invited – perhaps the free food and booze were the club's way of making up for the agony we endured slogging round the course pre-season. It was a popular day out with the boys and an opportunity for some of them to sink a few pints and have a bet. I just remember feeling sorry for the horses because I understood what they were going through.

Mainly, though, we trained on the recreation ground at Pilkington's Glass factory, a 15-minute drive away from the ground. There were three good pitches looked after by a couple of full-time groundsmen – decent facilities for a club in the lower divisions in those days.

Dave Cusack was a player-manager. A big no-nonsense centre-half, he had presence both on and off the field. When he spoke, you listened. He knew what he wanted from his players and was a good communicator. We all knew where we stood with Dave. Micky Stead, his number two, was also a player and a decent one, too. They worked well together. Micky played directly behind me on the right of a 4-4-2 formation and made sure I saw plenty of the ball. So did the gaffer. He had a good left foot and always aimed his clearances out to me on the right. Belle Vue was a massive pitch – I think it was the biggest in the League at the time – with a good surface. I was young and fit, strong and confident. I knew where the goal was and I felt I was more or less certain of a place in the starting line-up every week.

We had some good players, including Neil Woods, who played up front and later moved on to Rangers, Ipswich, Bradford City and Grimsby, goalkeeper Andy Rhodes and Dave Rushbury at left-back. Jim Dobbin, who'd come down from Celtic when Bremner was in charge, was a very useful midfield player and he went on to have a good career in the First Division with Barnsley and Grimsby. He went back to Doncaster in 1997, early in the season they dropped out of the League. It was the year Barnsley were promoted into the Premiership and soon after the end of the season, Yorkshire Television did a programme talking to the two captains about the contrasting fortunes of their clubs. John Helm came to interview me at home and also talked to Jim. The programme switched between our interviews and action shots of both teams and it was obvious that relegation and Doncaster's plight had hit Jim hard.

I finished up playing in all of Doncaster's 46 league games, scoring 14 goals. In a few months, I went from being the new boy and just another member of the squad to star man, and I soon heard on the grapevine that one or two clubs were watching me. Stories to that effect appeared in the papers, too. Leeds were having a look, no doubt through the eyes of Dave Blakey, Wimbledon were interested, so were Watford and one or two more. One club who never got a mention during the season was Crystal Palace – and that's where I finished up.

The first manager to make a formal approach was Allan Clarke, who was in his second spell at Barnsley after leaving Leeds in 1982 – the same Allan Clarke who, five years earlier, had told me I wouldn't make it. Towards the end of the season, Barnsley offered £50,000 but there was no love lost between the two South Yorkshire clubs at the time and the last thing Rovers wanted was to sell their prize asset to Barnsley. So I stayed put and the speculation died down for a while with people thinking Doncaster weren't going to sell.

The second-to-last away game of the season was against Bolton. They'd struggled over the previous couple of seasons and needed to win to stay up. We'd been mid-table or just below for most of the season but had finished really well and were quietly fancying our chances for the following year. We'd nothing to play for and nothing to lose and were looking forward to a good day out in front of a big crowd. All the pressure was on Bolton. In the end, the turnout wasn't that good but the 4,838 fans gave me some stick from the word go. I was booed just about every time I touched the ball. I couldn't work it out because I'd never let them down as a Bolton player. It didn't bother me, though. In fact, it had the opposite effect and I was pretty fired up all through the game.

Bolton played really well. Phil Neal, the former Liverpool and England full-back, was their player-manager. He slotted in beside the centre-half and they played it around from there. Steve Thompson, my mate while I was at Bolton, played in central midfield and they kept pushing and pushing but the goal wouldn't come – not for Bolton, anyway. With a couple of minutes left, we launched a counter-attack. I was in my usual slot, backing up the front men, and when the ball reached me 15 yards out, I hit it perfectly. Smack! It screamed into the top corner. For a split-second you could have heard a pin drop. That goal sent one of the most famous clubs in the land into the Fourth Division – and was scored by a former Bolton player.

Did I have any regrets? No. It wasn't a bad way of sticking up two fingers to those fans who had jeered me for the previous 88 minutes. I was sorry for Steve Thompson and the staff who had made me feel at home when I played for Wanderers, but relegation is decided over a season, not 90 minutes. I just happened to be the man who dealt the final blow. The press boys were waiting for me when I left the dressing room, wanting to know how it felt to send my old club down. I wasn't used to giving interviews but I made all the right noises about how sorry I was for the club and the players. I received a few phone calls from reporters the following week, asking me to talk about it in more detail, but I didn't want to get involved. These days I'm always happy to give interviews and I don't mince words. Then, I was still feeling my way and didn't want to say the wrong thing. When all was said and done, Bolton weren't the first big club to hit the rocks and they wouldn't be the last.

A few days after the final game, I called into Belle Vue to tie up a few loose ends and was chatting in the office when I got word that the manager wanted to see me. He didn't mess about.

'You'll be getting a couple of calls this afternoon,' he said. 'The first will be from Bobby Gould at Wimbledon, the second from Steve Coppell at Crystal Palace. We're asking £120,000 and they're both prepared to meet that figure. See what they say and let me know what you think.'

It wasn't entirely unexpected because of all the previous speculation but it was still a shock. That fee of £120,000 sounded like a hell of a lot of money. My immediate reaction was a combination of excitement and disappointment. I was thrilled about the chance to move up the ladder and the possibility of playing in the top flight if I chose Wimbledon. On the other hand, I felt a bit upset that Doncaster hadn't put up a fight to keep me. I'd found a club where I really enjoyed myself. I liked Dave Cusack and he liked me. He played me every week and picked me in a position where I could do what I was good at. I enjoyed the training, we lived in a nice home in a lovely area and we'd just about got the house as we wanted it. We weren't loaded with money but we were getting by. Above all, we'd just learned that Sue was pregnant. Even though a transfer would mean playing at a higher level, nothing would have suited us more than to stay at Doncaster for another season. In football, though, things don't always work out like that and when it's time to go, you go.

Gould rang more or less on cue. Wimbledon weren't exactly fashionable but they were in the old First Division – they went on to win the FA Cup in 1988 – so I had to be interested. Gould did a rotten job of selling the club. For starters, the money on offer was poor. OK, it was a lot more than I was getting at Doncaster but not much for a top division London club. I told him it wasn't enough and that Palace were also interested and I'd promised to talk to them as well.

'Look, do you want to play in the First Division or not?' he replied.

'Of course I do, but I've got to be able to make ends meet. My wife's pregnant and won't be working and I need more money.' He told me to take it or leave it, asked me to call him back if I was interested and rang off. I wasn't impressed.

Coppell was completely different. He took time to talk about my season at Doncaster and asked about Sue and how we would handle a move to London. He outlined his plans for me, told me what kind of money I could expect and suggested I should think things over and then give him a call back. Before ringing off, he said, 'Is there anything you want to ask me?'

There was. Before he rang, I'd done a bit of homework on Palace, who were in the Second Division but well fancied for promotion the following season. They seemed to be strong right through the squad and I wondered where I would fit in. I voiced those concerns to Coppell.

'Don't worry about that,' he said. 'That's my business. You leave me to worry about the team, the system and the results. I want to sign you because I think you can do well here. So just come down, play to your ability and enjoy yourself.'

That's what I wanted to hear. I knew that if I went to Palace, there would be no pressure on me because of the £120,000 fee. I would have a manager who would handle that.

That approach typified Coppell. Over the years I've played for a lot of managers who are more than happy to take the plaudits when the team is doing well but will gladly offload the brickbats on to the players when things are going badly. Coppell was never like that. As a player, he'd done it all. He'd won trophies with Manchester United and collected 42 England caps, but there was no big ego in Coppell the manager. When I put the phone down, I had no doubt which club I would be choosing.

A couple of days later, Cusack and I met Coppell at Toddington Service Station on the M1. We shook hands and got straight down to the business of discussing money. I didn't have an agent – not many players did in those days – so I did all my own negotiating. The money on offer was good, far more than I was earning at Doncaster, but I pointed out that house prices were four times higher in London and so was the cost of living. Ron Noades, the Palace chairman, had drawn up a contract that released a bit of money to put down as a deposit on a house and a club car was thrown in, too.

Sue and I talked it over. I suppose I could have dug my heels in and told Doncaster I didn't want to leave just yet, but the more I spoke to Coppell, the keener I was to join Palace, and the prospect of living in London appealed to us both. We had no fear or apprehension – just eager anticipation. Lincoln and Doncaster had been good for us. Now the big-time beckoned and we were ready.

I always kept an eye on how Doncaster were doing, though, and still do. I'd been there for just a season but I could see that the club was a bit of a sleeping giant, with a big enough catchment area to attract reasonable crowds. They'd been a decent Second Division side in the fifties and unearthed a potential superstar in Alick Jeffrey, who broke his leg playing for England Under-23s in 1956 and was never the same player again. The fans were knowledgeable and, with a bit of success on the field, I thought the place might just take off. Cusack was putting together a useful squad and they had a good youth programme in place under Steve Beaglehole, who had a couple of years as manager in the early nineties. One of the players to roll off his production line was Brian Deane, who made a name for himself with Sheffield United. He went on to do well with Leeds, Middlesbrough, Leicester and West Ham and also had a spell in Portugal with Benfica. He was just starting out at Belle Vue when I was there. So were Mark Rankine and Neil Richardson, who both played a lot of league football.

The Doncaster Rovers I left in the summer of 1987 should have been the basis of a strong football club. Yet ten years later, Rovers came within a whisker of collapse and reached the point where relegation to the Conference in 1998 was regarded as making the best of a bad job. I suppose the seeds of their collapse were being sown while I was there. A lot of people at the club were Doncaster Rovers through and through. They desperately wanted Rovers to do well and were not interested in personal kudos. Unfortunately, others saw it differently. It seemed that some were in it for themselves, happy to take out more than they put in.

If John Ryan, the current owner, had not arrived on the scene in 1998, shortly after relegation to the Conference, Doncaster would have gone out of business. Ryan was a lifelong Doncaster fan and you could see a mile off that the only thing that mattered to him was success for the club. He appointed a forward-thinking young manager in Dave Penney and left him to get on with what he was good at – managing a football team. Meanwhile, Ryan stuck to what he knew best, the business and commercial side of the operation. He put a structure in place that gave the club a real platform for success and, unlike so many businessmen who come into the game, he wasn't looking for personal glory.

It never ceases to amaze me that men with a good business record come into football thinking they can wave a magic wand and turn a club around, making a load of money in the process. It rarely happens that way because football isn't just any old business – it's about people and opinions, and change is usually a slow and sometimes painful process. In the end, as we've seen so often, those self-appointed saviours decide they've had enough and walk away, usually leaving the club in a bigger financial mess than when they arrived. Call me old-fashioned but I believe anyone taking over a club has to have a real feel for that club and be prepared to put something in without much prospect of taking anything out. A football club isn't a rich man's plaything – it belongs to the community and, above all, to the fans.

Doncaster recovered and came bouncing out of the Conference at the end of the 2002–03 season. The following year I played against them for Boston and they were by far and away the best side in Division Three, going on to win promotion at the end of the season. Doncaster are a shining example to every struggling club in the land, and vibrant proof that relegation from the Nationwide League is not the end of the world. In fact, if the authorities had any sense, they would make the Conference an official bottom division and introduce three up and three down with what is now Coca-Cola League Two. Two-thirds of the Conference sides are already full-time with a professional structure on and off the field that is just about every bit as good as most clubs in the lower reaches of the League. If and when they are finally promoted, they will be fully geared-up for the challenge. Most sides promoted into the League have done well, yet every season we hear how clubs are facing the 'spectre' of relegation to the Conference. That's so wrong. Relegation should not be seen as a stigma because the evidence shows that clubs are going into a league that is not too different from the one they are leaving.

6 SUMMONED TO THE PALACE

I CAUSED A SENSATION ON MY FIRST DAY AT CRYSTAL PALACE but not necessarily for the right reasons. Blame my Ford Capri. When I swept into the training ground in Mitcham, everything stopped, heads turned and for a few seconds the world stood still. I seem to recall that even Ian Wright and Mark Bright were lost for words, and that didn't happen too often. As far as I was concerned, the Capri was everything an upwardly mobile young pro could aspire to. It was a bright red automatic with a powerful engine, sunroof, radio-cassette player, leather seats, the works. OK, it maybe looked a bit down on its luck and the exhaust wasn't all it might have been, but it had been a class above most of the motors in the car park at Belle Vue, Doncaster. It didn't cut much ice in Mitcham, though.

Andy Gray, who was to play alongside me in midfield and went on to appear for England, was the first to react. After shaking hands, he offered to have a chat with a few of his mates and arrange for someone to torch the Capri if I agreed to split the insurance pay-out. I assumed he was joking. That was just the first example of the non-stop stick the new kid from up north was to receive about his wheels from his team-mates on that first day of pre-season training.

I suppose they had a point. The local garage owner in Doncaster, who used to service our cars in exchange for a few match tickets, had already labelled the Capri a death trap. I'd gone through several motors since my first purchase, the Citroen Visa that carried me, my mum and my L plates across the Pennines from Bradford to Bolton. I was never much good at bargaining and always seemed to get the rough end of the deal, lumbered with a worse car than the one I'd traded in. The Capri was last in a none too illustrious line of dodgy deals that had also included the acquisition of a Ford Escort and a big old 2.6 litre Rover, a real gas guzzler.

Near the end of the previous season, the garage had been sponsoring a game at Belle Vue and when the owner presented me with the Man of the Match award afterwards, I took the opportunity to raise the subject of my Capri.

'If I bring it in, will you have a look at the brakes?' I asked. 'They seem to be grinding a bit. I don't think it's much to worry about, though.'

'Aye, no problem, lad. Bring it in on Monday and we'll have a look.'

I did as he asked but when I called to find out how things were progressing, he seemed less than impressed with my knowledge of motor engineering.

'Brakes, what brakes?' he thundered. 'This car hasn't got any bloody brakes. The shoes have completely worn away. You're driving a death trap.'

The necessary repairs were carried out and the Capri eventually passed a late fitness test to transport Sue and me down the M1 to start our new life in the big city. A club car had been part of the Palace deal, so the Capri was destined for the great scrapyard in the sky soon after we arrived.

Mind you, Palace's idea of a sponsored car wasn't exactly what I'd had in mind. At the very least, I'd expected something along the lines of the Capri but ten years younger, something like the sleek models that adorned the car park at the training ground and transported my new team-mates to and from work. Instead, when I strolled on to the forecourt of one of the local used-car dealers, I was shown a Vauxhall Chevette with plenty of miles on the clock. Colour? Champagne gold. I wasn't impressed, so I rang Ron Noades and explained my predicament.

'I'm very grateful and all that,' I said, 'but I was hoping for something a bit more stylish. I don't mind putting in a bit of extra cash if it means a better car.'

Ron was happy with that arrangement. I agreed to put up an extra five hundred quid and, after trundling around in the Chevette for a week, I went back to the garage and collected a Vauxhall Cavalier – younger and with considerably more street cred than its predecessor.

Despite the Capri – or perhaps because of it – I fitted in quickly with the Palace players. I wasn't the only new boy. Steve Coppell had also signed Geoff Thomas from Crewe for £50,000. Geoff had started his career at Rochdale and after leaving Palace, moved on to Wolves, Forest, Barnsley and Notts County before returning to Crewe. He appeared in nearly 600 games and won nine England caps. In 2003, he was diagnosed as suffering from leukaemia and after undergoing a bone marrow transplant, devoted himself to raising money for leukaemia charities. In 2005, he completed the Tour de France course, a distance of nearly 2,200 miles, raising over £150,000. Later that year, he received the Helen Rollason Award, presented annually at the BBC Sports Personality of the Year show to a sportsperson who has shown courage and achievement in the face of adversity.

Geoff was from Manchester and we had to stand firm against a barrage of mickey-taking about our northern accents. The players seemed to see me in particular as a bit of an 'eh bah gum' rough diamond from Yorkshire and I soon acquired the nickname Casper, courtesy of Billy Casper, the central character in the film 'Kes' about a Barnsley lad who trained his own kestrel.

It was the first time I'd been part of a dressing room that included a lot of black players and quite a few people outside the club asked if I was finding it hard to settle in. That may seem a strange question now but my time at Selhurst Park coincided with an era when racism was rife among supporters at quite a few clubs, and black players were frequent victims of taunts from the crowd. Race was a talking point in football, so it was a valid question, but in the Palace dressing room, colour was never an issue. However, this was very much a London club, with many of the players born in and around the capital, and I was aware that, as a northerner, I was moving in to their territory. It was up to me to fit in with them, not the other way round. Geoff and I took all the jokes on the chin, gave a few back in return and got on with the job. We must have played it right because we were soon accepted into what was a close-knit dressing room.

However, while I adapted quickly to my new surroundings, it was clearly not going to be easy for Sue – five months pregnant and a long way from home. Normally, she would have had her family around to keep an eye on her but although both sets of parents visited as often as they could, it was a long journey from Yorkshire and basically, we were on our own. Having your first child is a big thing at the best of times. To be 250 miles away from home and family and trying to fit into new surroundings made it even harder.

At first we rented a one-bedroomed flat on the outskirts of Croydon, more or less in the middle of nowhere. It wasn't a problem for me because I was off at crack of dawn to join the commuters in the ten-mile, bumper-to-bumper crawl to Mitcham that could take anything up to an hour and a half. Sue was stuck on her own all day in a pokey flat in an unfamiliar town, relying on public transport to get around. We didn't stick it for long and soon moved to a two-bedroomed house in Shirley, a few miles down the road from Croydon. It was nothing special, with pretty basic furniture and fittings, and we missed having our own things around us. Both rental homes were a far cry from the home we had left behind in Doncaster. We didn't know the area or the shops, and had to go out to buy all the gear for the baby when I got home from training – although the club shop helped us out with a load of Crystal Palace babygrows and bibs.

Aimee was born in May Day Hospital, Croydon, at eight o'clock in the morning on Friday, 27 November 1987. It would have been nice if she'd been born back home in Yorkshire but that was obviously going to be a non-starter. I was always determined to be present at the birth, even though in those days quite a lot of prospective dads still preferred to leave it all to their wives. That was never going to be our style. Not being there would have been a crime. I'd been the only person around for Sue for the last few months of her pregnancy and I wasn't going to let her down when she really needed me.

Being there when Aimee was born was a life-changing experience for me. Like most men, I vaguely appreciated that giving birth was a tough business for a woman but until I witnessed the trauma that Sue went through, I'd absolutely no idea of what was involved. I knew she was tough – but not that tough! I wouldn't have missed it for the world and I've never been able to understand why some men don't want to be present. Similarly, I always felt it was important for me to play an active part in bringing up both Aimee and Lois, who was born five years later when I was at Barnsley. Nappy changing and feeding bottles were never a problem for me.

Sue had gone into hospital soon after I arrived home from training on the Thursday afternoon. I called Steve Coppell and explained the situation, saying that I might be struggling to make training on the Friday, and Saturday's game against Leeds United, of all people, was also looking a bit iffy. Steve just said, 'Get yourself down to the hospital and stay with Sue, never mind about training or Saturday. We'll sort that out. If everything goes OK and you want to come in on Friday and do a bit of work on your own, that's fine by me. Then give me a ring and see how you feel about playing on Saturday.'

The birth went well. I rang up Sue's parents straight away and then gave Mum and Dad a call to give them the good news. Unfortunately, they were out and they'd left my nan, my mother's mum, in charge. Her memory was starting to go but I told her the news and she was thrilled to bits. I repeated it for good measure.

'Nan,' I said, 'Sue's had a little girl and they're both fine. Have you got that?'

'Yes, I'll tell your mum and dad when they get in.'

I felt reasonably confident that she had taken the message on board and I was able to do a bit of training as planned on the Friday. I felt fine about playing and told Steve I would be OK. He named me in the starting line-up and opposite me, in midfield for Leeds, was a young lad called David Batty, playing his second first-team game at the age of 18. Ten years later, we'd be crossing swords again in the Premiership.

We won 3–0 and, after the game, I rang home again. This time Dad answered.

'What about the good news, then?' I asked.

'Yes, 3–0 against Leeds, great result.'

'No, not that. What about the baby?'

'Baby?'

'Yes, Sue's had a little girl. I rang and told Nan yesterday.'

'Well she never told us.'

Soon after Aimee was born, we finally moved into a house of our own in Caterham, just off junction seven of the M25 and on the main road from London to Brighton. Back in Doncaster, we'd paid £28,000 for our three-bedroomed detached in a country village and lived there for a year. Now we were paying something like £80,000 for a two-bedroomed, end-of-terrace property. Welcome to the real world, London-style! There were six houses in the terrace and up north we would have called them weavers' cottages, but I don't suppose too many weavers had lived in that part of Surrey. We loved Caterham. It had much more of a small-town atmosphere than Croydon and some nice shops within walking distance. Anneka Rice, who was a major television personality at the time, had a place in Caterham-on-the-Hill, just up the road. A little old couple, Connie and Dave, lived next door and the day we moved in they called round with a big tray of tea and biscuits. They'd got out the best china. They were a lovely couple and really took to us. They kept an eye on Sue when I was off on away trips.

I'd never really expected to play for a London club. As a kid, London meant Wembley, the Cup final, England international matches and huge clubs such as Arsenal and Spurs. I'd always set my sights at a top northern club because that's where my roots were, but it didn't take us long to adapt to London life. Just about every Sunday, we'd drive into the city, park the car near Waterloo Bridge and stroll into the West End. Covent Garden was our favourite. We loved all the different shops, market stalls and cafés and we'd wander round for hours. Sometimes we almost had to stop and pinch ourselves to make sure it was all really happening. A few years earlier, I'd run away from Nottingham Forest because I was homesick; soon afterwards we'd been delighted to move from Lincoln to Doncaster because it meant we could be nearer home and our folks. Yet here we were, ambling around central London, almost as if we owned the place.

The football side was great. The standard of coaching was higher than anything I had experienced before and I learned quickly, moving on to a new level as a player. I had a lot of respect for Steve Coppell from day one and I got on well with his assistant, Ian Evans, too. Ian had played and coached at Barnsley, so he knew northern ways and took to me immediately. Mind you, he wasn't averse to joining in the general stick that flew in the direction of Casper. Ian was tactically very aware and his training sessions were always organised and interesting but perhaps his greatest asset was his man-management. Some pretty strong, hotheaded characters inhabited that dressing room, resulting in quite a few flare-ups. Ian was a master at defusing the most difficult situations. He earned a lot of respect from all the players.

Pre-season work started with the usual two weeks of running and building up the fitness levels. In those days, pre-season really was a hard slog. Players would report back after three months and be thrown straight into a regime of long-distance running. At Lincoln, we used to run around the local municipal golf course, dodging wayward drives and trying to avoid horses that had strayed on to the course from the nearby travellers' camp. There was also an equine element at Doncaster, thanks to all that running round the racecourse. Basically, clubs were trying to make players fit for a season in the space of two weeks, and all that work in such a short time can't have done us any good. I always worked hard at keeping fit over the summer and did quite a bit of groundwork on my own, but some players used to hit the beer and chips as soon as the last ball was kicked and report back for training overweight and out of condition. We had a laugh about it. Nowadays, players have to be more disciplined and woe betide anyone who reports back carrying a few extra pounds and an extra inch around the waistline. The emphasis is on a much lighter, more gradual build-up to produce fitness levels that last a whole season.

After the first two weeks, we flew off to a training camp in Sweden. That trip was different from anything I'd experienced before. I'd played abroad with the youth team at Forest and travelled to Italy with the first team, but this time I was a fully fledged member of the first-team squad and a major signing into the bargain. We played half a dozen games, including a match against Malmo, who were one of the top sides in Europe and had been beaten by Forest in the final of the European Cup eight years earlier. These were serious matches against decent opposition, starting with non-league sides and moving up the ladder to the Malmo game. At my previous two clubs, pre-season warm-up games usually involved playing against local part-time sides, most of whom were more interested in kicking full-time pros than providing competitive match practice. The Swedes adopted a completely different approach and technically they were good. When we returned to England, we were just about ready, physically and mentally.

One thing that really came across during pre-season was the harder, more professional attitude of my team-mates. At Lincoln or Doncaster, I could miscue a cross or make a hash of a through ball without too much comeback from the rest of the lads. Expectations were not too high and if the cross wasn't spot on, too bad. The manager would have a go at half-time or the end of the game but that was usually as far as it went. That changed big-time at Palace, particularly where Wright and Bright were concerned. If they were making runs and not receiving the ball, they would let me know in no uncertain terms – on the pitch and in the dressing room afterwards. No one minced words and at first it took me back a bit, but it was nothing personal – just an expression of their professionalism and will-to-win. Before long, I was giving out the verbals, too. It was a ruthless, cut-throat environment, very different from the football world I had grown up in, and it didn't take me long to realise that I would have to be part of it if I was going to climb any higher up the ladder.

I was back in Yorkshire for my first league game as a Crystal Palace player, against Huddersfield Town at the old Leeds Road stadium. Sue's dad had always been a very big Town fan so needless to say there was strong support from the family when I emerged from the players' tunnel. Our starting line-up, in 4-4-2 formation, was George Wood; Gary Stebbing, Jim Cannon, Gavin Nebbeling, Paul Brush; Neil Redfearn, Andy Gray, Geoff Thomas, John Salako; Ian Wright, Mark Bright. Gary O'Reilly was the sub. Alan Pardew, John Pemberton and David Burke were also around during that first season, so we had some decent players.

The pitch was immaculate, just like a bowling green, and I can still see those famous blue-and-white striped shirts emerging from the tunnel. We were in our away strip, all yellow, and I remember thinking it didn't look much compared with their strip. Two goals from Bright should have been enough but Huddersfield pulled a couple back and it ended 2–2. Simon Trevitt came on as sub and scored their first goal. He was a useful player and would have made a big-money move to Coventry soon afterwards but for a serious knee injury. He later became a postman in Cleckheaton.

The Huddersfield game wasn't the last time we found ourselves struggling defensively that season. With Wright and Bright up front and me, Gray, Thomas and Salako in midfield, we were always going to score goals. We were a bit too attack-minded for our own good and we left gaps that were inevitably going to be exploited at that level. Coppell believed in attacking football, even to the point where team talks tended to be more about how we would demolish the opposition than an assessment of their strengths and weaknesses. Often we'd gallop into a lead only to be hauled back – a two-goal lead never felt enough. At Leicester, for example, we drew 4–4 after leading 4–2 at half-time. At

Blackburn, in my second season, we lost 5–4 after leading 4–1. Great stuff for the fans but not good news for Palace.

The squad was full of top players and real characters. If I'd been a betting man, I would have put a load of money there and then on Ian Wright going on to become a major force at the highest level and playing for England. I would class him as a great player, and if you don't learn from people like that you're wasting your time. If I was to list all the players I have learned from in my career, Wright would be near the top, even though he wasn't much older than me.

He had what I used to call likeable arrogance, and was totally confident in his own ability on and off the field. He had massive talent and was the quickest player I'd ever seen. I'd knock the ball into the channels for him and sometimes he could give a defender a 10- or 15-yard start and still win the race. Talk about turning an average ball into a good one! His enthusiasm was infectious and to be around him in a working environment was a football education. He helped to change my outlook on my own career. As a player, he had so many assets, first and foremost his blistering pace – and he could also produce such high skills at pace. That took some doing but it was only part of his armoury. What people often overlook about Wright is his bravery. He had the courage of a lion and if he thought he might score, he would go in with his head or feet, apparently oblivious to the risk of physical damage. He would chase down defenders relentlessly and I lost count of the number of times he turned what looked like an easy clearance and a lost cause for Palace into possession in the danger zone. He used to go sliding in on defenders, hook the ball away and then he'd be up on his feet like lightning and homing in on goal. No wonder he went on to play 33 games for England and become the leading scorer in Arsenal's history, until overtaken by Thierry Henry.

He and Bright were a tremendous pair – the classic combination of the big strong front man alongside a player with genuine pace. Opposing sides would sometimes play five at the back or employ a sweeper to keep them quiet but it was virtually impos-

sible. Bright finished my first season with 25 league goals, Wright
with 20, and our total of 86 goals in 44 games was evidence of the
threat they posed. They knew they were a class act and weren't
afraid to let everyone else know it, too. After a while, I didn't
need to look up to know where they would be. I'd simply knock
the ball into the danger areas and one of them would be there,
Wright moving on to a through ball, Bright peeling off at the far
stick to wait for the cross. I knew what they wanted; they knew
I could provide it. It gave a new dimension to my game. It was
like telepathy.

A few years after I left Palace, when I was at Barnsley, I was
chatting to our centre-half Mark Smith on the bus to a match and
the subject of Wright and Bright cropped up. Mark said, 'Do you
remember that day when you were at Palace and I was at
Plymouth? You beat us 5–1. I was marking Bright and struggling
a bit. In fact, I was struggling a hell of a lot. After about twenty
minutes, Wright called over to Bright, "Come on, don't hog him
all to yourself, let me have him for a while!" They switched positions and Wright scored a hat-trick.'

The last time I came up against Wright was when I was at
Barnsley and we played Arsenal in the Premiership. They beat
us 5–1 at Highbury and he notched the last goal. We shook
hands at the final whistle but I didn't really have an opportunity for a proper chat before the Barnsley team coach set off. The
following season, I moved to Charlton and who should be
kingpin in the dressing room at The Valley? None other than
Mark Bright – only this time there was a difference. Bright was
on the way down the ladder by then while I was the million-
pound new boy – and I wasn't going to let him forget that for
a single second!

Off the field, everyone seemed to like Bright, both at Palace
and Charlton. He always had a smile on his face and as soon as
he walked in the room, people seemed to cheer up. You always
felt relaxed in his company, even as the minutes ticked away to
kick-off. It's no surprise at all to me that he and Wright have gone
on to forge careers for themselves in the media and entertainment

worlds. They always were larger than life characters but, above all, they were superb professionals.

George Wood, the former Everton and Scotland keeper, was another character. George was a keen bird-watcher and thought nothing of spending hours in the countryside, peering through his binoculars, waiting for a sighting of some rare species. He wore contact lenses when he wasn't playing and I found out the hard way that without them, he struggled a bit with his long-distance vision. The first time we practised set-pieces, I was instructed to stand in front of George at the near post for a corner. I was vaguely aware that the rest of the lads were trying hard not to laugh but couldn't work out what was going on.

The fashion in those days was for in-swinging corners to the near post, hoping for a flick on across the face of the goal. The near-post defender and keeper were there to make sure it didn't happen. So there I was, stationed at the near post, and in came the corner. The next thing I knew, I was picking myself up off the floor after being knocked almost senseless by George. Because of his sight problems, he couldn't pick up the flight of the ball early on, so he just went for anything that moved – in this case, my head. I later discovered that I wasn't the first player to receive a battering from my own keeper and I certainly wasn't the last. He struggled with shots struck from any kind of distance but his reflexes were spot on and he almost always got out of jail with a brilliant save. He'd have been the best keeper in the world if he'd been able to see the ball properly!

Gavin Nebbeling was another one-off. He was from Johannesburg, stood over 6ft tall and weighed in at 12 stone plus. He was what the match programme writers used to call a no-nonsense centre-back. In other words, if it moved, he kicked it. In those days, the pre-match warm-up was less intense than it is today and a lot of players had their own routine as kick-off approached. At Selhurst Park, there was a big open space under the stand and behind the dressing rooms, and before going out to warm up with the rest of the lads, Gavin and I used to go in there. He'd say, 'Come on, Redders, give me some headers,' and I'd throw him a few gentle lobs. Gradually, I'd start to throw the ball a bit harder, then harder still and then at full pace as Gavin wound himself up for the kick-off. He'd send these rocket headers flying back at me, I'd catch the ball, hurl it back in his direction and he'd return it with interest. He must have had a head like a rock.

Unfortunately, the ceiling, which was held in place by a series of concrete struts, wasn't too high and one day the inevitable happened. Gavin soared feet off the ground for his final pre-match header but instead of making contact with the ball, cracked his nut on a concrete strut. He collapsed in a heap and, to my horror, I saw blood pouring from a big gash in his forehead. I dashed into the dressing room and shouted, 'Quick, Gav's cracked his head open!' There wasn't much more than half an hour to kick-off and David West, our physio, rushed into the warm-up area, where a dazed Nebbeling was rising groggily to his feet. David took one look at the damage and sent for the doctor. I couldn't see that Gavin had any chance of playing but the man himself had other ideas. 'Put some stitches in,' he growled. The doctor obliged and Gavin went off to rinse away the dried blood. A few minutes later, he took his place in the line-up as we prepared to leave the dressing room and within minutes of kick-off, he was powering away the clearance headers. Over the years, I've seen plenty of players leave the field with blood seeping from a cut head. Gavin was the first and only person who actually kicked off in that condition – tough character.

We had a good season. We won 22 of our 44 games but a tally of 13 defeats and nine draws spoke volumes. We finished sixth, three points behind Villa, who were runners-up, and two points behind Blackburn in fifth place. That would have been good enough for a play-off slot these days but in 1988, the top two were promoted automatically and the next three clubs played off with the club finishing fourth from bottom in the top division. (That year, the bottom three clubs in the First Division were automatically relegated.)

So we missed out. We would have been more than capable of holding our own in the top flight, even with our dodgy defending.

Wright, Thomas, Salako and Gray all went on to play for England and there was a lot of talent right through the side. I felt that my game had moved on to a new plane over the season and I said cheerio to the lads for the summer break confident that Neil Redfearn and Palace would do even better next time around. I was right on one score. Palace were promoted via the play-offs in June 1989 but by then I was a Watford player. I had made just 15 league appearances for Palace at the start of that season, so I wasn't eligible for a promotion medal but the club had a special plaque made for me. A smashing gesture.

7   WATFORD GAP YEAR

ON THURSDAY, 22 AUGUST 1988, I HANDED A WRITTEN TRANSFER request to Steve Coppell. I had started the first five games of the season and been substituted three times, even though I'd performed well. I was young, ambitious, naïve and a bit hot-headed and that's a pretty volatile combination. I decided enough was enough. It was the first time that I'd really crossed swords with a manager but it certainly wouldn't be the last.

That first transfer request marked the beginning of a three-year phase when I was either playing regular first-team football or knocking on the manager's door, asking difficult questions. All through my career I've played alongside people who were content to be in and out of the first team. They'd have a run of nine or ten games, find themselves on the sidelines for a few matches before coming back for another nine or ten towards the back end of the season. They'd settle for around 20 games a season plus a few substitute appearances and not make any bother as long as it meant another contract. They were happy to accept the tag of 'good clubman'.

Not me. I was as good a clubman as the next person but if I was fit, I expected to play. My target at the start of each season was to have my name on the appearance list in the programme 46 times by the beginning of May. From my point of view, I was easy to please. All I wanted to do was play first-team football and when that was happening, I wasn't a minute's bother. If I was left out or substituted on a regular basis, I would want to know why. As I saw it, I was either in the starting line-up or on my bike and if I wasn't in the first team, it was time to start making noises.

That was because I never doubted my ability and I was always confident I would succeed. I believed there was nothing I couldn't achieve if I was given the chance, and when I was denied the opportunity, I reacted aggressively. That level of confidence in a young player can seem like conceit and perhaps some managers picked up the wrong impression and started to doubt their instincts. They signed me because of what they saw on the pitch but maybe when they encountered me as a person, they became a little wary. Perhaps they failed to recognise my attitude for what it was – ambition, not arrogance.

For me, it was a question of pride. No doubt Coppell, and later Steve Harrison at Watford and Joe Royle at Oldham, had a different take on the situation. They probably saw it as pig-headedness or downright stupidity. I realise now that in the space of three seasons at three clubs, I acquired a reputation for being an awkward customer. Managers saw me as a good player and, without boasting, they were right. At that level, I could add some-thing to any side and score a few goals. They also saw a player who was likely to be truculent and hard to work with, and they probably had a point but, for me, everything was black and white.

I couldn't see the bigger picture. As an ambitious young player, I was totally focused on my own game and all that mattered was being involved every week. When I moved on to the coaching side, I saw plenty of young players knocking on the manager's door. I knew what the expressions on their faces meant and I realised how I must have looked all those years ago. I had to resist the temptation to pull them to one side and tell them I'd been down the same path myself and it would probably all end in tears. It's a lesson they have to learn for themselves. You can't put an old head on young shoulders.

Nowadays I realise that there is always a middle ground and,

A chip off the old block? Dad (left) in action for Bradford Park Avenue against Grimsby Town in the early fifties

Watch the birdie! Posing for the camera in my primary school days

Birkenshaw Middle School. That's me, third from the right on the front row. Steve Parrish, our keeper, later played rugby league for Bradford Northern

On the mark for Watford against Derby in the FA Cup. The goalkeeper out of shot was Peter Shilton and my team-mates are Nigel Gibbs (left), Tim Sherwood and John McClelland

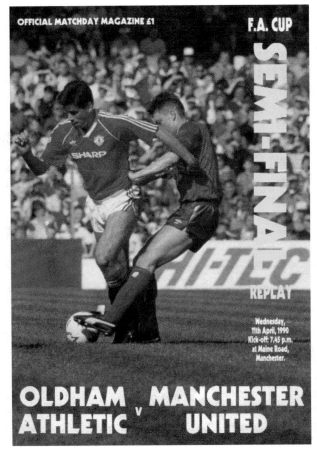

The match programme for Oldham's FA Cup semi-final replay against Manchester United, 1990, featuring my challenge on United's Neil Webb

in many ways, that's the sensible place to be. I'm wiser now and I see that I should have played the managers at their own game, bided my time and waited for an opportunity to show them they were wrong. Instead, I went at it like a bull at a gate and upset people in the process. In my defence, though, every decision I made, rightly or wrongly, was my own decision and I didn't rely on other people to do my dirty work. I was ready to fight and scrap for what I believed in and I didn't stir up trouble behind the manager's back. If I had anything to say, I said it face to face.

As a manager, would I sign the young Neil Redfearn? Yes, because I would know I was getting a good player. I would do my research and be told there was a bit of baggage. He would be knocking on my door if he wasn't in the team, but I would back my ability to handle him and demonstrate that I was on his side. If I could make him an ally, I would have found a real asset. If I rubbed him up the wrong way, he would be a headache. I could always get rid of him if things didn't work out. If Count Dracula was the best striker in the world, a guaranteed 30 goals a season man, I'd sign him. It might upset people but it would be up to me to find a way to make people like him for as long as I needed him. When he'd served his purpose, I'd move him on.

There were no sign of storms on the horizon when I reported back for the start of the 1988–89 season. We'd had a family break in Spain but stayed in Caterham for most of the summer, getting to know the area a bit better and spending a lot of time in London. Aimee always came along. There was never any question of leaving her with a babysitter for the afternoon. She was part of the family so she came with us. As time went by I became a master in the art of negotiating escalators and swing doors with a buggy and we discovered a network of places in central London where bottle-feeding and nappy changing were accepted without raised eyebrows from staff and customers. It was a good summer. We popped up north a couple of times and both sets of grandparents came down to visit and check up on Aimee's progress. We were feeling more and more at home in our new surroundings.

I trained regularly to make sure I was in decent nick for pre-season and when we reported back in July, I was ready for lift-off. I wasn't the new boy this time. I was part of the set-up and, one way or another, I was convinced this was going to be a big season for me and for Palace. We started with a 1–1 draw against Chelsea at Selhurst Park. I scored the goal. In the following game, a 2–0 defeat at Watford, I was substituted. I was disappointed but decided not to make a fuss, assuming it would be a one-off. Two games later, I was taken off again during a 1–1 draw with Shrewsbury at Selhurst Park.

I couldn't understand why. It seemed so harsh, particularly as in those days teams had only one substitute on the bench. In both games, I'd been playing well but for some reason I seemed to have become the main option when Coppell decided to make a change. If I'd been playing badly, I could have accepted the decision, got my head down and worked hard to put things right, but I'd been having a good time and it seemed so unfair. I was playing for a side that was clearly going places and I wanted to be part of it, one of the main men, not the odd man out. My reaction was to knock on the manager's door on the Monday, just before the team bus set off for a midweek game at Sunderland the following day.

'Have you got a minute, Gaffer?'

'Course, Redders, what can I do for you?'

'You keep taking me off,' I replied, coming straight to the point.

'Yes.'

'But I'm playing well.'

'Yes, you are.'

'So why do you keep taking me off?'

'Well, sometimes I need to change things around tactically and that might involve bringing off a player who is doing well.'

'I don't get that. Why not take someone off who isn't having a good game?'

Patiently, Steve explained the previous weekend's tactical switch and why I was the only person who could logically be taken off to accommodate the change. He assured me how well I was doing and after 20 minutes, I walked out of the room agreeing with everything he'd said and feeling like a million dollars again.

We drew 1–1 at Sunderland, I played well and I was taken off again. We had the Wednesday off but after training on Thursday, I was knocking on Coppell's door once more. This time I was armed with a written transfer request that I plonked down on his desk. I told him I was unhappy about being substituted three times in the first five games, even though I'd been performing well. I didn't accept his reasons and I wanted away. He didn't try to dissuade me.

For nine league games after handing Coppell my written transfer request, I played out of my skin. Perhaps that was because I believed I had a cause, a point to prove to the manager and anyone out there who might be considering an offer – and surprise, surprise, I stayed on for the full 90 minutes in every game. I was aware that several clubs were keeping an eye on my situation, including Watford, Bournemouth and Blackburn. Funnily enough, Blackburn seem to have made enquiries about me just about every time I've been available but for one reason or another, I've never signed on the dotted line. My 15th and last Palace appearance of the season was at Bournemouth on 12 November. We lost 2–0 – and I was substituted.

Early the following week, Coppell called me in. He said Watford had offered £175,000 and the Palace board were prepared to accept that figure. He said he didn't want me to go, that Palace were going places and I would be better off staying. He also said he understood my reasons and if I saw a move to Watford as a better chance of regular first-team football, he wouldn't stand in my way. I liked and respected Coppell and I now see that he had my best interests at heart. I also realise he was probably right and I was wrong.

When I signed for Watford in November 1988, they were top of the old Second Division, ten places above Palace. On the face of it, I'd made a good move but I was perhaps too young to realise that I could easily be facing exactly the same scenario in the not too distant future. Watford, like Palace, were an ambitious, progressive club with a strong squad. One blip in form would open the door for another member of the squad to show what he could do. No one was certain of a first-team place.

I linked up with Steve Harrison at a junction off the M25 and followed him all the way back to Vicarage Road. We went into his office to discuss terms. There were no problems, I signed the contract and once the formalities had been completed, we started chatting about the club in more general terms. Inevitably, the conversation turned to the chairman, a gentleman by the name of Elton John. Steve told me what a great guy Elton was, how easy he was to get along with and how good he was for the club. Elton always liked to meet new signings but he wasn't around that day. So Steve opened a drawer in his desk and said, 'You'd better have these instead.' He produced a couple of LPs, signed by the man himself. They must have been worth a bob or two and Sue and I reckoned they were a pretty good welcome gift. I was lucky to get my P45 when I left 14 months later.

I met Elton soon afterwards. Despite the stage image, he was a pretty ordinary, down-to-earth guy around the club and kept a very low profile. Apart from wearing big fedora hats he never dressed in anything remotely resembling his stage outfits. At first I was in awe of him. Well, you would be, wouldn't you? He was a genuine megastar, known all over the world. I'd always liked his music and been a fan so it was odd to find him stopping me in the corridor to pass the time of day or ask how the family were settling in. That was typical of him. He seemed genuinely interested, although obviously he was closer to the players who had been around a long time.

When he wasn't touring abroad, he never missed a game, home or away. He always used to come in the dressing room before a match and wish us luck, and he'd pop in afterwards, either to congratulate or commiserate or have a quiet word with the manager – all very low-key. He knew his football too, more than a lot of chairmen I've been involved with, but he never made any attempt to interfere with tactics, team selection or anything like that. Basically, he was a fan who happened to have enough money to bankroll his football club. Over the years, he did a tremendous job for Watford. He kept his finger on the pulse and when I fell out with the manager after a few months, he must have known what was happening but he never let it affect his relationship with me.

The name of Graham Taylor still dominated everything at Watford. He had lifted the club from obscurity to the upper reaches of the old First Division. They had finished second in 1983, qualified for Europe and reached the FA Cup final the following year. They were big news. When he left to take over at Aston Villa in 1987, Watford brought in another big name, Dave Bassett, but that didn't work out. Bassett stayed for a year or so and when he left, Harrison took over. I suspect that in many ways, he was trying to copy the Taylor style.

I went straight into the side and played 11 league games in a row. We won five, drew three and lost three. Then I began to feel that the manager was becoming a bit cool towards me. Why? I've no idea. He had gone out and paid £175,000 for me. Surely that meant he rated me as a player and had looked into my background as a person. There was no bad blood between us but I was left out after being substituted in a 3–0 home defeat by Nottingham Forest in the fifth round of the FA Cup. I'd played in 17 league and Cup matches on the bounce, including a third-round dust-up with Newcastle that went to three replays, and I thought I'd done well, but after a while it was pretty obvious that Harrison wasn't going to pick me again in the immediate future.

I was tempted to tackle him about it but, in the end, decided to take it on the chin. I went away to play in the reserves and did well. By any standards, my performances earned me a recall but I knew it wasn't on the cards and I resigned myself to playing out the season on the outside looking in.

Then, out of the blue, Harrison called me up for the final league game at Oxford. I couldn't believe it but perhaps he saw how well I was playing and decided I might just be the man to make the difference in the play-offs. We were virtually certain of our place but a win would guarantee a home game in the second leg. We rolled Oxford over 4–0 to earn a play-off semi-final against Blackburn. We drew 0–0 at their place and then, after Simon Garner had put Blackburn in front early on in the second leg, I equalised before half-time with an absolute cracker. I picked up a loose ball 25 yards out, hit it perfectly and Terry Gennoe, Blackburn's goalkeeper, never had a chance as it flew into the top corner after taking a tiny deflection. That's how it finished, though, and we went out on the away goals rule. Blackburn lost to Palace in the final.

When I arrived home after the match, Sue was waiting. 'Come and watch your goal on the telly,' she said. I wasn't that bothered, to be honest, but she insisted and switched on the video. There I was, collecting the loose ball, hammering it past Gennoe, turning away in celebration and being mobbed by my team-mates as the fans went wild. Then the camera switched to the bench where the celebrations were less than ecstatic. Perhaps they didn't want to get carried away too much too soon and wanted the players to keep their feet on the ground, but it looked to me as if they were saying, 'Yes, we wanted to score – but why did it have to be him?' It was weird.

I expected to be moving on during the summer but nothing had happened by the time we reported back for pre-season training. Neither Harrison nor I said anything. An unwritten understanding seemed to exist between us that we'd draw a line under the events of the previous season and start with a clean sheet. I'd worked hard through the summer to make sure I was really firing when the season began. I hardly had a day off and if I'd competed in the 10,000 metres at the AAA Championships, I wouldn't have been far off the pace.

What's more, I was trying to convince myself that I couldn't spend my life falling out with the manager because that was the road to nowhere. This season, though, Harrison had options. Coming through the ranks was a kid called Rod Thomas, who had played for England at schoolboy level and was being hailed as the best young player since Adam was a lad. In the end, he made more than 300 league appearances but never really made it right to the top. Harrison probably reckoned that if Redfearn started to cut up rough, Thomas was waiting in the wings.

I started well, played in the first six games and it seemed the hatchet had been buried. Then things started to go downhill. I missed the next four, came off the bench in the next two, missed another two and then played four on the roll before being taken off in a 2–1 defeat at Leeds on 18 November 1989. I wasn't chosen against Wolves the following week and it seemed pretty obvious I was out in the cold again. This time I'd had enough. I slapped in a written transfer request straight away and maintained a regular flow of requests over the next few weeks. I used to knock on Harrison's door, walk into his office and drop the request on to his desk. Each time, I also wrote to the chairman and club secretary informing them that I had made a transfer request. The letters had to go by registered post so it ended up costing me an arm and a leg. Harrison never looked up. He just took the letter, put it to one side and that would be the last I heard of it. It didn't bother me. I just thought, sod it, I'll go somewhere and prove him wrong.

I never sulked and didn't do anything in the dressing room to rock the boat but things came to a head at a team meeting soon after my first transfer request. It seemed Harrison was under the impression that I'd been leaking inside information to local reporters. He was wrong. I didn't know the local press boys too well and giving off-the-record tip-offs to reporters has never been my style. If I have anything to say, I say it up front. Harrison thought otherwise and as soon as he walked into the room he singled me out.

'I'm not happy with you,' he said.

'And I'm not happy with you, either,' I replied.

At that point we should have called a halt and sorted out the problem in his office later. Instead, we went at it head-to-head, trading insults in front of the whole squad before the exchange ended in an awkward silence and the team meeting got under way. We were both partly to blame – me because I was naïve and inflexible and Steve because he was a young manager trying to find his way and hadn't faced this situation before.

Soon afterwards, when I arrived at the club's training ground in Stanmore, Tom Walley, Harrison's number two, called me over and said, 'Redders, the gaffer says you've to warm up on your own. Three laps of the training ground.' Three laps? It was a massive area and three laps would have taken me the best part of an hour, never mind a 20-minute warm-up period. I didn't argue and set off. Half an hour later, soon after the start of my second lap, I came across Ray Graydon and Stuart Murdoch, who were working with the kids. They were a strong unit. Ray later went on to have a successful spell as manager of Walsall, and Stuart, a highly innovative coach, has managed Wimbledon, or MK Dons as they are now known.

'What the hell are you doing?' asked Murdoch.

'Warming up,' I replied. 'The gaffer's sent me round on my own. Three laps.'

'Three laps? Don't be bloody silly. Come and train with us.'

So I dropped off the treadmill, joined the juniors for their five-a-sides and an hour or so later returned to the dressing rooms, showered, changed and went home. No one missed me.

To be fair to Harrison, his approach wasn't unusual in those days. If a manager bombed out a player, that player just faded into oblivion. It would have been far better for us to have had a face-to-face confrontation and cleared the air. Then he could have monitored me to see how hard I was working, whether my attitude was right and if I was causing problems among the rest of the squad. Anything less than total commitment from me and he would have been justified in getting rid. Instead, we entered a period of cold war. It was a ludicrous situation, as if Steve had decided to lock the door on me and throw away the key.

The impasse finally ended around Christmas, 1989. I'd played for the reserves against Chelsea at Stamford Bridge and as I was coming out of the players' entrance after the game, I spotted Joe Royle, the Oldham manager, in the car park. He looked up, saw me, smiled and nodded. I thought to myself, 'I wonder . . .' The following day we had another reserve game at Barnet in the Hertfordshire Cup. Afterwards, Tom Walley said the manager wanted to see me first thing the following morning. I assumed it would be for some kind of bollocking. Instead, Steve said, 'Come in. Sit down. We've accepted an offer from Oldham. I assume you'll want to talk to Joe Royle.'

'Tell him I'm on my way,' I replied.

I rang Sue, drove home and picked up her and Aimee, hit the M1, dropped off Aimee with my mum and dad and arrived at Boundary Park mid-afternoon. We sat down in Joe's office and his secretary brought in a tray of tea – china cups, silver milk jug and sugar bowl. Joe played mum and poured the tea. He came over really well and was obviously keen to have me on board. Oldham were having a great season – they would go on to reach the final of the League Cup and semi-final of the FA Cup – and I was equally keen to be part of it. There were no hassles on either side and eventually Joe said, 'OK, have you any questions?' I was just about to say no when Sue beat me to the punch.

'Yes. If you're going to leave him out, will you tell him why?'

I thought, 'Fair play, good point, why didn't I ask that?' Joe was a bit taken aback. I suspect he'd always regarded footballers' wives as part of the furniture rather than an element in the decision-making process. Sue had seen how my in-and-out life at Watford had affected me and wanted at least an assurance that I would be kept in the picture.

'Yes, I'll do that,' Joe replied and, a few minutes later, I signed for Oldham. My Watford gap year was over.

I don't bear Steve Harrison any ill will. It's all water under the bridge now. He was always an excellent coach to work with and had some great ideas. It doesn't surprise me that he's gone on to have a good career as a coach. We bump into one another every now and then on the match circuit and there doesn't seem to be any bad blood on his side, either, I'm glad to say. In fact, I'd dearly love to sit down with him and find out what he was thinking all those years ago. We were both wrong and both too proud to back down but we've probably learned from one another's mistakes. I've realised that sometimes you have to step back and look at the broader picture, and maybe Steve has discovered that the secret of good management is keeping players happy and ambitious, even if they are not playing regular first-team football. It isn't easy. Harrison allowed two players, Rick Holden and me, to leave the club and join Oldham and over the next two seasons, we were part of an Oldham side that reached the final of the League Cup, the semi-final of the FA Cup and, above all, won promotion to the top flight. We might so easily have done the same for Watford.

Even though I had major problems at Watford, it certainly wasn't all doom and gloom. I made a point of not letting my absence from the side get me down. I trained hard, gave 100 per cent when I played in the reserves and tried to stay positive. The rest of the lads in the dressing room helped enormously. They were a great bunch. Later, when I started a business management course run by the League Managers' Association at Warwick University, it was like a Watford Old Boys reunion. Stuart Murdoch was there along with Tony Coton, Kenny Jackett, Nigel Gibbs and Glyn Hodges, all of whom had been at Vicarage Road with me. We had some real laughs as we remembered the old days.

If you made a random selection from the players I worked alongside at Watford, you might come up with Coton in goal, Gibbs, Glenn Roeder, David Holdsworth and Kenny Jackett in defence, me, Lee Richardson, Gary Porter and Hodges in the middle of the park and Paul Wilkinson and Dean Holdsworth up front. Add Holden, Iwan Roberts, Wayne Allison, Willie Falconer, Paul Miller, John McClelland and Tim Sherwood to the mix and you'll see that the club had some pretty useful players. A lot of us have moved into coaching and management.

Coton, who played for Birmingham before joining Watford, went on to have a great career with Manchester City and Sunderland and later became a goalkeeping coach at several top clubs, including Manchester United. Jackett, who played 31 times for Wales, had a spell in charge at Watford and was number two at QPR before returning to management with Swansea a couple of years ago. Roeder also had a spell in charge at Watford, as well as managing Gillingham and West Ham. He was part of the England coaching set-up for a while and was Newcastle's caretaker-manager after Graeme Souness's departure in early 2006, becoming manager in the close season. Hodges, another Welsh international, became the Welsh Under-21 coach under Mark Hughes after a spell as caretaker-manager at Barnsley. Glyn was fantastically talented with one of the best left feet I've ever seen. Wilkinson, who played alongside me in the Barnsley side that won promotion to the Premiership in 1997, has coached at several clubs, while Gibbs was Watford through-and-through. He was born down the road in St Albans, and from day one he was only ever going to play for Watford. No other club interested him. I'm sure that if Manchester United had come calling, Nigel would have stayed at Vicarage Road. Inevitably, he moved on to the coaching side at Watford when he retired from playing.

Surprisingly, three players on the Watford staff – Richardson, Allison and Holden –had first started to make an impact when playing for Halifax Town. Like me, all three were born in Yorkshire so there was no shortage of White Rose influence in the dressing room. They all went on to have good careers. Holden became a physiotherapist when he retired from playing. He'd played at the top level with Oldham and Manchester City, and eventually linked up with another ex-Oldham man, Andy Ritchie, at Barnsley. Richardson played all over the place – including Blackburn, Aberdeen, Oldham and Huddersfield – before joining Chesterfield as player-coach and later assistant manager. Allison, or The Chief as he has always been known, was the classic big, strong striker and was always in demand. He moved to Bristol City, Swindon, Huddersfield, Tranmere and Sheffield United before linking up with Richardson once more at Chesterfield. The Chief was still going strong into his late thirties.

So was Iwan Roberts, who's been a mate ever since those Watford days. He's collected 15 Welsh caps and played for some great clubs. I was thrilled to bits for him when he won the First Division championship with Norwich in 2004. He was 35 at the time and had already played over 600 matches at the sharp end, many at the top level, for six clubs, but he was still able to compete. Sue and I are godparents to his son, Ben, and after leaving Watford

for Huddersfield in 1990, Iwan stayed with us for a few weeks. I
was at Oldham at the time and we had a spare room in our house
at Slaithwaite, near Huddersfield. Iwan's wife Julie stayed down
in Watford, trying to sell their house. For the first three months
of his stay at Huddersfield, Iwan had been able to use his reloca-
tion allowance to stay in a hotel, but after that, they still hadn't
sold their place, so Iwan had nowhere to live. He didn't really
fancy renting a place on his own.

We'd been in a similar position ourselves and knew how hard
it was to find the right place. So I said to Iwan, 'Come and stay
with us for as long as you want. The only condition is that you
cook dinner every now and then.' He had no problem with that
and when his turn in the kitchen came round, he didn't mess
about. He was a big lad and didn't go in for too much salad or
pasta. His idea of a square meal was a full roast chicken dinner
and we certainly didn't go short when Iwan was in charge. He
used to walk the dogs with me down by the canal and we'd have
a real old natter about football and cricket – for a Welshman, he
was a decent cricketer – and generally put the world to rights.
They were good days.

A lot of people inside the game claim that players never make
any real mates but move on from club to club, turn the page and
start all over again. I don't agree. I dread to think how many
team-mates I've had since that first game for Bolton in February
1983, but I'm still in touch with a lot of them, and when I bump
into colleagues from the old days, we usually hit it off straight
away – off the pitch, that is. Even though I was at Watford for a
short time, I made some good friends there. I made a few at my
next port of call, too – Boundary Park, Oldham, known during
the winter months as Ice Station Zebra.

8 THE ROYLE FAMILY

The date: Saturday, 11 May 1991

The time: 4.45 p.m.

The place: Boundary Park, Oldham

The match: Oldham Athletic v. Sheffield Wednesday

The prize: the Second Division championship

It's deep into injury time, the scores are level at 2–2. Andy Barlow, our left-back, plays a one-two, goes into the box and is tripped – clear penalty, at the Chadderton End, the Boundary Park kop. I've been taking the penalties all season so I pick up the ball and put it on the spot. I look towards the goal. People are massed along the dead-ball line and packing in behind the goal, pressed up against the net. They have climbed over the perimeter wall and are waiting for me to score.

Kevin Pressman is in goal for Wednesday. Three years earlier I'd played for Crystal Palace against Wednesday in the Football League Centenary Trophy tournament. Pressman had been in goal then and I'd scored a penalty, the first goal by a Palace player at Wembley. I'd hit the ball low to his right and he'd gone the wrong way. Will he remember that now? Definitely. The guessing game is on – for me, which way to go, for Pressman, which way to dive.

Decision time – I choose the same option as at Wembley and so does Pressman. The ball hits the back of the net and rebounds off the wall of delirious fans. Oldham are champions. The crowd pour on to the field and it takes stewards and officials several minutes to clear the playing surface. Eventually, the referee blows the whistle to restart and seconds later he blows it again for the end of the match. It's all over. I'm a hero.

I never kicked another ball in anger for Oldham Athletic. Three months later, when my team-mates opened the season at Liverpool in the new FA Premier League, I was on the outside looking in, kicking my heels in the reserves after another fall-out with another manager.

I sometimes reflect on my 20 months at Boundary Park and wonder how it all went wrong – how, once again, I fell out with a manager, this time Joe Royle, a man for whom I had such enormous respect for most of my short stay. Yes, I was volatile and, with the great gift of hindsight, I might have acted differently. But I also felt let down by him.

At first, joining Oldham had been like a breath of fresh air after my problems at Watford, even though Sue and I had to endure some pretty hairy moments away from the football. When I left Palace for Watford, we'd doubled our money in a year on the house at Caterham. It was boom and bust time on the property market and we rode the boom, slapping down a big slice of the profit as a deposit on a house at Leaverstock Green, near Hemel Hempstead. It was a one-time council house that had been refurbished but we'd spent a fair bit more money to make it feel like home.

When we came to sell after I moved to Oldham 12 months later, the bottom had fallen out of the market and we couldn't recoup any of the money we'd put in. It was devastating. We'd invested a lot of time, money and effort to improve the house and we were left with nothing to show for it. We didn't even have enough to put down as a deposit on a house in the Oldham area.

After the hard times at Lincoln and Doncaster, I'd earned decent money at Palace and Watford and I was given a reasonable deal at Oldham, although Sue had given up work before Aimee was born so we just had the one salary coming in. We certainly didn't need reminding that I was in a precarious profession in which one bad tackle or a single freak injury could have ended my career there and then. We were walking a tightrope. We both believed in my ability to reach the top level and earn good money. The house and the lifestyle would follow, but those early days at Oldham were a worrying time off the field. We weren't in debt but we had to start all over again.

My contract allowed us to spend the first three months in rented accommodation and we soon found a bungalow on Tandle Hill, not far from the ground. Oldham did their pre-season running in a park nearby. The sale of the house in Leaverstock Green dragged on and we ended up staying in the bungalow for longer than expected. The club knew about our predicament and turned a blind eye to the exact terms of the contract. After about nine months, we finally tied everything up down south and found ourselves the house in Slaithwaite, just a few minutes' drive over the Pennines from the Oldham ground.

Understandably perhaps, people have the impression that professional footballers are never short of money, but as long as I've been in the game, only a small élite have earned the really big money. I haven't been involved with too many players who could afford to shrug aside the kind of loss we suffered on the house in Leaverstock Green.

On the field, though, Oldham were going like a train in the League and in the League Cup, known as the Littlewoods Cup in those days, and Royle was rated one of the best young managers in the country. I'd always had a lot of time for his approach to the game and the way he liked his sides to play. His right-hand man was Willie Donachie, the former Scotland full-back who had played alongside Joe at Manchester City. Willie was still involved on the playing side at Oldham but doubled up as first-team coach, and while he was a pretty dour character, he was already becoming one of the best coaches in the country. His knowledge of the game was massive and he and Joe were in the early stages of what has become a successful managerial team. To make life even easier, my mate Rick Holden had joined Oldham from Watford just a few months before me. Rick and I had both done reasonably well at Watford and I don't think our transfers to a rival Second Division club had gone down too well with the fans at Vicarage Road.

I later learned that Joe had asked Rick about me and he'd put in a good word. At the time, I fancied Steve Coppell would have had something to do with my Oldham move, too. He and Royle had always been pals and I couldn't believe Joe would have pushed ahead with the signing without asking Steve's opinion. I later heard that my old boss at Palace had said I was a good lad – as long as I was in the side! That must have been enough for Joe. That sort of thing goes on a lot, both inside and outside the club environment, as managers do their homework about a signing. Over the years, quite a few people have given me a call and told me they're thinking about buying a player I once worked with. They fancy him as a player but need the low-down on what he's like in the dressing room or on the training ground, whether he's got the right attitude. They want to know if there are any skeletons in the cupboard. Does he like a drink? Is he a womaniser? Nobody knows more about a player than his team-mates and, if asked, I always give an honest opinion. If I fail to mention something significant, it will reflect badly on me when the manager discovers the truth, so my own credibility and reputation are on the line as well.

From day one, Joe went out of his way to make me feel part of the squad. The side were doing so well in the League and Littlewoods Cup, he could easily have left me on the sidelines for a spell, but even though I was cup-tied, he made sure I was involved and worked me into the league side on a regular basis. Between signing in January and the end of the season, I started 15 league games, came off the bench twice and played in six of our nine FA Cup ties. Before one of our big FA Cup games, the *Daily Express* carried a feature in which both managers assessed their own players in the form of a pen picture. Joe forecast that I would go on to play for England. No wonder I was flying!

I'd endured some difficult times with my previous managers but in Joe Royle I felt I had found someone I could really relate to. I respected and admired him and this showed in my relations with him. I didn't fly off the handle as soon as I was substituted or left out of the starting line-up and if, during that first season, he called me in and said I wouldn't be playing, I took it on the chin. I went back to the training ground and worked and worked until another opportunity came along. In the end, it always did. Joe was almost a father figure and I bought into it. I thought, 'This fella's on my side.' He encouraged good habits and I shared his thoughts on how the game should be played.

I had come into a successful club and everything about the place was positive. Even though I had worries about the house down south, I couldn't wait to report for training every morning, and when I arrived the work was innovative and stimulating. Everyone was pulling in the same direction on and off the field and the atmosphere was marvellous. Players didn't really want to go home after training. They were happy to hang around for an extra five-a-side or some shooting practice, a sure sign that the club was going places. Believe me, if things aren't right, players can't wait to get away after training. It was a cracking little club.

Every Thursday, a gang of Joe's pals would come along to watch us train and when we had finished, they would get changed and have a work-out of their own, followed by a five-a-side. Strengthened by old pros including Frank Worthington and Len Cantello, our physio Ian Liversedge, and sometimes Joe himself, they played Friday night games on Oldham's plastic pitch, taking on all-comers. I can't imagine many clubs having such an easy-going set-up, even 25 years ago, but the Thursday Club just about summed up the laid-back atmosphere around the place.

I was accepted into the dressing room straight away yet it might easily have been so different. The other players were all close and they could have been forgiven for seeing me as a threat. Instead, I was welcomed with open arms and within a few days I felt as if I'd been at Boundary Park all my life. Obviously, Rick Holden was glad to link up again and I soon made a lifelong friend in Andy Barlow, who moved on to the coaching side when he retired and eventually became a regional coach for the Professional Footballers' Association. Nick Henry played alongside me in midfield and 14 years later we were reunited at Scarborough, Nick as head coach, me as his number two.

We were a great side going forward with some smashing attacking players. As well as Rick Holden and Nick Henry, we had Andy Ritchie, Ian Marshall, Roger Palmer and Paul Warhurst. Then there was the plastic pitch. Even though we were a talented outfit, there is no doubt at all that our synthetic surface gave us a massive advantage. I'd played on it for Watford the previous season and scored – a good goal, too, and afterwards Royle was quoted as saying I had impressed him. He must have had his eye on me even then and he would have spotted that I didn't have any real problems with the pitch. In general, though, opposing sides were understandably less than chuffed about the prospect of coming to Boundary Park.

In an effort to reduce our advantage, visiting teams were given special dispensation to train on the plastic on the Friday afternoon before a home game. The idea was to give them a feel of what was involved but everyone knew they would need more than a brief work-out to feel at home. The players' tunnel at Boundary Park was above the level of the pitch and as soon as their session started, we used to nip out into the tunnel and take a peep from a hidden vantage point behind the dug-out. Sometimes we used to kill ourselves laughing at the way they struggled to come to terms with the surface and how quickly they started moaning. We knew that however much practice they did, psychologically they were more or less beaten before a ball was kicked in anger. Game after game, teams found themselves two goals down and on the ropes after 20 minutes or so. Often they would start well and then, all of a sudden, bang 1–0, bang 2–0 – game over.

We knew every inch of that surface and how it worked because we trained on it every day of our working lives. As soon as my dad saw the plastic, he said, 'Look, you've got to take advantage of this. It's a firm surface with a true bounce. It was made for you.' He was dead right. Opposing defenders were uncertain of their footing and uneasy about committing themselves to the tackle, so there were always going to be loads of chances around the edge of the box, and I could be totally confident about the bounce and pace of the ball. A chance popped up and bang, the shot went in. It was like shooting fish in a barrel. I wanted to kick on in my career and enhance my reputation as a goal-scoring midfield player, and that plastic surface presented me with the perfect opportunity.

There were four plastic pitches around at the time, at Oldham, QPR, Preston and Luton. The one at QPR was terrible. You could actually see the cracks and joints. Quite honestly, it was dangerous. Ours was OK, no more. To kill the bounce a bit, the groundsman used to put sand down on a Saturday morning and water it in for half an hour or so. Quite often, sod's law being what it is, the wind would get up and by kick-off time half a gale would be blowing off the Pennines on to Boundary Park. The sand would have blown away, the surface dried out and players who weren't used to the conditions found it almost impossible to control the ball. Some sides struggled even to keep it on the pitch. Not us! We knew all about the wind and how the ball reacted, and we knew for a fact that the opposition would be frightened to death trying to defend against an attacking side like Oldham.

What we didn't appreciate were the possible long-term effects of training and playing on such an unforgiving surface. I got away with it but a few of my former team-mates have paid the price. Frankie Bunn, who played up front, is a prime example. By the time he was forced to quit in the early nineties, his knee was wrecked. It had a hole in the middle the size of a 10p piece. Andy Barlow and Andy Ritchie have suffered, too, and so have one or two others. I'm not necessarily blaming the plastic because there are a lot of ex-pros around with bad knees who never even saw a synthetic pitch, but the constant banging and jarring must have taken its toll on vulnerable players. It didn't occur to us at the time that there might be a problem.

Should the plastic pitch have been allowed? No. It gave us an unfair advantage. Our home record in the championship season was played 23, won 17, drawn five, lost one. With form like that, all we had to do was keep ticking over on our travels and we were home and dry. For one game in a season, our opponents had to play on an unfamiliar surface in unfamiliar footwear against players who trained on the same pitch every day and played there every other week. I used to wear trainers. Footwear was a matter of personal preference but wearing boots with studs was out of the question. It was like trying to play in high heels, although of course I've never actually worn a pair of high heels.

Even back passes could be a nightmare for visiting goalkeepers, unsure of the pace and bounce and not 100 per cent certain of their footing. When we played Watford, I scored an absolute beauty, chipping the goalkeeper from 25 yards. That was David James, who would be England's first choice 12 years down the line. I knew David from our Watford days – and he knew me. He was expecting a shot but when I saw him off his line, I decided to chip. David saw it coming and might just have got back to it on grass but he slithered around on the plastic and ended up in a heap in the back of the net, where the ball was already nestling. He picked me out afterwards. 'I always thought you were a mate, Redders. That will have worked wonders for my reputation – a six foot five keeper chipped from twenty-five yards!'

However, goalkeepers and everyone else will have to get used to synthetic surfaces eventually. They were not up to much 15 years ago but in the 21st century it's a different story. They feel like grass and play like grass and they are almost certainly the future. FIFA are determined to continue expanding the game into less-developed countries, where it isn't always possible to prepare grass pitches or keep them in good condition. Those countries will be allowed to use artificial surfaces and before too long, we will all have to play on the same type of pitch. Let's be thankful that the new pitches are a million miles away from the Boundary Park version of the early nineties.

My stay at Boundary Park was the longest period of consistent success I have experienced. For the best part of two seasons, big game followed big game and the fans responded. Home games were often a sell-out. While we were living at Tandle Hill, I used to give myself an hour and a half for what was basically a ten-minute drive to the ground. It was bumper to bumper all the way and sometimes I used to panic like hell that I wouldn't report on time.

We reached the semi-finals of the FA Cup, beating Birmingham after a replay in the third round, Brighton in the fourth, Everton after two replays in the fifth and Aston Villa in the quarter-finals. We genuinely felt we could win the competition. The Littlewoods Cup run – Oldham were beaten in the final 1–0 by Nottingham Forest, their fourth victory in the competition – had proved we could beat anyone on our day and as we rolled over some big clubs in the FA Cup, we became more and more convinced it was going to be our year. Manchester United were our opponents in the semi-final at Maine Road. It finished three apiece and United beat us 2–1 in the replay, also staged at Maine Road, Mark Robins scoring the winner. Fourteen years later we were both on the same League Managers' Association course at Warwick University. Small world.

Those two games were tremendous occasions. We were up against top players, including Bryan Robson, Paul Ince and Mark Hughes, but we matched them all the way. My abiding memory is from the replay – a shot by Nick Henry gave Jim Leighton in the United goal no chance, hit the underside of the bar and bounced down. All the players within range were convinced the ball had crossed the line and video evidence later proved we were right, but the referee said no goal. If that goal had stood and we had gone on to win the match, Alex Ferguson would probably have been sacked as United manager. He had been in the job for four years without winning a major trophy and United finished 13th in the League that year, way below expectations. They held on to beat us, though, defeated Crystal Palace in the replayed final and

Ferguson had turned the corner. So you could argue that the goal that never was from Henry was the catalyst for the enormous success Ferguson and United enjoyed from 1990.

The build-up to the semi-final provided me with my first real taste of blanket media coverage. The rest of the boys had experienced it on the way to the Littlewoods Cup final but, having been cup-tied, I hadn't really been involved. I was determined not to let it pass me by, either during the build-up or in the games themselves. I tried to savour every minute and at times it felt surreal, almost as though I was detached from reality and it was another Neil Redfearn out there giving interviews in front of a camera, or on radio, and talking to reporters from the big national papers.

The full glare of the publicity machine was turned in our direction and, by and large, they seemed to be on our side. We were the underdogs – the small-town team taking on the big city giants. Television crews seemed to cover our every move in training and a posse of radio reporters and newspapermen would be waiting for interviews afterwards. I'd never sampled anything like it and, at first, I was a bit wary but I soon got the hang of it and began to enjoy talking to the media. It proved to be excellent grounding for the media frenzy that surrounded us at Barnsley a few years later. We also made a record, 'The Boys in Blue', with comedy duo Cannon and Ball. It was rubbish and predictably failed to disturb the hierarchy at the top of the charts, but it was all part of the ballyhoo that used to be such a big part of the FA Cup's allure.

Even after our defeat by United, the big games kept coming as we spent the closing weeks of the season pushing for a play-off place, eventually missing out in eighth position, two places and three points adrift – so near but so far. Our failure to make the top six was definitely a knock-on effect from the two Cup runs. We were certainly as good as any other side in the division. In all, we played 65 games with a squad of 21 players and something had to give. In the end, it was the final run-in to the play-offs when we won four of our last nine games, losing three times in the process. Some people said we caved in under pressure but I would beg to differ. We were just knackered.

In that first season, I nicked a couple of goals in the League and another one in the FA Cup. That was not a bad return but I knew I could do better and that if I delivered the goods, Joe couldn't possibly leave me out. So I went away and worked even harder in training than I had the previous year at Watford. I could have run the legs off any midfield player in the country. I felt as if I had three lungs. Physically, I was at the height of my powers and I had energy to burn. I knew I was going to be a dangerous proposition to opposing defences. When I reported back for pre-season training there was never any doubt in my mind that I would be in the starting line-up from the word go. Once the season started, I used to do extra running in the afternoons, pounding up to the monument in Tandle Park and looking down at the ground. I even used to go for a run on the morning of a match. If we were staying in a hotel overnight before an away game, I'd take some extra kit with me, get up around ten o'clock and head off for a 20-minute run, at a good pace to make sure I got a sweat on. Joe would sometimes be in the hotel foyer when I returned and he'd be laughing his socks off. 'You're crackers!' he'd say, but he never tried to stop me. It wouldn't be allowed under today's strict training regimes, of course.

The extra runs were all part of my basic philosophy: 'Stay fit, score goals and you'll play every week.' So it proved. I started in each of the first 38 games and scored 12 goals. No manager could have asked for more, although there were times when I overdid the running out on the park. In the first 20 minutes I'd be making runs here, there and everywhere, often without a hope in hell of receiving the ball. Joe would come to the touchline and shout, 'Redders, bloody well stand still. Give people a target to aim at.' He was right, of course. If a defender is under pressure and looking for an outlet, he needs a stationary target, not some guy belting off into the middle distance calling for an almost impossible pass. It took me a while to take that particular lesson on board.

Joe didn't seem to have any complaints, though, until with

promotion within our grasp he started messing me about. In early February, he'd brought in another midfield player, Paul Kane from Aberdeen. Paul Barnard, an England youth international, was also knocking on the first-team door. Kane was a decent player but, with all due respect, he wasn't going to give a manager anything like 15 goals a season, and while Barnard was promising, he was still just a kid. In contrast, I was in my pomp and as I warmed up before the start of the home game against our promotion rivals West Ham on 29 March, my 36th consecutive league appearance of the season, I'd no reason at all to suppose my days as an automatic choice were numbered.

I was substituted during that game, a 1–1 draw, and again two matches later against Millwall. The following week I was on the bench against Leicester and I started just three of the last eight games of the season. At the same time, I sensed a change in Royle's attitude towards me. All of a sudden he seemed cold and distant, not warm and friendly any more. Perhaps, after signing Kane and seeing Barnard's progress, he was playing mind games to keep me on my toes but it had the reverse effect. I simply couldn't understand what was going on. I had never felt so let down by a manager, a man I had trusted totally. I felt double-crossed.

With promotion in our sights, this clearly wasn't the time to rock the boat, so I put on a brave face in the dressing room, but I was bitterly disappointed when once again Joe named me as sub for that final game of the season against Sheffield Wednesday at Boundary Park. We'd already won promotion but were two points behind West Ham at the top. To clinch the title, we had to win and hope West Ham would go down at Notts County, who were in fourth position. Wednesday were certain of the third promotion slot, so all was set for a carnival occasion. The only thing missing was the trophy – the authorities had decided to take it to Meadow Lane in the expectation of a West Ham win.

Boundary Park was absolutely packed to the rafters with nearly 19,000 fans crammed into every nook and cranny, but Wednesday decided to spoil the party and took a two-goal lead through David Hirst and Danny Wilson, my boss at Barnsley when we won promotion six years later. We must have been bad if we let Danny score! His goal prompted Joe to change things around and I was sent on with about half an hour to go. We drew level with goals from Marshall and Bernard. A draw was not going to be enough, though, even if West Ham lost. The atmosphere was white hot when, deep into injury time, Barlow made that fateful run into the box and the referee blew his whistle for the penalty.

That goal is written into Oldham folklore but I honestly didn't feel any pressure. We were promoted anyway and that was the big thing. The championship was a bonus. As I prepared to take the spot kick, my only thought was to score another goal for Neil Redfearn and prove a point to Joe Royle. The title never entered my head. Selfish? Yes, I suppose so, but professional, too. If I'd started to think about anything other than hitting the net, I wouldn't have been totally focused and I might have missed.

Soon afterwards, we played Manchester City in a testimonial for Roger Palmer, who had started his career at Maine Road. The trophy was presented before the game and we did a lap of honour in front of 17,500 fans, making it a good night for Roger! As we were going round the ground, the trophy was passed from player to player and with perfect timing, my turn came as we reached the 'Chaddie' End, where I had scored the penalty. The whole terrace erupted. It was an incredible experience, as if the fans were waiting for me and saying, 'You're one of us.' A lump rose in my throat all right because I felt the same way about them.

Since leaving Oldham, the fans have always given me a special reception when I've returned to play at Boundary Park. I went back a few times with Barnsley and scored a couple of goals, one a free kick and the other a penalty. And a few years ago, when Oldham played QPR in the Division Two play-offs, I was invited back as guest of honour. I agreed to take a penalty in front of the Chadderton End with Chaddie the Owl, the club mascot, between the posts. When I was introduced, the crowd went mad and started chanting, 'There's only one Neil Redfearn!' Then the MC said, 'Do you want Redders to take a penalty at the Chaddie End?'

That was greeted with a great roar of approval. So I trotted over, put the ball on the spot and confronted Chaddie.

As it happened, I'd rung Andy Barlow before the game to tell him I would be guest of honour and I mentioned the penalty. He was less than impressed. 'Have your wits about you,' he said. 'That bloody owl's not a bad keeper. I've taken a penalty against him as well. Don't make a fool of yourself.' Little did he know that by prior arrangement, Chaddie was going to dive one way and I was going to go the other. So the ball finished up in the right-hand corner and Redfearn strutted off with pride and reputation intact.

Afterwards, one or two fans took me to one side and said, 'They should never have sold you. Royle had a nightmare there. We'll never forget that penalty against Sheffield Wednesday.' One supporter was less than impressed, though.

'You got a lot of goals for us all right, but don't forget you took the penalties,' he said.

'Aye, I did,' I replied. 'And don't you forgot that one of them won the championship.'

However, the champagne had gone flat for me by the time we reported back for pre-season training in the summer of 1991. Maybe I should have knocked on Joe's door and sorted everything out face to face but I still had that stubborn streak and I felt I had been wronged. I believed he had kicked me in the teeth and I took refuge in my old ways. I thought, 'Sod you, Joe, I'm not going to be the one to make the first move.' Obviously, he felt the same way. During the summer, he had gone out and re-signed Mike Milligan, one of the heroes of earlier FA Cup and League Cup campaigns. Things hadn't really worked out for him at Everton after a £1 million transfer. Milligan's return suggested Joe was going to switch things around and revert to an orthodox 4-4-2 formation instead of the three-man midfield of me, Donachie and Nick Henry. Inevitably, my situation was raised in the press during the countdown to the new season.

Joe's response was to say that if Redfearn was prepared to play wide right, he would be in the starting line-up. My answer was that I'd scored 14 goals from central midfield during the promotion season so why should I be shunted out to make way for Milligan, a good honest pro who would work all day but never score anything like the same number of goals? In fact, Milligan scored three goals in 36 league games that season. I would have backed myself to do a lot better than that.

The stand-off continued, amid speculation that I would be on the move, right through the build-up to the new season. I don't think Joe wanted me to leave but he was determined that if I stayed, it would be on his terms, not mine. I didn't really want to leave, either. If Joe had called me into the office and gone out of his way to convince me I was part of his plans, I would probably have agreed to stay. After all, Oldham had reached the top division. This would have been my first chance to play against the best teams and players in the land, but there was no dialogue. The nearest he came to a peace offering was naming me as man of the match in a pre-season friendly against Rossendale and presenting me with a bottle of champagne afterwards. He kept telling the press that I was still in his plans but he never told me, and when Oldham played their first game at Anfield on 17 August, I wasn't involved.

A couple of weeks later, he called me into his office and said three clubs had made approaches for me – Barnsley, Blackpool and Port Vale. Blackpool were in the old Fourth Division, so that move was clearly a non-starter. Both Port Vale and Barnsley meant dropping down a division but I could handle that. For me, only two things mattered. First, I had to get away. Second, I had to play first-team football again and prove a point to Royle. Barnsley wanted me on a month's loan, a deal that would put me in the shop window even if they decided not to take me on full-time. They had played six games and were bottom of Division Two. Oldham were in the top division and due to play Sheffield United at Boundary Park the following weekend but it was no contest. I signed for Barnsley and on my debut we drew at Derby, doubling our points tally for the season. Four weeks later, the move was made permanent.

I learned afterwards that Blackburn had also made an offer. Jack Walker had just started to pour his millions into the club and they were clearly going places, but Oldham didn't want to sell a player to potential local rivals. I didn't have an agent at the time and I was totally unaware of what was going on behind the scenes. So I joined Barnsley, who had just sold their central midfield man, Steve Agnew, to Blackburn.

People told me I was mad and I suppose they had a point. The argument went that I'd had a good season and Oldham had won the championship. I'd fallen out with the manager but I was still a hero to the fans, and I was being presented with a golden opportunity finally to play in the top flight, even if it wasn't in my favourite position. My chance to switch to a central role would surely come along eventually. Why drop down again after working so hard to make it to the top? Looking back, that argument made sense. Oldham did survive that first season among the big boys but they didn't break any pots and, at some stage, an opportunity would have arisen for me to show what I could do at that level. Not for the first time, I couldn't see the bigger picture.

But I'm not complaining – just think what I would have missed if I'd stayed! Little did I know, as I drove to Oakwell to begin my loan spell, that I was about to embark on a magical mystery tour, a trip that would take unsung Barnsley into the Premiership seven years later and transform a little-known Yorkshire club into one of the most talked-about teams in the land.

I will always look back on my days at Oldham with massive affection, however. I even managed to make a big impression on a future England star – Paul Scholes, later of Manchester United. A while ago, I watched a television interview with Paul and when he said, 'Oldham Athletic,' in answer to a question about which club he supported as a kid, I sat up and started to take a bit more notice. 'I used to cheer them on from the Chaddie End,' he went on.

'Who was your favourite player?' the interviewer asked.

'Neil Redfearn,' came the reply.

So, fame at last. Mind you, if I was still his favourite player by the time we got around to crossing swords in the Premiership, he had a funny way of showing it. People used to say Paul was a mild-mannered lad on the field, the kind of player who wouldn't say boo to a goose, but he always seemed to reserve a few crunching tackles for his one-time favourite!

I still admire Joe Royle. I always have. He and Willie Donachie are a fantastic pair. Joe had a remarkable ability to make his players feel at ease and lose their fear. He brought in decent footballers, created a good atmosphere and encouraged them to go out and play. Not many managers have that gift.

Joe and I have not really had much to do with one another since I left Oldham, although he brought his Ipswich team to play Boston when I was assistant manager there in 2003 and I desperately wanted to have a chat. For one reason or another, we were never in the same place at the same time and didn't have a chance to talk. After the game Neil Thompson, the Boston manager, told me he'd had a word with Joe, who had wanted to know how I was getting on. Tommo told him I was playing well, still battling, working hard on the training ground, and how pleased he was to have me on board. 'That's great,' replied Royle. 'I'm pleased for him. Redders did a really good job for me at Oldham, you know.' If only you could have said that to my face, Joe. Some other time, perhaps.

9 REDDERS ON THE REDS

FOR THE FIRST TEN YEARS OF MY PROFESSIONAL CAREER, I followed the golden rule – never fall in love with a football club. Then, on 6 September 1991, I walked through the players' entrance at Barnsley to start a month's loan and that was me for the next seven years. My life would never be the same again. It wasn't a passionate affair at first. You might say we were just good friends. After a series of ups-and-downs at my three previous clubs, Barnsley offered me a warm welcome and the growing conviction that I was needed and appreciated. As the years went by, we grew closer and closer and by the time Barnsley were promoted to the Premiership on 26 April 1997, we were head over heels in love.

By then, I was club captain and the longest-serving first-team player. I'd missed just 15 games in six seasons and I had my own column, 'Redders on the Reds', in the programme. Above all, I had played my part in helping Barnsley achieve the impossible by winning promotion to the Premier League. After the victory over Bradford City that secured Barnsley's place in the Premiership, when I saw the faces of people who had been involved with the club all their lives, I was overwhelmed with emotion. The hard-nosed pro had a soft centre after all.

I saw delight in the face of chairman John Dennis, the man

who had inspired the transformation that converted the club from the First Division's oldest inhabitants into the most unlikely new recruits in the Premiership's history. His father Ernest had been chairman before him and had dreamed dreams of his own. I saw raw emotion in the face of Eric Winstanley, a tough Barnsley man who had served the club as player and coach for nearly 40 years and had been the master strategist behind our success. I witnessed amazement on the face of Norman Rimmington, who had spent most of his 73 years at Oakwell, the loyal servant who would do anything and everything asked of him if it would help Barnsley Football Club. I saw the ecstasy on the faces of the thousands of fans who lived the dream that had begun with the formation of the club 110 years earlier.

A little over 12 months later, when Barnsley were relegated, I saw on those same faces a crushed, defeated expression. In some cases, the tears flowed. Inevitably, I suppose, our affair ended soon afterwards and the parting of the ways turned out to be a pretty acrimonious business, but for me, the passion never really died. The same people who say you should never fall in love with a football club would also no doubt insist that you should never go back, but if Barnsley fluttered her eyelashes in my direction again at some time in the future, I would find it very hard to resist her charms.

When I signed for Barnsley, I was craving a club where I could settle down, feel part of a football family, play every week and develop my game. I was 26 and, including my apprenticeship at Forest, I'd already played for seven clubs. I was conscious that I needed to put down some footballing roots and finally show people what I was capable of doing over a long period. I thought I had found that place at Oldham but it wasn't to be.

In many ways, Barnsley was a very similar set-up and for only the second time in ten years, I was back among my own kind in Yorkshire. The people spoke my language with an accent that wasn't a million miles away from my own. Yorkshire folk are straight talking and honest and they don't mince words. It's all for one and one for all and if a player is giving them everything, they will respond and back him, even if he's having a bad time. Their attitude was one of the reasons why Oakwell felt like home from day one.

It was a ramshackle old place, nothing like the redeveloped Premiership-class stadium that dominates the Barnsley skyline today. I sometimes wonder if the modern, state-of-the-art stadium was one of the underlying causes of the club's decline after losing their Premiership status. Visiting teams love Oakwell these days. The players take a look at the arena and think, 'We'll have some of this.' Playing at Barnsley gives them a lift. It didn't in my day. I knew from my time at Palace, Watford and Oldham that a lot of players used to detest going to Barnsley. It was usually cold, always cramped and the fans could be distinctly inhospitable. 'Barnsley away' was one of the fixtures players liked to get out of the way early on before the weather deteriorated and the natives became too hostile.

Travelling fans probably felt the same way, too, for the away end was open to the weather – and stayed that way during our Premiership season, much to the dismay of sodden supporters on wet days. Accommodation for home fans was a bit iffy as well but no one seemed to care too much. The main stand had five or six blocks of seating with a terraced paddock in front. Opposite was a covered standing enclosure, originally named the Oakwell Ales Stand after the local brewery that produced the famous Barnsley Bitter. When John Smiths took over the brewery, their logo appeared on the roof. Behind, you could see the pithead machinery of the local collieries, long gone now, of course, just like the stand, which was demolished in 1994. The home terrace was the Pontefract Road Stand, otherwise known as the Ponty End. Again, it was standing room only and it bit the dust before the start of the promotion season.

The playing surface used to slope slightly from left to right and players reached the pitch down a sloping concrete runway. At first, the incline was pretty gentle but the gradient gradually became steeper and it could be absolutely treacherous. It was no fun trying to negotiate the slope with metal studs at the best of times but on a slippery day, a bit of local knowledge came in very handy indeed. I've seen many an opposing player end up on his backside going out for the warm-up. They hated it. Throw in the baying, hostile fans who used to gather in the paddock on either side of the runway and you'll get an idea of what those first few tentative steps on to the Oakwell pitch were like. It must have seemed like walking the plank to some visiting players.

Even the club cats disliked footballers, although unfortunately they didn't differentiate between Barnsley and the opposition when they decided to have a go at a passing pair of ankles. They were a couple of stray toms, born on a farm in Hooton Pagnell, a little village between Barnsley and Doncaster. Joe Joyce, the former Barnsley defender who went on to become head of coaching at the PFA, brought them to the club as kittens. They were never named, although they were called plenty of different things in their time. They had obviously been around a bit and one of them had a dodgy ear that flopped forward over its eye, no doubt the result of a late-night brawl. They were perfectly friendly with the groundsman and his team, the office staff, players' families and the directors, but for some reason, they never took to the senior pros. If they were around when we went through the players' entrance, they'd arch their backs, hiss and take a swipe as we walked past. The click of studs on tarmac was like a call to arms and we were all a bit wary.

They even caused us grief when we went to the club offices to collect our wages. The offices were housed in a little brick building between the main stand and the away terrace and the cats seemed to have a sixth sense that told them when we'd be arriving. They'd be sitting on the counter waiting for us and would have a bit of a go at us as we signed the receipt for our hard-earned brass. They took a particular dislike to Andy Rammell, one of our strikers. Andy was over six feet tall and weighed in at around 13 stone so he was quite a handful on the pitch, but he used to dread facing those two cats and would always check if they were around before going in for his wages. If he hadn't been collecting his money, he'd never have set foot in the office.

For the players, the nerve centre of the club was the ground floor of the main stand, another structure that had seen better days. It was basically a long corridor, running from end to end, separated by the players' entrance and tunnel. One side of the corridor was rough and ready and the preserve of the playing staff, the other was carpeted and mainly the province of the non-footballing fraternity. The dressing rooms were at the farthest end of the corridor towards the Ponty End and, by and large, facilities in the home dressing room were pretty good. When I joined the club, we had a couple of baths and a few showers but it wasn't long before more baths were installed, the walls were tiled and by the time we reached the Premiership the place had been completely refurbished.

The same could not be said of the away dressing room. That had barely enough room to swing one of the club cats let alone accommodate 11 players, subs and all the gear. When we played Manchester United in a Cup replay during the Premiership season, they had to leave all the skips out in the corridor, where they clogged the place up completely. Opposing teams who knew the form tried to operate a rota system for getting stripped. Half the squad would go into the dressing room first, change and then go out for the warm-up. As soon as they left for the pitch, the rest of the players would nip in and put their kit on. Sometimes, half the players would just get changed in the corridor. It was all a bit chaotic and, like the slippery slope leading on to the pitch, a big psychological advantage to the home side. Often visiting players were sick to death of the place before a ball was kicked.

Between the dressing rooms and the tunnel were the boot room, a small gym area, where we used to do our weight training, and the physio's room. At the top of the tunnel was the hallway from the players' entrance, where the teams lined up before going out on to the pitch and where the press used to gather after the game to buttonhole the managers and players. The referee's room was in this area, too, perfectly placed for angry managers wanting to vent their spleen on the officials.

Leaving the hallway and moving away from the dressing-room

area, the manager's office was the first door on the left, while the entrance to the press box, in those days precariously attached to the front of the stand and open to everything the weather had in store, was on the opposite side of the corridor. Then came the boardroom, strictly men only, and ladies' room, where the wives of directors and guests were entertained on match days. Next along the corridor was a little boiler room where the press used to gather before matches and again at half-time in an effort to thaw out over a cup of tea and a range of tasty snacks. I'm reliably informed that there was often a marked reluctance to leave the warmth of the boiler room and return to the frozen wastes of the press box, although the media, unlike most opposition teams, enjoyed their visits to Oakwell. The kitchen and supporters' club lounge were right at the far end of the corridor, at the opposite end to the dressing rooms.

A warm, friendly atmosphere pervaded the whole place and everyone, from chairman John Dennis down, went out of his way to make me feel at home. John had been chairman for just a year or so when I arrived but he saw the club into the Premiership and was still there after I moved on in 1998. He eventually left the club in 2003 but continued to go to games as a season-ticket holder. He is a lifelong Barnsley fan who has a wholesale fruit and vegetable business in the town, founded by his father. The rest of the directors were all dyed-in-the-wool Oakwell fans, too.

John was a relatively young man when he took over and, from where I stood, he seemed to know what made Barnsley supporters tick. I saw him as a chairman who was always prepared to sit down and listen to the fans. He wanted the best for them and was happy to explain where he and his fellow directors wanted to take the club. He ran a tight ship, which meant there wasn't a lot of money around to pay players big wages, but we respected John and his directors and appreciated what was involved. They were accessible, happy to share a laugh and a joke and always gave the impression that they cared about us. It was a good atmosphere and John Dennis deserves a lot of credit for that.

Before every game, he used to pop into the officials' dressing room and ask the referee and his linesmen what they would like to drink after the match, an Oakwell tradition that no doubt went back to his father's days as chairman. An order would be placed and sure enough, ten or 15 minutes after the final whistle, the chairman would amble through from the boardroom carrying a tray laden with foaming pints of Barnsley Bitter. As the years went by and a stricter fitness regime for refs crept in, fizzy orange or even mineral water started to replace the ale but a few diehards still ordered a refreshing pint. I can't believe it happened at many other clubs, if any. John would leave the tray with the officials and, on his way back to the boardroom, pause for a cosy chat with the press. He knew all about good public relations long before clubs even thought of appointing full-time press officers to keep the reporters informed.

Little things counted for the players, too. Every year, for instance, we received a frozen turkey at Christmas, although one festive season, when finances were tight, we had to settle for a capon. We said that if we were down to a chicken the following year we'd call in the PFA! The turkeys were usually delivered late morning, a week or ten days before Christmas, and left in the supporters' club bar, which was always cool because it was only used on match days and the radiators were turned off for the rest of the time. The players would just be finishing training when the birds arrived and after a pot of tea and a shower, we'd go along to the bar to collect our Christmas dinner.

One year, things didn't go according to plan. The birds were delivered first thing in the morning, way ahead of schedule and before most of the players had arrived, and it was a particularly cold day. Anyone who has spent some time at Oakwell on a cold winter's day will know how inhospitable that can be. The central heating under the stand was on full bore and, as luck would have it, no one had remembered to turn off the radiators in the supporters' bar. It was like a furnace in there and the frozen birds didn't stand a chance. We were given the seasonal good tidings that the turkeys were ready for collection when we reached the warmth of the dressing room after training and, as usual, a fair

bit of banter was flying around as the first group of players saun-
tered off to collect their birds. The mood changed when they
returned to the dressing room empty-handed.

'Where's your turkeys, then?'

'Running around in the bloody bar. They've thawed out.'

This news was greeted with a stunned silence. None of us was
in the Gordon Ramsay class as a chef, although our right-back
Nicky Eaden always claimed to be a dab hand in the kitchen, but
we knew enough about the risks of salmonella poisoning to know
that re-frozen turkeys can be bad news for the family at Christmas.
With over a week to go before the big day, the birds currently
warming up nicely in the bar were going to be well past their best
by the time Christmas morning came around. We had no choice.
We took them home, had an early Christmas dinner and made
hurried plans to find a replacement for the big day.

Like the chairman, Norman Rimmington had been involved
with the club for almost his whole life. He was a rugged old
Barnsley man who called a spade a spade and he'd done just about
every available job at Oakwell – player, first-team coach, physio,
kit man, general odd job man. He had hands like shovels and if
any of the players went to him for a rub down, he'd soon find the
sore points and work on them with his massive thumbs.

Down below the stand was Norman's empire and, after training,
he used to hold court in the kitchen, next to a gas-fired geyser, full
of boiling water. The players operated a rota system for making
the tea. A few tin teapots littered the dressing room, great big things
that had seen better days and taken a few kicks in their time. They
weighed a ton when they were full and there was an unwritten
rule that before putting the tea bags in, we had to make sure no
old studs or lumps of mud were lurking in the bottom of the pot.

The duty player would pick up a teapot, amble down to the
kitchen, bung in half a dozen teabags to ensure a maximum
strength Yorkshire brew and then return to the dressing room,
armed with tea, milk and sugar. Straightforward? Yes, unless
Norman happened to be in the kitchen – and he usually was when
I was duty tea boy.

'Sit down, lad,' he'd say.

'Nay, Norman, I'm brewing up. The lads are waiting for their tea.'

'Never mind those buggers. Sit thissen down. Nah then, what's tha' reckon to this 'ere business at Old Trafford last neet?'

Off we'd go, chewing the fat about the big midweek incidents on and off the field. Eventually, I'd find a natural break and put the teabags in the pot, by which time Norman had moved on to cricket.

'They'll never win t'Ashes with that bloody lot they've got out there,' he'd say, and off we'd go again . . .

Next up would be politics, after which he'd come full circle and would be ready to return to football. So it would go on – until one of the lads came storming down the corridor, shouting, 'Where's our bloody tea, Redders?' Norman would smile an innocent smile and ask what all the fuss was about. I wasn't the only one he collared on a regular basis, either.

Even after escaping Norman's clutches, we had to run the gauntlet of Margaret and Janet, the cleaners who were responsible for keeping the corridor area spick and span. I'll swear they had supernatural powers. When I was on the tea run, I usually couldn't be bothered to change my boots first and took my chance that the cleaners would have either gone home or be having a sandwich and a mug of tea in another part of the ground. I'd check that the coast was clear and all the cleaning equipment had been put away and set off at a gentle trot. The outward journey to the kitchen always passed without a hitch and, after bidding farewell to Norman, I'd set off back with a fully laden tray. Halfway back, Margaret or Jean would materialise out of thin air and shout, 'Don't go fetching that bloody tea with your boots on, Redfearn. I'll have to vac this carpet again now.' They ruled that corridor with a rod of iron and even the manager would have copped for a telling-off if he'd done the tea run without taking his boots off first.

Eric Winstanley was another member of the backroom team who was Barnsley through and through. He'd been a talented young player, a footballing centre-half who attracted a lot of interest from the big clubs but struggled with one or two bad injuries. Even so, he made the best part of 500 appearances for the club. He was youth-team coach when I arrived but he'd already been an apprentice, senior player, club captain, chief scout, reserve coach, first-team coach and even caretaker manager. One of his stints in charge, before my time, coincided with a visit from Newcastle United, who were flying high at the top of the division and managed by Jim Smith, football's original Bald Eagle. No doubt spurred on by Eric's words of wisdom, Barnsley rolled over Newcastle with a bit to spare and afterwards a proud Eric announced to the world's press, 'We've knocked the Bald Eagle off his perch today!'

In the early days, I sometimes used to join in the kids' five-a-sides and watching Eric work with them was an education. Andy Liddell, Nicky Eaden, Adi Moses and Dave Watson were four of Eric's production line who helped the club win promotion to the Premiership. Chris Morgan soon followed them into the side. They all performed well in the top flight and went on to have decent careers. It was fascinating to watch Eric working with the young lads and I used to think to myself, 'You're wasted here, Eric lad.' Fortunately, two years down the line, Viv Anderson thought so, too, and appointed Eric first-team coach. In November 2005, when I was appointed player-manager at Scarborough ten years later, the first thing I did was to bring in Eric as my number two.

For me, Eric was the brains behind the Barnsley passing game that had the fans drooling during promotion year. He made his training sessions interesting, innovative and enjoyable. We did loads of possession work and he preached attacking football from the start. He convinced us we could outplay any team in the top flight and by the time the first ball of the promotion season was kicked, we were convinced he was right. He gave us creativity and scoring power and we honestly thought that if the opposition scored three, we'd get four. He was so positive in everything he did.

Eric, John Dennis, Norman, Janet and Margaret were just a

few of the people who quickly convinced me my future lay at
Barnsley and as soon as my loan period was over, I made the deal
permanent. There had been no problems settling into the dressing
room — we'd won three games out of six and moved up four
places during my loan so I think the lads were keen to see me
stick around. It was a bit of a scrap at first but we turned things
round in the New Year and eventually finished in 16th place.

Mel Machin was manager and I always got on well with him.
He was a complex character, an introvert who found it hard to
communicate away from football, but his knowledge of the game
was very deep. Sometimes, during team talks, he'd analyse our
previous performance and I used to think he'd been watching a
different game. He seemed to spot things no one else even thought
about. He'd tell us to have a think about what he'd said and almost
always he was spot on. It was easy to drift off during his team
talks because, like I say, he wasn't a forceful personality, but I
listened hard and learned a lot during my two seasons under him.

Machin was also shrewd in the people he had around him. John
Benson, who had a long career in coaching and management and
was in charge at Wigan when I moved there in 2000, was his assistant and John Deehan his first-team coach. Deehan has also gone
on to become a top-class coach and had one or two stints in management. We played a 5-3-2 formation and we had some good players.
What's more, with a Bishop and an Archdeacon in the squad, we
weren't likely to go short of spiritual guidance! The 'clerics' in
question were otherwise known as Charlie Bishop, a central
defender, and Owen Archdeacon, who played wide on the left.
We even had Adi Moses playing for the juniors. Archie, as Owen
was inevitably known, was a Scotland Under-23 international. He
had been signed from Celtic in 1989 and played over 250 games
for the club before returning to Scotland for family reasons before
our promotion season. He was a class act – cultured left peg, good
in the air for a little chap and a genuinely nice guy. He would
have done OK in the Premiership.

Two Northern Ireland internationals, Gary Fleming and Gerry
Taggart, were at the heart of the defence while Mark Robinson

and Archie, the wing-backs, were both excellent crossers of a ball. I operated in the centre of midfield, breaking up the play, getting things moving but without the licence to go forward that I had enjoyed at Oldham. It was a solid, well-balanced side that was unlikely to go down. On the other hand, we weren't going to go up either. In fact, that just about summed up Barnsley Football Club at the time. We were the longest-surviving inhabitants of the old Second Division and unless something sensational happened, that's how we would stay. In the comfort zone? Yes, maybe, but with an average home gate of six or seven thousand, anything more ambitious looked like pie in the sky.

A lot of fans didn't like Machin, claiming that we were too defensive and didn't play good football under him. I disagreed and for my money, Machin was unlucky. In my second season, we started badly and were bottom of the table at the end of September, but we picked up and at the beginning of April, we were up to ninth after winning four out of six games. The play-offs looked a real possibility until we picked up a few injuries in the run-in and slipped back to 13th. Machin left in the summer of 1993.

In his place, the board went for the young option, bringing in Viv Anderson as manager and Danny Wilson as player-coach. I'm sure one of the big attractions for the board was that Viv was planning to continue playing on a regular basis, but after appearing in 16 of the first 18 games, he struggled with injuries and in the end managed 20 league appearances all season. Danny, on the other hand, missed just three league games.

Anderson was very much his own man. He had been the first black player to win an England cap and was only the second black manager when he was appointed. He'd played over 700 games at home and in Europe, for Nottingham Forest, where he collected a couple of European Cup winners' medals, Arsenal, Manchester United and Sheffield Wednesday. He'd done well out of the game and perhaps for that reason he didn't feel under too much pressure to produce results immediately. Unlike a lot of managers at the time, he knew that he could walk away if things didn't work out and would still have plenty to fall back on. He wasn't prepared to compromise his beliefs about the way the game should be played and from the start, he insisted on a passing game. He believed in total football, building from the back and passing, passing, passing. We played countless games of five-a-side in training and carried that style of play into matches. If ten passes had added up to a goal we'd have won every game 6–0 and been top of the League.

Significantly, he took away the fear factor. Towards the end of Machin's time, some of the players were apprehensive. The crowd were on their backs and they were afraid to take risks. Viv blew that away and we were better, more confident players as a result. Understandably perhaps, he seemed a bit naïve at first. It was his first management job and he appeared to take a lot of advice on board from a lot of different people, which isn't always a good thing. OK, talk to one or two people whose opinion you really value but, in the end, a manager stands or falls by his own beliefs.

I liked Viv and the way he went about the job, even though he began by playing me wide on the right. I wasn't happy about that after performing well in central midfield for Machin but, unlike the young Neil Redfearn from Palace, Watford and Oldham days, I didn't kick off about it. Eventually, Viv opted for a three-man midfield, gave me licence to push forward and I was back on my true stamping ground again. I played in all 46 league games under Viv and scored 12 goals, a big step up from the totals of four and three I had notched in my first two seasons. I felt that as Viv came to terms with the system he wanted to play, I was becoming an integral part of the machine.

The Barnsley fans were ready to give him a chance at first but when we won only four of our first 20 league games and slid to 23rd, they grew restless. It wasn't just the opposition who took a load of stick when they trotted out on to the pitch between those diehard supporters in the paddock. The Barnsley crowd have always appreciated good football but they like a bit of steel as well – particularly when things are not going well. They didn't think Viv was giving them enough of the hard stuff and eventually rounded on him. 'Get it bloody forrard!' was a familiar clarion call as we passed it around at the back and tried to play the ball through midfield. As Viv's right-hand man, Danny came in for more stick than most of us but that never bothered him. Viv wasn't worried, either. He just kept urging us to pass, pass, pass and eventually we picked up a bit after the turn of the year – but an 18th place finish was definitely not what the board had in mind when they appointed their high-profile managerial dream team.

What the directors and the fans didn't appreciate was that Viv's total football regime was beginning to pay dividends. Results weren't satisfactory but the players were starting to feel at home and, with Eric Winstanley pulling the strings as coach, we knew we were moving in the right direction.

Then, after just a single season in charge, Viv left. Bryan Robson, his former team-mate with Manchester United and England, needed an assistant manager at Middlesbrough, offered Viv the job and away he went. It was a hell of a shock for the players, who were growing into Viv's style of football, although I suspect that quite a few fans, disgruntled about the previous season's low finish, weren't too sorry to see the back of him. Inevitably, there was a load of speculation about who would take over. All sorts of names were being bandied around but one man who didn't feature too strongly in the betting was Viv's right-hand man, Danny Wilson.

However, the bookies and the pundits reckoned without Danny's stubborn, determined streak. Wilson wanted the job, knew he could do it and nothing was going to get in his way – not even a board of directors who were not entirely convinced about his credentials to succeed Anderson. Danny refused to take no for an answer, pleaded with the board to give him a chance and finally on 2 June 1994, they made him the 20th manager in the club's 107-year history. Barnsley Football Club was about to change forever.

10 COPACABARNSLEY!

Sunday People, 27 April 1997
'Let's all have a party,' chanted delirious Barnsley fans as Danny Wilson's little big shots charged into the Premiership.

Or should that be carnival for the club whose fans have been chanting 'It's just like watching Brazil!' throughout the most momentous season in their 110-year history?

Golden goals by Paul Wilkinson and Clint Marcelle gave Barnsley a 2–0 victory over Bradford City in front of a full house that included celebrity fans Michael Parkinson and Dickie Bird. And when West Indian whizzkid Marcelle hit that late clincher, the Oakwell fans really hit the roof.

Champagne corks popped as the players took a lap of honour and then saluted supporters from the safety of the directors' box.

Not bad going for a club written off as no-hopers by Mark McGhee, manager of vanquished promotion rivals Wolves.

Wilson joined his players for champers before emerging to quip: 'Celebrate? Perhaps I'll have an extra lump of sugar in my coffee tonight!

'This is just fantastic – for the club and everyone in the town. People here have experienced some hard times over the last decade so perhaps we've given them something back.

'At the start of the season, no one gave us a chance but we won our first five games on the trot and we've gone from strength to strength ever since.

'People expect the bigger clubs to do well because they have money – but we have a great spirit.'

Wilson, who has just signed a new three-year contract, added: Look at Wimbledon. We can emulate them. We will have a bit of money to spend but it's important to spend it wisely.'

Former Middlesbrough striker Wilkinson said: 'I've scored only one in about 20 games so this was well overdue.

'I never felt coming here was a backward step and who knows, we could be passing Boro on the way up. I hope not – I'd like to go back and play there next season.'

Chairman John Dennis, whose late father Ernest was also chairman at Oakwell, said: 'It's a dream come true for the town and the club and we're going to enjoy every minute.

'Don't ask me about next season. We've got a whole summer to celebrate promotion first.

'But don't worry, things won't change in the Premiership. We'll always be just little old Barnsley!'

Ada was waiting as usual when I drove into the players' car park. She'd been in charge of that parking area for as long as anyone could remember and she ran it like a military operation. She wasn't much more than five foot tall and not in the first flush of youth but nobody argued with Ada. Over the years, many a disgruntled visiting dignitary had been moved on because he didn't have the right pass.

She also used to sell the club's Super Six draw tickets and tried to cajole the players into buying a few as we left the car park. Sometimes I did, sometimes I didn't. If I decided against it, Ada was not at all impressed by my lame excuses about not having any change or leaving my wallet at home. On this day of days, she was ready for me.

'Now then, Redfearn,' she said. 'Are you going to buy a ticket for a change?'

'Sorry, Ada love, I'm clean out of brass.'

'Well in that case, make sure you bloody well go up this afternoon. Then they'll 'appen give you a rise and you'll be able to buy some of my tickets next season.' There was no answer to that.

We'd been under the microscope all week. The whole country seemed to want a slice of Barnsley Football Club and we lost count of the interviews Danny Wilson and the players gave to the press, radio and television, not to mention photo-shoots. It was never-ending. The game was a sell-out and when I arrived there must have been nearly 10,000 people milling around waiting for the turnstiles to open, even though it was a miserable, rainy afternoon. It was as if they were scared of missing a single second of what they were convinced was going to be the greatest day in the club's history.

I travelled across with Sue and the kids and as I walked the couple of hundred yards from the car park to the players' entrance, I could feel the tension and expectation among the fans. Usually, there were a few cheerful calls of 'Good luck, Redders!' and autographs to sign. This time it was much more intense. People came up to me, touched me on the arm and muttered, 'Come on, Neil, you can do it, lad.' The pressure was certainly starting to crank up a few notches and it was a relief to reach the dressing room.

I've never had a match-day routine so there was no set ritual for me to follow. Some players always drink their morning tea out of the same mug, set off at the same time each week, take an identical route to the ground, put their left sock and right shinpad on first or have to be in a certain place in the line going out on to the pitch. Not me. I just take it as it comes. In fact, I believe superstitions put added pressure on a player. I have a light breakfast, take it easy in the morning, set off in good time, exchange a bit of banter in the dressing room and then go out for the warm-up. I honestly cannot say which sock or boot goes on first.

Paul Wilkinson, who joined us from Middlesbrough at the start of that season, was even more laid back than me – he didn't even bother with a warm-up. He just ran a hot bath and climbed in, bidding a cheerful farewell to the rest of the players as they went out for their work-out. At ten to three, he climbed out of the bath, put on his gear and lined up. Carel van der Velden, a Dutch midfield player who'd joined us at the start of the season but never really featured on a regular basis, once asked him why he didn't warm up before a game. 'I am warming up,' replied Wilko. 'It's a bloody sight warmer in this bath than it is out on the pitch.' He was an experienced professional who knew what was best for him and he felt that a strenuous warm-up took a bit of edge off his game. Fair enough.

He wasn't the only Barnsley player who wasn't totally convinced about a tough warm-up routine. We had one particular session that involved walking, jogging and sprinting across the width of the pitch, time after time after time. It was hard work and on one occasion, Darren Sheridan sidled over to me and said, 'What the bloody 'ell's going on? This would be all right if we were having a day off tomorrow – but we're supposed to be playing a match in half an hour!'

When we went out to warm up before the Bradford game, the atmosphere was absolutely electric. We did our best to treat it as any other warm-up but that was impossible. There was a bit of light relief for me when I was presented with the Player of the Year award before we returned to the dressing room. When I raised it aloft to say thanks, the roar was deafening, almost as if I'd scored the winner in the Cup final. Back in the dressing room, there was the usual joking around before we went out. Danny always enjoyed coming in and having a laugh before the final team talk and Sheridan and John Hendrie usually had a few jokes to liven things up. On this occasion, it was all a bit forced. Even though we still had an away game to play against Oxford, we all knew that this was the day. We just needed to be out there. It was almost as if we wanted to get the game over with.

We were expected to win, which only added to the tension. Barnsley were second, Bradford third from bottom. No contest – on paper, that is. While we needed to win to go up, they needed points to stay up. Bradford were not going to roll over. They were fighting for survival and it was a twitchy, nervy affair until Wilko headed us in front in the 20th minute. That should have settled us but, even though we might have had two or three more, we never really flowed. The crowd were edgy, too, and suddenly, in a Bradford counter-attack, Ole Sundgot, their Norwegian striker, hit the post. That was an awful moment. Surely it wasn't all going to go wrong? We needed the second goal and at last Clint Marcelle, who had come on as substitute in the second half, did the business with a couple of minutes left. Bradford were beaten and they knew it. It was time to party.

At the end of the match, the crowd piled on to the pitch as we headed for the dressing room. I had no chance of making it ahead of the invading force. Once, when I was at Palace, I'd been surrounded by celebrating fans as I tried to leave the field and made the mistake of handing over my shirt. Next it was my shorts, then my socks and I ended up leaving the field with next to nothing on. I wasn't going down that road again! As I battled my way towards the tunnel, I was confronted by a giant of a man in a Barnsley shirt. He must have been six foot five or six tall, with a shaven head, and he was built like a Californian Redwood tree. He gave me a bear hug, lifted me above his head like a toddler, sat me on his shoulders and tottered off in the general direction of the players' tunnel. The crowd loved it – but I wasn't 100 per cent convinced I was in safe hands.

Almost as soon as we made it into the dressing room, John Dennis burst in. He ran around, hugging each player in turn – and one or two ended up with a second helping. He was a big bear of a man, too, and for the second time in ten minutes, I nearly had all the breath crushed out of my lungs. There were hugs all round and I made a point of singling out Neil Thompson, who had been a second-year apprentice when I was at Forest all those years before. Tommo and I had never lost contact and we'd shared the dream for Barnsley. It was good that he was around in our moment of triumph.

After a few minutes, all the players were ordered back on to the pitch for what felt like a never-ending a lap of honour and as soon as we disappeared down the tunnel, the fans invaded the pitch again, demanding an encore in the directors' box. Michael Parkinson and Dickie Bird, lifelong Barnsley fans, were already there. We hadn't seen too much of Parky in the last few years but he shook hands with some of the lads as we pushed our way through the press area to the front of the directors' box. Dickie usually sat in the stand when he came to matches. He just blubbed away happily and talked Barnsley to anyone who was prepared to listen.

The press and television cameras were allowed into the dressing room for more interviews and pictures as the champagne and beer flowed like water. When we finally emerged after a shower, the party was still in full flow in the boardroom and corridor. Everybody seemed to be carrying a bottle of champagne and already empties were scattered all over the place. Some of the lads were making plans to party the night away in town but I didn't fancy that. I linked up with Sue and the kids and left the ground with Lois on my shoulders, Aimee holding one hand and Sue holding the other. A fan took a picture as we walked out of the players' entrance and back to the car park – Ada had gone off to celebrate by this time, I suppose. We climbed into the car and drove home for a quiet night. Well, we still had another game to play the following week, didn't we?

To be honest, I just wanted to sit back and savour the moment at home. I was happy to slip away from the limelight until Monday morning and reflect on Barnsley's incredible story, and how, at the age of 31, with eight clubs and over 600 games in the bank, I was going to become a Premiership player at last.

In three seasons, we'd been transformed from a club that was going nowhere fast into arguably the most talked-about team in the country. Danny Wilson must take most of the credit. Danny is without question the most successful manager in Barnsley's history, yet he had to overcome major problems with the fans when he first arrived as Viv Anderson's assistant. He played in a holding role in central midfield and they really gave him a hard time. Players such as Danny often end up getting stick from the crowd. They have a lot of possession so inevitably they are going to make more mistakes than players who only want the ball when they're in good positions. Supporters don't always appreciate what's involved.

They used to boo the name of Wilson when the team was announced over the Tannoy during the warm-up. The jeers would begin again as soon as he made his first mistake and we couldn't fail to hear the calls of 'Rubbish, Wilson!' and 'Get him off, Anderson!' during the game. If the boos affected Danny, he never let on. He just concentrated on his own game. He had enormous self-belief and no fear, and he took pressure off other players with his unselfish approach. I never saw him shirk a challenge or fail to be available to a team-mate in trouble. He is not a tall man but he has a massive heart and his strength and confidence were infectious.

He epitomised everything that was good about Barnsley as we grew more and more successful and I never had any doubts about his appointment as manager after Anderson left. While I can't speak for the rest of the lads, I think it was generally accepted in the dressing room that Wilson was the man for the job. We wanted stability and continuity because even though Viv's season had been unexceptional in terms of results, we felt things were beginning to come good.

As a manager, Danny was up front, in your face, and the only time he would criticise his players was if they didn't want the ball. Individual mistakes weren't a problem, provided you fought to win the ball back, but woe betide anyone under the Wilson regime who took the easy option or failed to give 100 per cent all the time. There were one or two among the squad at first but they were no longer around by the time we were running for the Premiership. Danny and Eric Winstanley were a perfect combination. Wilson, the battler who would run through a brick wall for his club; Winstanley, the loyal clubman, cultured coach and hardened old pro with a gift for bringing out the best in his players, a father figure who knew instinctively when to put an arm round a player's shoulders or when to give him a kick up the backside.

The players soon bought into it. When professional footballers sit down over a mug of tea in the dressing room, one or two will usually raise doubts about the way things are being done in training or how the team is being asked to play out on the park. That never happened under Danny and Eric. Of course, players who found themselves on the sidelines weren't happy and there were plenty of people queuing up to knock on Danny's door to ask why they weren't in the starting line-up, but I can't remember anyone having misgivings about the overall direction we were taking.

I saw a lot of myself in Danny. Both of us were single-minded, determined, ambitious, and we didn't suffer fools gladly. We were never particularly close but we shared the same approach to the game and we'd combined well together on the field. We'd also spent enough time together in the dressing room and out on the park for him to see what sort of character I was, and he was the first manager to tune in to my ambition and really use it to his advantage. He knew that he had to harness that ambition and nurture it, not try to stifle it. So he made me captain and said, 'Right, go out and lead my team.' It was a turning point for me and perhaps for Barnsley. I was thrilled to bits.

I suppose the names of Wilson and Redfearn will always be linked with Barnsley's climb but the idea that Danny and I shared a special relationship and were the driving force behind Barnsley's success is wide of the mark. The real power behind the throne was Eric Winstanley, not Neil Redfearn. Danny kept me in the loop as club captain but I was always at arm's length on a personal level. He didn't confide in me and I suspect the same applied to most of the backroom staff – even Eric, sometimes. That's a good thing in my book. A manager should be approachable but he should never be one of the lads. Danny earned the respect of his players and staff by the way he did the job during his first couple of seasons in charge, not because we felt he was a mate.

He soon proved himself to be a shrewd operator in the transfer market. He wasn't afraid to take a chance on non-league players and brought in Martin Bullock from Eastwood Town and Darren Sheridan, younger brother of Irish international John Sheridan, from Winsford Town. Both went on to play Premiership football. He paid a few thousand quid for Bullock and what a signing he turned out to be! At 18, he stood 5ft 4in and weighed just over 10 stone sopping wet, but on his day he was devastating, either playing wide or tucked in behind the front two. So quick! He used to go past defenders as if they weren't there. It must have been like trying to tackle smoke.

Darren was probably the most underrated member of the squad. I would go so far as to say he was a better player than his brother, who played a lot of games at the top level and won 34 international caps. I always rated John highly – but not as highly as Little Shez, as we called him. In some ways, he was one of the unlikeliest-looking professional footballers I've ever seen. The first time he turned up for training I wasn't alone in wondering, 'Who the hell's this?' Small, bandy-legged with a forties haircut, he looked like a throwback to another age, but he had one of the sweetest left pegs you could want to see, and a crunching tackle. I've seen many a player take on Shez, thinking he wouldn't present much of a problem. Seconds later, the player would be picking himself off the floor and wondering what had hit him. Shez was aggressive, afraid of no one and didn't bother too much about reputations.

His never-say-die spirit typified that Barnsley side and he soon became one of the characters of the dressing room. He lived in Manchester and when he first signed, he couldn't drive and had to travel over on the train every day. That meant changing at Huddersfield and I wish I had a pound for the number of times Shez called on a Sunday night, asking if I could pick him up at Huddersfield station the next morning. We could almost set the clock by him. I'd always say yes without thinking because he was such a good lad. Then one day I worked out how many extra miles I'd done by diverting to the centre of Huddersfield every day instead of taking the direct route from home to Oakwell. When I started dropping a few subtle hints about the cost of petrol, Shez contrived to change the subject – until it was time to confirm that I was OK for a lift next morning.

At least with me in charge of transport, he used to report for training on time but once he'd passed his test and bought his first little motor, there was no telling what time he might come staggering in. He'd always have some excuse about the M62 being clogged or something more obscure like a burst water main in Ashton under Lyne. It used to drive Danny mad. As the deadline for reporting arrived, Danny would be prowling around, asking if Shez was in yet. Usually Darren would contrive to make it with a few seconds to spare but plenty of times he bumped into an angry manager and collected a fine.

Eventually, after three successive days of bad weather and fines, Shez decided enough was enough and vowed to mend his ways. He set the alarm for the crack of dawn, beat the traffic and stunned Barnsley's early birds by arriving at the ground soon after nine. The lads couldn't believe it when they strolled into the dressing room to find Shez sitting reading the paper, looking very pleased with himself. Inevitably, it was too good an opportunity for our prankster-in-chief to miss and once he had established that the gaffer was in his office, Shez crept into the corridor, eased past Danny's door and dialled the manager's number on his mobile. Danny answered.

'Gaffer, it's Shez. Look, you're not going to believe this but I'm stuck on . . .'

'I don't care where you're bloody stuck, Shez. Get yourself in here on time or there'll be big trouble.'

At this point, Shez nudged open the door with his foot and Danny looked up to see Darren, mobile phone in place, grinning from ear to ear.

Danny went into Europe for another of his most successful signings, Arjan de Zeeuw, a central defender who was combining life as a medical student with a career in the Dutch First Division. He played for Telstar, based in the town of Ijmuiden. Arjan had never heard of Barnsley when he was first approached but he didn't need long to work out that something a bit special was in the air. He picked up a Yorkshire accent in no time and acquired the nickname of Chester – as in Chester Zoo. A colossus of a lad,

Chester was as fit as a butcher's dog and a tremendous athlete. Not many centre-halves finish at the front in pre-season running but Chester usually did. He played a major role in winning promotion, always looked at home in the Premiership and after leaving Barnsley, had a successful time with Wigan and Portsmouth, where he played top-flight football once more before rejoining Wigan on their arrival in the Premiership in the summer of 2005.

Two more foreign signings arrived in the build-up to promotion year. Striker Clint Marcelle, a Trinidad and Tobago international, came from Portuguese club Felgueiras. Jovo Bosancic, a former Yugoslav Under-21 midfield player, had also been playing in Portugal, with Uniao Madeira. Initially, they came in on trial and both of them impressed straight away, although it took a while for Jovo to get the hang of English football life off the field. He was given a club house as part of his contract and after a couple of days he asked to see the chairman.

'I want bed,' he said in his broken English.

'Fair enough,' replied John Dennis, and patiently explained where he could find the nearest bedroom furniture shop.

'No,' insisted Jovo. 'Club buy me bed.'

'Club don't,' replied Dennis, or words to that effect.

Jovo got the message and before long, he worked out that he would have to fend for himself like the rest of us.

Clint was a mercurial character on and off the field. He must have been hellish to play against because he was so tiny, so quick and had such good feet. He usually arrived for training in a baseball cap and dark shades, spoke with a hint of an American accent and tried to come over as a pretty cool character. He nurtured a bit of a tough guy image but didn't quite have the physique to match. Like Jovo and Arjan, he soon became part of the furniture and an important member of the squad. Add home-grown young guns Liddell, Eaden, Watson, Moses and Morgan, throw in a bit of spice in the shape of seasoned pros including Matty Appleby, Steve Davis and me, and the mixture was almost complete.

However, Danny realised that if we were going to sustain a

promotion bid, we would need a hardcore of experienced players who knew about the promotion game. So he brought in Peter Shirtliff from Wolves, Neil Thompson from Ipswich and John Hendrie and Paul Wilkinson from Middlesbrough. All four had played at the highest level after winning promotion with good clubs and totalled over 1,700 league games between them, a lot of them in the top division. Most important, they still had something to offer – they were up for a last hurrah, if you like. Their signings were masterstrokes.

Thompson, Shirtfliff, Wilkinson and Hendrie didn't have an impact just on the field, though. They were senior players and commanded immediate respect because of what they had achieved in the past – but that would have soon evaporated if they hadn't shown straight away that they were still prepared to put in the hard work on the training ground. All four were excellent professionals and they hadn't come to Barnsley to run down their careers. They were still hungry.

Wilko had done well for Everton, Forest, Watford and Middlesbrough before joining Barnsley on a free in the summer of 1996. He and Hendrie had forged an effective partnership at Middlesbrough and, sure enough, Danny managed to persuade John to move in at Oakwell about three months after Wilko's arrival. At a stroke, he had given the club a proven strike partnership who had performed in the top division – a superb piece of business. Wilko created a load of goals for Hendrie and me. Eaden would drive in diagonal crosses from the right, Paul would knock the ball down and I was already on my bike to pick up the pieces. If I didn't, John would.

Hendrie's arrival proved to be the final piece in Danny's jigsaw, although by the time John played his first game, against Crystal Palace on 12 October, we were already established among the frontrunners. In fact, we'd laid down our marker on the very first day of the season, winning 2–1 at West Brom, one of the pre-season promotion favourites. As the team bus pulled away from The Hawthorns, Andy Liddell announced, 'We'll go up this season, you know.' No one argued. Lidds had played well, scored one of the goals and was entitled to be upbeat. He was voicing the previously unspoken conviction most of the squad had felt since the start of pre-season training. Confidence and inner strength seemed to flow right through the club and the performance at The Hawthorns sent out a clear warning to the rest of the division that Barnsley were going to be a force. As I was leaving the field, I'd shaken hands with Andy Hunt, the Albion striker, later a teammate at Charlton. 'Bloody hell, you lot have played well,' he told me. 'We're supposed to be the promotion favourites but you've blown us away today.' I was thinking exactly the same thing.

We proved that our opening performance was no fluke by winning our next four league games on the bounce, beating Huddersfield, Reading and Stoke at home and Manchester City away. We felt like the Harlem Globetrotters – good enough to beat anybody – and from that point the season seemed to have a momentum of its own. Even when we played below our best, we were usually too good for the opposition. True, we lost ten games, one of them after promotion had been secured, but nobody outplayed us. Both 2–2 draws against Bolton – who were promoted as champions and rightly regarded as the best side in the division – were among the best matches I have played in, and not just because I scored twice in each match! The Oakwell game against Bolton at the end of October was televised live, the critics raved about our performance and it was impossible not to believe that we were on the verge of something really big.

People have said that the return game at Burnden Park five weeks later was the first time our fans chanted, 'Brazil, it's just like watching Brazil!' I can't vouch for that but that chant stayed with us all the way to the Premiership. It was typical of our fans' tongue-in-cheek humour. After all, you can't get much farther away from Copacabana beach in Rio than Barnsley, can you? If the samba soccer wasn't quite flowing, they'd sing, 'Ryhill, it's just like watching Ryhill!' which is a former pit village just down the road from Oakwell. It wasn't long before the media caught on, and so did opposition supporters, who chimed in with their own version of the song if their side scored first.

Despite the Brazil chants, it took our supporters a while to accept that we might actually be going into the Premiership. They'd seen a few false dawns in their time and weren't going to be carried away on the back of a decent start to the season. So it wasn't until we were top of the League at Christmas that home gates really started to pick up and cries of, 'Up the Football League we go!' began to ring round Oakwell on a regular basis.

On a personal level, every game was pure pleasure. We weren't beaten away from home until mid-November and week in, week out, we lined up knowing that we were a top side, convinced that we were going to play some great stuff and more than likely, we were going to win. It was a bit a like waking up on Christmas morning – you can't be certain what's in store but you know it's going to be fun. Things didn't always work out to plan, of course, and once or twice we came a cropper, but that promotion season at Barnsley felt just like the year Oldham went up. I was flying. I felt invincible.

Media attention grew all the time. The Premiership was huge and here was a little South Yorkshire club who thought they played like Brazil trying to break in. Things like that aren't supposed to happen, are they? As the captain, a lot of the focus was on me. I was performing well, scoring goals and it seemed that all of a sudden the world was waking up to the fact that Neil Redfearn could play a bit.

I didn't have a problem with the increasing number of inter-views. I've always believed it's important for players to talk to the press because they are the link between players and supporters. I never saw myself as the star of the team and I'm sure Hendrie, Wilkinson and de Zeeuw, who also came in for a lot of media attention, would say the same thing. The team ethic in that dressing room was so strong that we genuinely felt we didn't have any individual stars. Media interviews came with the territory but we were all far happier back in the team environment. It was a case of all for one and one for all. Promotion would be won or lost in the dressing room and on the pitch, not talking in front of tele-vision cameras or chatting to reporters. As captain, I was determined not to come across as 'The Big I Am', either with the media or supporters. I wanted to lead by example, not by waving the big stick or hogging the media limelight.

As well as the two draws against Bolton that proved we could compete with the best side in the division, one or two other games will always stick in the memory. Four days before Christmas – on the day after the Redfearn family moved house from Slaithwaite to Holmfirth – we won 1–0 at Sheffield United in front of nearly 25,000 fans. That was a massive result. I picked up a hamstring injury and missed two games, including another big one, a 2–0 home win over Manchester City at the end of December. Over Easter we beat Charlton 4–0 and Oldham 2–0 and we were so nearly there. Then we could only draw at Crystal Palace and lost 4–2 in a rearranged game down at Portsmouth, meaning we had to beat Bradford City on that fateful day at Oakwell to guarantee promotion.

The last match of the season was at Oxford, with a lunchtime kick-off, on the Sunday after we clinched promotion. We were given a guard of honour by the Oxford players and the match officials as we took the field to a tremendous reception from both sets of supporters. Thousands of Barnsley fans had made the trip and the away end at the Manor Ground simply wasn't big enough to hold them all. So hundreds clambered into the trees behind the terracing and watched the match from there to chants of, 'Stand up if you're in the trees!'

To say we weren't fully focused would be a huge understatement and we were thumped 5–1 – I scored the goal to bring my tally for the season to 19 – but nobody seemed to mind. A fair bit of drink flowed on the coach back to Barnsley and when we arrived at Oakwell, the directors had laid on a buffet for the whole squad with loads to eat and drink. I was well-oiled by the time we hit town for a few more bevvies. Fans were everywhere, all wanting to shake hands and tell us how much promotion meant to them and to the town. Times had been hard in Barnsley because of the miners' strike 12 years before, followed by pit closures. Now we'd given the town something to smile about.

That night is all a bit of a blur, to be honest. A Monday morning hangover was looming. I vaguely remember being loaded into a taxi with Matty Appleby, who was definitely the worse for wear – or worse than me, anyway. Matty lived in Wakefield so I asked the driver, inevitably a Barnsley fan, to drop me off at home and then carry on to Wakefield with Matty. I think the driver would have taken us to the moon if we'd asked him. All he wanted to do was talk football but after a while I realised that the conversation was two-way traffic. Matty was a sleeping partner alongside me in the back seat. When we reached Holmfirth, I checked that the driver was OK about ferrying Matty to Wakefield, even though he didn't have an address to aim for, and staggered off into the night. The next day we reported at the ground by mid-morning and Matty pulled me straight away.

'Bloody hell, Redders, you lumbered me there.'

'How do you mean, Matty?' I replied, putting on my most innocent expression. He paused for a moment.

'We did get a taxi home last night, didn't we?'

'Aye, of course. Don't you remember? The driver dropped me off in Holmfirth and last I saw, he was setting off to Wakefield with you fast asleep in the back. There wasn't a problem, was there?'

'Only that I had to pay the full bloody fare from Barnsley to Wakefield via Holmfirth.'

The official civic reception was held the following week. We were driven from Oakwell to the Town Hall in an open-topped bus and it absolutely bounced down with rain. That was never going to stop thousands of supporters turning out, though, and the whole town seemed to be a sea of red and white. The players were led on to the Town Hall balcony and introduced one by one. We were given a fantastic reception but, for me, the day really belonged to John Dennis, Ada, Eric, Norman and all the other people who'd been at the club for most of their lives and were an integral part of the Oakwell fabric. The players had enjoyed a great season and written the name of Barnsley Football Club into the history books but players come and go. That's the name of the game.

For two of those who'd played a big part in Barnsley's success, Gary Fleming and Steve Davis, the promotion celebrations must have left a bitter-sweet taste. Gary had totted up over 250 league and cup games for Barnsley after spells with Nottingham Forest and Manchester City. He'd won 31 caps for Northern Ireland and been an automatic choice for club and country for six seasons, but on the day we were promoted, he was sitting in the press box, working as a radio summariser, on the outside looking in. Nearly two years earlier he'd picked up a serious knee injury and six operations in the following 18 months could not save his career. He was forced to retire before the promotion season and started a university physiotherapy course. The club awarded him a testimonial and we played Manchester City four days after the Oxford match. Over 5,000 turned up and Gary will have done well out of it, but it was a sad way for such a good career to end.

Steve Davis was one of the first-choice central defenders for the first half of the promotion season. He was a great professional and I could never really work out why he hadn't been picked up by a Premier League club before Barnsley launched their charge. He could read the game, pass, head and tackle. He was dangerous in the box at set-pieces and would usually come up with four or five goals a season. He was one of the best defenders I played with and I'm sure he would have been a revelation in the Premier League, but on 11 January he broke his leg at QPR and missed the rest of the season. Steve was never the same player again. He fought his way back and at one stage looked as if he might make it, but the damage was done and eventually he had to settle for life in the lower divisions. Fit and well, both Steve and Gary would have strengthened us in the Premiership. Football can be a cruel business.

For the rest of us, though, the 1996–97 season was Utopia. None of us will ever forget it. We'd played great football, picked up the results and won promotion to the promised land of the Premiership. What more could any Barnsley fan ask for? The Maracana Stadium in Rio instead of Oakwell? Maybe, but then again, maybe not.

11 LIVING THE DREAM

WE REPORTED BACK FOR PRE-SEASON TRAINING TO DISCOVER Oakwell under siege from the media and undergoing a major refit. The new season would start with the away supporters' end still open to the elements but, like the rest of the stadium, it was now all-seater. The area underneath the stand had been completely refurbished and re-carpeted and Margaret and Janet left us in no doubt about what would happen if we dared to cross their threshold with our boots on. Barnsley Football Club had clearly gone up in the world and the players returned from their summer break to discover that their first Premiership perk had come rolling in – a McDonald's Gold Card. Welcome to the big-time!

The cards were part of a sponsorship package with the Premier League and entitled every registered player in the Premiership to one free meal each day. As the nearest McDonald's was just a few hundred yards away from Oakwell, some of the lads wasted no time in taking advantage of their new-found status as celebs of the fast-food world. Regular customers were bemused to find themselves standing shoulder to shoulder with the local heroes in the queue for a Big Mac with fries.

The staff at McDonald's in Barnsley soon cottoned on to the idea but, unfortunately, not all the outlets were quite up to speed and sometimes the card caused a bit of a panic behind the scenes.

I discovered that for myself when I stopped off at the McDonald's drive-through on Leeds Road in Huddersfield, just round the corner from the McAlpine Stadium, Huddersfield Town's home. I pulled up and placed my order, which was passed on to the kitchen, or wherever the orders were dealt with. So far, so good, but when I presented my card, the girl behind the counter looked at me as if I'd come from another planet. Trying to keep my voice down, I explained that it was a Gold Card, part of a special deal that entitled Premiership footballers to a free meal every day.

'Are you trying it on or what?' she boomed back. 'I've never heard of these Gold Cards you're on about. This is the first I've ever seen.'

'Well it would be, wouldn't it?' I countered. 'This is Huddersfield and Premiership footballers are a bit thin on the ground round here!' That went down like a lead balloon. Either she was a very big Huddersfield fan or the joke was completely lost on her.

'I'll have to clear this with the manager,' she said.

Her superior was also a bit sceptical when she arrived on the scene, by which time quite a queue of cars had built up behind me. She said she would have to call head office to check me out. Could I run the details past her again? So I had to explain once more that this was a McDonald's Gold Card, a special deal for Premiership footballers, and I was Neil Redfearn from Barnsley Football Club. She went away to make her phone call and the customers in the main restaurant area tuned in as she started, 'I've got this chap in here who says he plays for Barnsley Football Club ...' By the time she finally cleared the transaction with the powers-that-be, my meal was stone cold but I didn't really have the heart to ask for another.

Our physio Mick Tarmey cringed visibly when he saw the cards, which clearly threatened to put a spanner in the works of his care-fully laid plans for the Premiership. He'd worked tirelessly through the close season to prepare a strict diet regime for each player and, as usual, we were going to be weighed every week and have our fat levels checked on a regular basis. Players who failed to match up would be fined but he must have wondered if the temptation of a daily Big Mac would prove too hard to resist for one or two of the boys. As it happened, the cards weren't seen as an 'open sesame' to a daily trip to the nearest drive-through, but they were very useful for us to have in our back pockets if we were in a bit of a rush and feeling peckish after a hard morning on the training ground. Our families thought they were the best thing since sliced bread. The deal was still running when I moved to Charlton the following year but I gave my card to Richard Rufus, Charlton's England Under-21 defender. He must have spotted that I was an old softie at heart. Another card was waiting for me when I moved on to Bradford City 12 months later.

Fortunately for the Barnsley players, none of the reporters who flocked to Oakwell during the countdown to our Premiership season actually clocked any of the lads standing in the queue at McDonald's – what a great story that would have been! They uncovered just about everything else, though. It was an unrelenting time for us all, particularly Danny Wilson, who seemed to be giving more or less round-the-clock interviews to an insatiable media pack.

We did our best to meet all the demands but I sensed a bit of an edge to our relations with the press this time. In previous years, and particularly during the promotion campaign, there were a lot of familiar faces in and around the press box and also among the reporters wanting an interview after training. We knew them, they knew us and, by and large, we trusted one another. In fact, some of the match-day regulars were decidedly less than neutral observers by the time we beat Bradford City to clinch promotion. However, our arrival in the Premiership wasn't big news only in Barnsley, Yorkshire and the north of England. A lot of the London press boys came calling.

I don't know whether or not they had a hidden agenda and were looking for Barnsley to go crashing straight back down, but on quite a few occasions a distinct whiff of hostility crept in to what they wrote. At best, some of the pieces about the club and the town were patronising; at worst they were downright insulting.

The players weren't exactly portrayed as keeping pigeons in the loft and taking the whippets for a walk after training but that seemed to be an underlying message in several features.

Many of the London journalists hadn't seen much of us the previous season, so they were shooting in the dark a bit about our prospects. Valid questions were raised about whether Redfearn would score goals in the top flight, whether Hendrie could still hack it, if de Zeeuw was all he was cracked up to be and whether the young lads who had done so well the previous season would cut the mustard with the big boys. Generally, the verdict was negative. We didn't know whether we would survive either, but we felt we deserved a fair crack of the whip before a ball was kicked. Even the bookies gave us a bashing. We were quoted at 1000-1 for the title while Crystal Palace, who had been promoted via the play-offs, were 250-1.

So much attention was coming from so many quarters that for the first time, I decided to find someone to handle all the press enquiries and deal with the countless requests from fans for autographs, pictures and so on. Margaret Cooper was a million miles away from the hard-nosed agents who handle a lot of Premiership players but she was a real support. A really sweet lady in her fifties, Margaret was based in Rotherham and she became a family friend. Every week I'd hand over a big bundle of letters and she'd take them away and sort everything out without any fuss. She worked with one or two more of the Barnsley players as well.

Margaret also handled my marketing and promotion. There were lots of opportunities out there and it was important to maintain a high personal profile now that Barnsley were in the Premiership. She arranged the interviews, let me know when and where they would take place and I made sure I was on time. My financial affairs and contracts were, and are, handled by Mel Stein, a lawyer based in London.

Four players were signed during the summer, three from European clubs. At £1.5 million, Georgi Hristov, a 21-year-old striker from Partizan Belgrade who had already played for Macedonia, was the most expensive player in Barnsley's history.

Eric Tinkler, a South African international midfield player, arrived from Italian *Serie A* club Cagliari for £650,000 and we handed over £450,000 to Maribor for Slovenian international defender Ales Krizan. The only British player to arrive before the start of the season was left wing-back Darren Barnard, a £750,000 signing from Bristol City, although Ashley Ward, a striker, was signed from Derby County for £1.2 million early in September.

Reserve goalkeeper Lars Leese had joined us from German club Bayer Leverkusen for £250,000 near the end of the promotion season, Peter Markstedt, a defender from Swedish club SK Vasteraas, was signed in November and Jan Aage Fjortoft, another striker, joined us from Sheffield United towards the end of the season.

None of the squad had really heard of any of the foreign imports but we trusted Danny. He had done so well for us and for the club that we assumed he was on a winner again. We had no reason to suppose that he hadn't brought in good players who would strengthen the side. He had a limited budget, he needed players and he opted to go mainly foreign. The key factor behind the decision was probably Arjan de Zeeuw, who had been a great success and hadn't cost much. It's difficult to bring in the right players when you don't have much money at your disposal, though, and in many ways, the choice of those foreign summer signings condemned us to a hard time even before a ball was kicked.

Hristov was supposed to be a potential world beater – and potential was all we saw. He never looked like carving out a niche for himself in the Premiership, although he has gone on to have a good career back home. He was a nice enough lad, although he blotted his copybook in a big way by taking a pop at Barnsley women. In what he later claimed was an off-the-record remark to a Macedonian reporter, he said they were ugly and drank too much. Needless to say, that didn't go down too well in the town, although I'm sure it was a case of naivety rather than malice. He was pretty upset about the whole business, apologised profusely and built a few bridges by posing for press pictures with a bevy of local beauties, but the damage had been done. That incident reinforced the message that, as Premiership players, we were under the microscope and one step out of line would land us in bother.

Tinkler was a good lad as well but as a player he was ordinary. Krizan would have struggled to win a place in the promotion side and when he arrived in November, Markstedt was no great shakes either. These four turned out to be peripheral figures when they should have been central.

It was hard for them because we were such a close-knit group of players, united by winning. Success is the strongest bond in football. Things like a night on the pop, a visit to an assault course or a paint-balling session are sometimes said to be great for team bonding. Nonsense! They're a bit of fun in their own right and help players to relax but they don't hold together a losing side. We'd struggled against the odds to gain promotion and we were very protective towards one another. Maybe we gave off the wrong vibes when the foreign contingent arrived but, then again, perhaps they didn't care enough. They never showed the same kind of passion as the players who had taken Barnsley into the top flight. Yes, it was difficult for them for all the obvious reasons – foreign country, new club, new team-mates and so on – but they were the big signings who were brought in to help keep the club in the Premiership and they didn't deliver. We were stepping into the unknown, into a League that was on a different planet, and we needed help and leadership. We didn't get them. The four outfield players – Hristov, Tinkler, Krizan and Markstedt – started 50 Premiership games between them. That figure should have been well over 100. They weren't being paid peanuts, either. They were on very decent money but in my view they never really showed the same kind of commitment as the other players.

On the other hand, the domestic signings did well. Barnard appeared in 35 league games, scored a few goals and proved himself at the top level. Ward was an asset, too. He arrived with a big reputation and just about lived up to it with eight league goals. Later, Fjortoft gave us some extra muscle up front, something we had been lacking since Paul Wilkinson had dropped out of contention early in the season, but basically it was down to the lads who had put Barnsley in the Premiership to keep them there – and deep down, we knew we weren't going to be quite good enough without a bit of outside help.

Should Danny have gone for English players with proven experience at that level – just as he'd signed Wilkinson, Hendrie, Shirtliff and Thompson when we were in Division One? With the wonderful gift of hindsight, yes of course he should. Summer signings are important for everyone connected with a club and if you bring in two or three recognised quality performers who are going to give the side an extra dimension, the whole club gets a lift. I'm sure some established Premiership players would have jumped at the chance to come to Oakwell. Instead, the club brought in four untried, untested and relatively unknown players. It was a big letdown.

We went down to Devon for our pre-season break. We'd been there the previous year, based at Exeter University, and it had gone well. The location was quiet, we were tucked away from the media and the public and Danny and Eric obviously thought it was the ideal place to concentrate our minds ahead of the season. They treated us like adults and we weren't confined to barracks or given a strict curfew. We had one day off when we were free to go out and have a drink together and if any of the lads wanted to pop into town in the evening, they were allowed to do so. No one took advantage and came rolling back in the early hours. If they had, Danny would have bombed them out, simple as that. We knew that – and he knew that we knew – so there were no problems. We played games against Yeovil Town, who were in the Conference in those days, and Tiverton Town before heading home for more warm-up matches against Rotherham, Chesterfield and Doncaster.

Our fans discovered what watching Brazil was really like when we played top club side Santos at Oakwell in our final pre-season friendly, eight days before the big kick-off. They beat us 3–0 but it could easily have been six or seven. They looked magnificent in an all-white strip and what a side! We couldn't get near them. To be fair to Barnsley, we were still in pre-season and not quite up to speed whereas they were well into their season and already had one tour game against Wolves under their belts. Perhaps it should have been a wake-up call about what we might expect from the top Premiership sides but frankly we weren't too bothered about the result. Twelve months earlier, we'd gone through a pre-season without winning a match but still came flying out of the traps with five straight wins. We'd won three of our six friendlies this time and we felt we were ready for what the Premiership had to offer.

The final part of the build-up came on the Sunday before our first game when Barnsley held an open day at the ground. It was a chance for the fans to meet the players, take a look around the stadium and spend their brass in the club shop. It was a sunny day and I decided to take Lois along. She was four and a half at the time and she loved Toby Tyke, the club mascot, who wore a bulldog suit and was massively popular with kids of all ages – from three to 73. This would be her chance to meet him face to face, as it were.

I thought a steady trickle of supporters would come along during the day and she would be able to have a good time with some of the other players' kids, but when we arrived at the ground, thousands of people were queuing to get in. It was manic and later estimates suggested that around 10,000 people turned up. It took us ages to make our way from the car park to the players' entrance. I was signing autographs and posing for pictures all the time. I'd never experienced anything like it and I soon realised that taking Lois was a mistake. The fans had turned out to meet me so I had to give them all my attention – and Lois had come along for a day out with her dad and a chance to meet Toby Tyke. All these people wanting my time weren't part of the equation for her but they were an indication of the frenzy that was building up around us.

We kicked off the season against West Ham at Oakwell on 9 August and it was a massive relief finally to play our first Premiership match. The build-up had seemed endless and apart from the trip to Devon we'd never really been free to concentrate

all our attentions on the job in hand, playing Premiership football. The weather had been good all week and I was keen for it
to cool down on match day – I've never enjoyed playing in heat
– but true to form, it was boiling. I was far more nervous than
usual, or perhaps anxious would be a better word. All morning I
was wondering, 'How will we perform? Will I be able to cut it
at this level? What if we get a real thumping?' I hated the nagging
doubts. I just wanted to be out there playing, enjoying myself,
responding to the atmosphere. I desperately needed my first two
or three touches to be good, to get an early shot on target and to
make a couple of decent tackles. I was very thankful that we
clicked more or less straight away and were well worth our ninth-
minute lead.

Attacking the Ponty End, we worked the ball out to Nicky
Eaden on the right. He crossed towards Wilkinson and I knew
instinctively what would happen next. Wilko climbed highest and
flicked the ball right into my path six yards out. I timed my run
as sweet as a nut and glided the header past Ludo Miklosko and
into the far corner. The Ponty End erupted in front of me, a wall
of red shirts hailing the goal. It was a fantastic feeling, an even
better moment than the penalty that clinched the Division Two
championship for Oldham six years earlier.

In that split second, I knew we were going to be all right in
the Premiership. We were playing well, we were 1–0 up and we
were showing the world that we could hold our own against a
pretty decent side who went on to finish the season in eighth place.
We had nothing to fear. I even forgot how hot it was. West Ham
shuffled things around at half-time and scored twice, through
John Hartson and Frank Lampard. We threw everything at them
but couldn't equalise.

At the final whistle I was physically and mentally shattered.
For the last 20 minutes I'd been running on adrenaline, using up
energy that my body didn't really have. When I looked in the
mirror before leaving the dressing room, I saw a gaunt, sunken
face. Sue said straight away that I looked terrible. I felt it, too. I'd
run through every emotion that day and just wanted to go away

and sit quietly on my own. I realised then how much nervous energy we had used up during the non-stop build-up to that first game. All the interviews had taken a toll. It was time to start thinking about Barnsley and Neil Redfearn and concentrate on football once again.

Losing was a huge disappointment and we didn't really deserve it. I wouldn't go as far as to say we should have won but a draw would have been about right, although Barnsley Football Club deserved to start Premiership life with a victory after all we had achieved and for the way we had handled the attention in the build-up to that first match. But there's no room for sentiment in football.

For the next nine months we were on a roller-coaster ride around the Premiership and, for me, three games against Manchester United defined our season. On 25 October, they hammered us 7–0 at Old Trafford. Afterwards, Alex Ferguson said in his press conference that he hoped Barnsley would survive. He described us as a smashing little club who did everything right on and off the field and said we might just be OK if we stuck to our beliefs.

In February, we returned to Old Trafford for a fifth-round FA Cup tie. This time we drew 1–1 and United got out of jail in the closing minutes when a clear penalty for a foul by Gary Neville on Andy Liddell was not given by referee Mike Riley. Afterwards, Ferguson was not quite so fulsome in his praise of little Barnsley. Ten days later, after we beat them 3–2 in the replay at Oakwell, he let go with both barrels. The pitch was a ploughed field, the ball was square, the ref didn't know what he was doing, the facilities weren't up to scratch. He can't have had a cup of tea or he'd have taken a pop at the tea ladies as well. That was exactly the response we were looking for. We wanted people such as Ferguson to have a go at us because they knew we were a good side who were likely to beat them next time out, instead of damning us with faint praise. We'd arrived!

If only we'd adopted that same aggressive, positive approach at the start of the season, I'm sure we would have survived in the Premiership. Instead, we gave our opponents, both teams and individuals, far too much respect. We worried about what they might do to us, rather than what we could do to them. We accepted as a compliment the patronising remarks about being a 'nice little club' and a 'smashing little side' when we should have been insulted. We were far too nice, far too polite – and by the time it dawned on us that the only way to survive was to adopt a more aggressive approach, it was probably too late.

The FA Cup was the catalyst for a mid-season sea change. Before the start of the competition we'd been giving away goals for fun – seven at Old Trafford, six at home against Chelsea, five at Arsenal, four against Everton, Wimbledon and Southampton – but after we knocked Bolton out of the cup in the third round, there was only one more drubbing, 6–0 at West Ham the following week.

In the fourth round, we beat another Premiership side, Spurs, after a replay. Then came the fifth-round tie at Old Trafford when, instead of sitting back and waiting for them to hit us with every-thing but the kitchen sink, as we had in the league game, we went for them. John Hendrie gave us the lead after their keeper, Peter Schmeichel, had completely miscued a clearance. The ball ended up behind him, ensuring a frantic chase as Hendrie and Schmeichel trundled after it. Hendrie got there first and poked the ball into the empty net.

United equalised but we were the better side and finished the job in the replay. But for that ludicrous penalty decision, we would have won first time around. Our run ended at Newcastle in the quarter-finals but, by then, the Premiership was seeing a different Barnsley, a Barnsley who believed they were up there on merit and were determined to contest every inch of ground instead of giving superior footballing sides the freedom of the park. This team comprised a bunch of players who said, 'Sod it, we're Barnsley and we'll do it our way. We'll let them worry about us for a change.'

The pivotal match was against Liverpool at Oakwell on 28 March. We'd beaten them 1–0 at their place in November and, clearly not in the mood to concede a league double, they were doing everything to wind us up from the start. I soon detected a feeling of real hostility among both sets of fans. Gary Willard, who had already booked more players than any other Premiership referee, never got a handle on the game at all. He unnecessarily booked Phil Babb of Liverpool and Darren Sheridan early on and after 53 minutes, sent off Barnard for tripping Michael Owen. When he dismissed Chris Morgan 12 minutes later for a foul on Owen, the crowd erupted. They were convinced Morgan never touched Owen. A fan ran on to the field to attack Willard, who promptly took the players off while the crowd cooled down. Just before the final whistle, he sent off Shez for a second bookable offence after a fracas involving Paul Ince and Steve McManaman. I'd seen Shez do far worse and stay on.

McManaman scored the winner from the ensuing free kick, sparking another invasion. Ince and I both had to step in to prevent supporters reaching Willard. The police were involved and for a while it was complete mayhem. An appeal for calm was broadcast over the public-address system and eventually the pitch was cleared for Willard to blow the final whistle. Barnsley fans were milling around near the Liverpool team coach afterwards and had to be restrained by police when the players climbed on board. It was two hours before the police decided it was safe for Willard to leave the ground. Amid the chaos, there had been a football match, too. I gave Barnsley the lead, Karlheinz Riedle equalised and then put Liverpool ahead. I scored a second while we were down to nine men and we looked like hanging on until McManaman's late goal.

That game marked the turning point for us. We'd beaten Southampton 4–3 the previous week and we were outplaying Liverpool when all the trouble started. If we'd kept 11 men on the field and beaten them four or five, they could not have complained. Until the dismissals of Barnard and Morgan, we had the perfect blend. We were aggressive, competitive and we played just about our best football of the season. Liverpool couldn't live with it but instead of winning by a mile, we lost 3–2.

That result was shattering psychologically because our

performance had proved that we could compete with the top Premiership sides. It was yet another game in which we'd played well and lost and, from that point, we desperately needed to nick a couple of wins when we played badly. It never happened and we ended up losing seven of our last nine matches, with just a single win over Sheffield Wednesday to give us a glimmer of hope.

Relegation was confirmed in a 1–0 defeat at Leicester in the penultimate game of the season. They scored with about half an hour to go. We piled bodies forward but it was one of those days when we seemed destined not to score, and somehow we knew it. The harder we ran and the more we tried, the more we tied up. Afterwards, I felt empty, hollow. For the sake of the fans we knew we had to lift ourselves for the last game, against Manchester United at Oakwell, and we played OK, even though we lost 2–0.

I believe the Premier League was poorer without us. We were a shock to the system. People looked down the list of Premiership clubs and there was the name Barnsley. What the hell were they doing there? Everyone loves an underdog and by the second half of the season, fans everywhere were rooting for us to stay up. Perhaps they were tired of seeing us kicked in the teeth by the critics. We were a one-off. We had the ability to match the best sides but at first we were too naïve and collected too many beatings, but we didn't buckle. We were a bit like a prize fighter. Time after time, we looked down and out, only to take a count of nine, get up and deliver a knock-out punch in the next round. If we could have just hung on, we would have got better and better.

I loved every minute of that season. It was my first taste of the top division and I'd waited a long time for the chance to pit myself against the best players. Before a ball was kicked, I had no idea how I would fare. I just knew I would give it my best shot. I felt at home straight away. I loved the big stadiums and the atmosphere and I soon discovered that the style of play suited me, too. Premiership sides didn't close me down as tightly as teams in Division One, although sometimes I was man-marked, just as I had been at Oldham and during Barnsley's promotion season. The opposition were frightened of me and knew they had to prevent me from getting into the danger zone.

At Oldham and Barnsley in the old Division One days, I used to play on it and talk to the marker during the game. I'd tell him, 'You'll have to stick close today. If you don't pick me up, I'll score.' He'd respond by telling me which leg he was going to break first or that I was slow and couldn't trap a bag of cement. That didn't worry me because I knew he was rattled. If I did score, I'd rub it in straight away. 'There you are, son. Don't say I didn't warn you! You'll get a right bollocking from the gaffer now. He'll probably take you off.' Arrogant? Maybe, but it was all part of the psychological battle between my marker and me, and I would use anything to give me an edge. It wasn't a tactic I employed too often with Premiership players, though. And generally the opposition preferred to close down my options and asked more searching questions about my next moves.

I found I could answer most of those questions and I believe that I finished the season as the best attacking midfield player in the Premiership. That sounds boastful, I know, but I'm not being big-headed. I'm making what I think is a realistic assessment of my season. I scored ten goals in 37 games, more than any other central midfield player, and I scored those goals for a struggling side that had just been promoted from the First Division. I'm very proud of what I achieved that year. My only regret was that I hadn't been playing at that level for a long time.

At the end of the season, my initial reaction was that I wanted to stay around and help Barnsley bounce straight back. I was convinced we were good enough. In fact, I was sure we could breeze it. At that stage, it seemed reasonably certain that Danny would be staying on as manager. Over the previous couple of seasons, Danny had been linked with several clubs and, after we were relegated, the rumour mill started again. There was even some speculation that I might succeed Danny if he left but, as far as I was aware at the time, Danny intended to stay.

My situation was straightforward enough. I had proved myself as a Premiership player and I wanted paying accordingly. It wasn't the first time I'd had a dispute over pay. Midway through my seven years at the club, I thought I was being taken for granted, not being paid what I felt I was worth, and considered moving on when contract talks looked like stalling. I spoke to Joe Jordan, who was manager of Stoke at the time, and Sue and I met him at Woolley Services on the M1 near Wakefield. He was very likeable and articulate and he made a lot of sense when he talked about football. I also had a word with John Rudge at Port Vale, but I never really wanted to leave and, eventually, a deal was ironed out. I suppose it was a bit like having a spat with the missus – you pack your bag, open the front door, discover it's pouring down with rain and think, 'Oh perhaps I'll go tomorrow instead.'

This time it was different. I had spent a season in the top flight on my old First Division wages, far less than some players in the Barnsley dressing room who had not contributed anything like as much. I didn't expect to be paid more than anyone else, all I wanted was parity with the top earners at the club and when I mentioned this to Danny, he didn't attempt to dissuade me from asking for a better deal.

If the Barnsley directors had taken me to one side and said, 'You've done a great job, we'll make it right for you financially,' I would definitely have stayed. However, the reluctance on their part was obvious and I suspect they were putting out one or two feelers to see how much they could get for a player who had cost them £150,000 and given them the best years of his footballing life. In the end, it boiled down to a simple issue – would I do what was best for Barnsley Football Club or for my family? No contest. I knew there would be Premiership clubs keen to sign me after my performance over the previous nine months and I knew they would pay me good money. So when Barnsley continued to hedge their bets, I asked Mel Stein to find me a Premiership club.

Charlton, newly promoted from Division One, were first in. They were ready to give Barnsley a million pounds and pay me four times what I was earning at Oakwell. Mel said they were very keen indeed. Charlton wanted me, Barnsley didn't. On the face of it, the offer was too good to be true, but I still couldn't make up my mind. The head said Charlton, the heart said Barnsley. I suppose that, deep down, I was hoping for a last-minute change of heart among the Oakwell directors. Also, and with no disrespect to Charlton, I wondered if some interest might surface closer to home. Apparently, Leeds had offered £500,000 for me around Christmas and I thought they might come back in, although they probably wouldn't have been prepared to pay a million pounds. After I had signed for Charlton, I learned that Everton and Sheffield Wednesday had also made inquiries. No one at Barnsley told me about those approaches and, frankly, I felt let down. I'd given everything for Barnsley but when I asked for something in return, they turned their backs on me.

I signed for Charlton on 25 June 1998, but it took me the best part of a month to get used to the idea that I had to start all over again somewhere else. Joining a new club with a chance to stay in the Premiership should have been an exciting time but I was absolutely gutted about leaving Barnsley and, for a while, I still wondered if I'd done the right thing. That kind of emotion was completely out of character. I've always believed that professional football is a short career and a player should earn as much as he can while he can, but I'd become deeply attached to Barnsley.

When I left, Danny Wilson told the media, 'I didn't want Neil to go but there was no way I would deny him the opportunity to remain in the Premiership.' A week later, Barnsley held a press conference at Oakwell to announce that Danny was leaving to join Sheffield Wednesday. Barnsley's golden age was over.

12 THE SOUND OF SILENCE

'SAY NOWT,' SAID MY DAD. SO I SAID NOWT. 'JUST KEEP QUIET and leave the talking to me,' was Charlton manager Alan Curbishley's advice. So I kept quiet and left the talking to Alan. Playing the strong, silent type isn't normally my style but on this occasion I was more than happy to keep my head down and let someone else deal with the flak.

The rumpus began after the Premiership game between Charlton and Arsenal at The Valley on 28 December 1998. Patrick Vieira, the Arsenal midfield player, had been sent off early in the second half for using an elbow. I was on the receiving end. Two days later, I was branded a cheat by Vieira's manager, Arsene Wenger, and that was enough for Dad and Curbs to order the vow of silence and for my manager to mount the barricades on my behalf. A furious war of words ensued, which ended with the two managers having their heads knocked together by the FA.

Now I've played with and against a lot of people in almost a thousand matches over the last 25 years and, as far as I know, Wenger is the only person who has labelled me a cheat. It hurt at the time and it still hurts today. I'm no angel, never have been, but I'm not a cheat. I play a man's game like a man and I like to think that just about every pro I have been involved with would tell you that I play fair. I don't elbow opponents, I don't spit in their faces, I don't dive, I don't try to con referees and I don't attempt to get opponents sent off, which was what all the fuss was about on this occasion.

It was a Christmas derby and a big game for both sides. Arsenal needed the points to maintain their championship challenge, we needed them to ensure we would still be playing Premiership football the following season. We had a lot of injury problems, particularly among the front players, and Curbishley had asked me to play farther upfield than usual, a little bit behind Steve Jones in a 4-4-1-1 formation.

The trouble started when Vieira won the ball off me as I was pushing forward in an attacking position, and set off towards our goal with me in pursuit. I knew from past experience that Vieira always wanted time on the ball and when he was put under pressure, he would get a bit flustered and start throwing his arms about. That had happened in one of Barnsley's games against Arsenal, when he was challenged by Martin Bullock and Darren Sheridan. One nibbled away at his left side, the other on the right, but Vieira ploughed on, swinging his arms around as he went. No damage was done because he was well over 6ft tall and Little Shez and Martin were the best part of a foot shorter. The flailing arms flew harmlessly over their heads as they continued to press home their challenge. I wasn't so lucky on this occasion.

There was the usual shoving and jostling between us and twice I tried to hook the ball away from him from behind. The first time he reacted by throwing his arm back at me but made no contact. When I tried again, Vieira responded in the same way, swinging back his arm to throw me off. His elbow did not hit me in the face but caught me at the top of my chest and under my chin. It wasn't a massive contact but my head was moving downwards at the moment of impact and the force of the blow was enough to rattle my teeth together and stop me in my tracks.

For a split second, it really hurt and I went down on to my knees with my hand to my mouth. There was no major damage, although my teeth had taken quite a clattering and I'd gashed the inside of my lower lip, so I started to get up again. Uriah Rennie, the referee, had already blown his whistle and was running towards us. I started to say, 'Come on, ref, don't book him for that,' but I was too late. He showed Vieira a red card and booked me for the original foul, a tackle from behind. Rennie clearly believed that Vieira intended to hurt me and the fact that he did not strike me in the face was irrelevant. The letter of the law says that if a player raises a hand towards an opponent, he is in trouble. It doesn't matter how much contact there has been.

I thought both decisions were harsh. I didn't really deserve to be booked for what were a couple of relatively harmless challenges and I don't think Vieira should have been sent off. OK, maybe the intent was there, but I hadn't been injured and a booking for Vieira and a talking-to for me would probably have been enough. Be that as it may, Vieira walked, the game ended in a 1–0 win for Arsenal and, afterwards, the big talking point was not the Vieira-Redfearn incident but a tackle by Charlton defender Eddie Youds on Dennis Bergkamp, Arsenal's Dutch international striker. Wenger was up in arms about the challenge and the tackle was the major subject for discussion on the television highlights and in the following day's papers.

It wasn't until Wenger had watched a video of the Vieira incident a couple of days after the game that I suddenly became back-page news and the full-scale war of words broke out. From that point, the situation mushroomed until it was totally out of hand. The two managers spent over a week firing off broadsides at one other, with me in the middle wishing it would end. It was daft. A player had been sent off, for heaven's sake. It wasn't the start of World War Three. The FA had supported the referee's decision. Surely that was the time to call a halt and get on with our lives, but no, Wenger wouldn't let it drop.

'My thought is that Patrick didn't deserve to be sent off and that Neil Redfearn cheated the referee,' he said. 'Usually, I think Redfearn is an honest type of player but maybe Charlton wanted so much to win the game that he was ready for anything to get Patrick sent off.'

Curbishley sprang to my defence. 'I can't see how Arsenal can make such a fuss. I suppose if the elbow had flattened Neil's nose they would have accepted the decision. The intent was there, no matter where Vieira's arm actually landed. Neil is the innocent party. Vieira is the one who was cheating because he was using violent conduct.'

Wenger's response was to name me as the dirtiest player in the Premiership, and so it went on until, on 8 January, Graham Bean, the recently appointed Compliance Officer at the FA, stepped in and advised the two managers to end the squabble.

The source for Wenger's allegation that I was the dirtiest player around was a league table based on the number of sendings-off and bookings for each player. At the time of the incident, I'd been booked more than anyone else, probably because I made more tackles, but that didn't make me the dirtiest player in the League. I can't think even Wenger seriously believed that I was. I suspect he might have been trying to distract some of the attention from his own side's disciplinary record, which didn't make particularly good reading for the Highbury hierarchy. Before the Charlton game, their players had received four red cards and picked up 36 cautions – and here was yet another blot on their copybook. Perhaps he chose to single me out in an attempt to divert some of the flak from his own player and, like so many managers, he was selective in what he saw.

To label me the dirtiest player was one thing and, to be honest, it was water off a duck's back, but to call me a cheat was, I believe, totally out of order. I've collected my fair share of bookings but I've never been cautioned for deliberately trying to hurt another player and I've only been sent off twice, both times during my spell at Halifax, long after I left Charlton. For a player who makes as many tackles as I do, that's not a bad record and it suggests that referees know my character. It certainly knocks on the head any idea that I was one of the dirtiest players around. The fact is that any competitive player is going to pick up a few bookings because, inevitably, there will be mistimed tackles or a split-second of over-reaction in the heat of the moment – and I am a competitive player. So, for that matter, is Patrick Vieira.

We play the game hard and we accept the consequences if the referee reckons we've overstepped the mark.

Looking back, I'm glad I took the advice of my dad and Alan Curbishley and avoided a slanging match with Wenger. I respected the man a lot and still do. It's a pity he didn't show a touch of respect for me back in January 1999. He knew when he called me a cheat that I had been a very good professional for a long time and had worked my way through the divisions to become a Premiership player. Surely he'd seen me playing often enough for Barnsley and Charlton to realise that I was not the kind of player to feign injury. If I really wanted to, I could rattle on at great length about Arsenal's disciplinary record under Wenger. We all know it isn't exactly the best in the game. I could delve into the number of times he has apparently been looking the other way when Arsenal players have got into trouble, but what's the point? Arsenal are a great side, Wenger is a top manager so why take a pop at him so long after the event? I'm just glad to have an opportunity to set the record straight as far as I am concerned.

The incident took place around six months after I'd arrived at The Valley as the first £1 million player in Charlton's 93-year history. If the price tag wasn't pressure enough, Curbs cranked things up a bit when, at the press conference to announce my transfer, he told the assembled media, 'I've brought in Neil because he's proved he can score goals from midfield in the Premiership. He scored fourteen times in all competitions for Barnsley last season and now I want him to do the same for Charlton.' I thought, 'Thanks, Alan! That's really going to make life easy.' Scoring 14 goals would have been a tall order if I'd joined Arsenal, Manchester United or Liverpool, let alone newly promoted Charlton. It was a big ask before I'd even kicked a ball.

It became even bigger when we got down to pre-season training and it was obvious Alan was going to stay true to the 4-4-2 formation that had won promotion from Division One. I couldn't help but wonder whether I would be able to get into the danger zone often enough to score the goals expected of me. I also had misgivings about whether the system would be sophisticated enough at

Premiership level. I knew from my experience at Barnsley that survival in the Premiership was about more than commitment and hard work.

Perhaps for that reason, I didn't find it particularly easy to settle and felt like an outsider at first, although that was probably more down to me than the other players. At Barnsley, I'd been an integral part of the dressing room for seven seasons and one of the senior players for the last two or three years. I'd seen players come and go and no one had seriously threatened my position as one of the main men. Now, for the first time since 1991, I was the new boy, even though I was a proven Premiership player and an expensive signing. I was apprehensive about how the established order would respond.

I knew there would be a strong feeling of togetherness among the players who had won promotion, just as there had been at Barnsley, and I also knew from my experience at Oakwell that some of the players would be uneasy about my arrival. They would be putting me under the closest scrutiny in pre-season training and in the warm-up games, saying to themselves, 'Let's have a look at this Redfearn. Let's see what he's got to offer that's so special.' They would be watching me in the dressing room to see how I fitted in with the banter and the practical jokes. They would be waiting to see if there was any edge on my part.

I was given the squad number four, previously the possession of Keith Jones, who had played 44 games in central midfield in the promotion season, and I felt uncertain about taking the shirt. He'd done the hard work the previous year and was entitled to hang on to the same shirt but instead, he found himself edged out by the new man. He wasn't the first person to discover the hard way that there's no sentiment in football but I would have been more than happy to take number 15 or 16, even though it was pretty obvious I would be in the starting line-up. I wouldn't have blamed him for being a bit resentful towards me – but he wasn't. In fact, everyone, players and staff, went out of their way to make me feel at home and I had no reason to be so apprehensive. Even so, I tried to play myself in slowly, testing the water as I went along.

Then, when I had more or less started to feel at home with a few games under my belt, I fell foul of the media, in this case a young freelance who was working for the *Daily Star*. He collared me after training one day and asked if I could spare a few minutes to talk about the differences between Barnsley and Charlton. As usual, I was happy to do so.

'You won promotion at Barnsley,' he began, 'and now you're playing at another newly promoted club. What's the difference between the two sides?'

'Well,' I replied, 'Barnsley played free-flowing, open football and scored a few goals but were a bit naïve at the back. Charlton are more organised, keep their shape, work hard at set-pieces but don't have as much flair.'

It was a fair comment, given in all honesty, and obviously I went into greater detail about the merits of the two sides, comparing Barnsley's flair with Charlton's organisation. I wasn't derogatory about Charlton, nor did I eulogise about a Barnsley side who, after all, had been relegated. Unfortunately for me, the reporter must have been out to make a bit of a name for himself. He no doubt knew that I was always open in my dealings with the press and sometimes spoke a bit too freely. He spotted an angle that I hadn't been aware of during the interview and chose to leave out the remark about Barnsley being naïve in defence. The following day's banner headline proclaiming 'Barnsley better than Charlton, says Redfearn' was the last thing anyone at The Valley, particularly me, wanted to read.

Curbishley was not best pleased. He called me into his office before I'd had a chance to read the article, threw the paper across the desk and said, 'What the bloody hell's that all about? What's going on?' I read the story, explained what I had, in fact, said and apologised if I'd put him in a difficult position. I also pointed out that I was an experienced professional and there was no way I was, knowingly, going to stitch up my club, my team-mates or a manager who had always been straight down the line with me. Alan's response was, 'Fair enough. I believe you. Leave it with me' – no fine or disciplinary action, just a sensible adult approach to what was basically a storm in a teacup. As far as he was concerned, that was the end of the matter.

I hadn't said anything out of turn, I hadn't criticised the manager or individual players. I'd just given what I considered to be an honest answer to a straightforward question, forgetting that the London media could be a bit sharp. Understandably, perhaps, the fans were less than impressed. 'If you think Barnsley are so bloody good, why don't you bugger off back there?' was the general theme of the comments hurled at me for the next couple of games before things calmed down again.

Curbs had brought in three new players. Chris Powell arrived from Derby and he fitted in straight away on the left side of the back four, alongside Danny Mills, Eddie Youds and Richard Rufus. John Robinson and Paul Mortimer were the wide players in midfield, with Mark Kinsella and me in central positions. Up front, we had Clive Mendonca and Andy Hunt, the third new signing, from West Brom. With Mark Bright, Shaun Newton, Carl Tiler, Steve Brown, Keith Jones, Anthony Barness and Steve Jones in the squad, we had a lot of good pros and were a solid unit. We started well, drawing our first game at Newcastle and then beating Southampton 5–0. I scored one of the goals. We might easily have hit ten and I remember thinking, 'I'll be all right with this lot after all.' We followed that with a 0–0 draw at Highbury and were up there with the front runners. Inevitably, reality kicked in when we went up to Old Trafford and were thumped 4–1.

The honeymoon was over and as the season developed, I couldn't escape a growing sense of personal frustration. I had a manager who liked me, trusted me and was giving me every opportunity to succeed. In return, I was prepared to give the manager, my team-mates and the supporters 110 per cent, but somehow it wasn't quite working, mainly because of personal doubts about my role in Alan's 4-4-2 system. He wanted me to play an orthodox central midfield role instead of giving me a free hand as Danny Wilson had done at Oakwell. I was expected to track back and defend deep. Fair enough – but if I did that, I wasn't going to be in a position to score 14 goals at the other end.

That isn't a criticism of Curbishley, for whom I have the utmost respect as a man and a manager, but I can't really believe Alan didn't do his homework and see how I'd been able to score so many goals for Barnsley, where the system had, in some ways, been built around my ability to make runs and get forward into scoring positions. Goals win matches and if you have a player who can score regularly, particularly from midfield, you protect him and play to his strengths. So having shelled out so much money for that type of player, it would surely have made sense for Alan to shuffle the system around a little bit to accommodate me. He didn't do that and to some extent I was a square peg in a round hole, a natural goal-scorer who didn't have the freedom to go out and score goals. I managed to score three times in 29 league starts and overall, I did a decent job. But I suppose the bottom line is that I wasn't the right player for that Charlton side.

Like everyone else, though, I went out and gave everything every week. No one at Charlton was going to roll over because, like any other promoted side, we knew from day one that survival was the name of the game and we scrapped for every minute of every match. Kinsella was a real presence in the middle of the park, Robinson an excellent wing-back, Rufus a quality defender and Youds never gave an inch. As I'd said in my ill-fated interview at the start of the season, we were never going to score a lot of goals but we weren't going to give too many away – and that's how it proved. We lost 11 of our 38 games either 0–1 or 1–2, we had five goalless draws and we drew four more games one apiece. If only we'd been able to nick the odd extra goal here and there, we would probably have survived instead of missing out by five points.

In the end, Charlton, like Barnsley, were relegated. Like Barnsley, we weren't quite good enough; unlike Barnsley, Charlton kept it together and learned from the experience. Curbishley stayed, most of the leading players stayed and I was certain that they would go straight back up with a realistic chance of surviving second time around. I was right. Charlton did exactly what Barnsley should have done and reaped the rewards, while

Barnsley plunged down two divisions and ran into serious financial problems.

To go down for a second season running was a real wrench. Even though I'd been at Charlton for just a year, I'd come to know my team-mates inside out and we were all hurting together. A professional player operates at full tilt all the time and in a tight dressing room, we see our team-mates for what they are. We share the highs and lows and we learn what makes one another tick. We see right inside each other and take responsibility for one another on and off the field. While it's tough for supporters when their side is relegated, it's very hard for the players, too. I shared the experience with my team-mates at Barnsley and Charlton and virtually all the players at both clubs were devastated by relegation. No one shrugged his shoulders and made light of it, knowing there was another payday just around the corner.

The Charlton players had spent nine months working their hearts out to keep their club in the Premiership and they almost succeeded. I could relate to how Curbishley, coach Mervyn Day, and the other coaches and players who had been at the club for a long time felt because I had gone through the same thing myself 12 months earlier. When the axe fell, it really hurt me, too. That may come as a surprise to some people because, Barnsley apart, I've never really showed my emotions at a football club, but I was gutted.

Almost as soon as Charlton were relegated, speculation began that I would be returning north in the summer, quoting my family's inability to settle in London as the reason. Nothing could have been further from the truth. Sue, Aimee and Lois loved just about every minute of our stay. So did the dog and cat, for that matter. We lived in Fyfield, near Ongar in Essex, in a house rented by the club. It was magnificent, a farmhouse-style property with six bedrooms, set in an acre of ground, with a long driveway up to the front door. We couldn't have asked for more. My fears that the move would be a big disruption for Aimee and Lois, who had settled in at school back home, were unfounded. They saw it as an adventure and adapted to their new school straight away. Lois even picked up a London accent. One day a couple of months after we moved, she and Sue were having a bit of a tickle and a rough-and-tumble on the sofa and Lois couldn't stop giggling. She was nearly helpless with laughter and finally managed to blurt out, 'Ooh Mum, you are a funny bunny!' in a perfect London accent. I couldn't believe my ears. No, the only member of the family who had felt unsettled was me.

Footballers enjoy the limelight during the good times but they tend to look for excuses when it isn't going so well and I was no exception. I'd done well at Barnsley but when things weren't working out at Charlton I needed to find a reason why. I knew the supporters expected big things – in other words, lots of goals – from their million-pound player but I wasn't come up with the goods. Instead of looking at myself, I tried to find other reasons, someone or something else to blame. So I pointed the finger at the 4-4-2 system that I felt was strangling my attacking instincts.

Sue saw it differently, arguing that I was the new man at a new club and couldn't expect everything to change for me. She said that if things weren't going well for the club, supporters would inevitably blame the newcomer rather than the players who had given them promotion. She was right but I refused to see it her way and grew more and more unsettled about the way things were going and my role in the side.

I tried not to let my feelings show in the dressing room and started to take my problems home. During that season, there were times when I wasn't much fun for Sue and the kids to be around. I should have tried harder to leave my work worries behind but that's never been my style. Unlike some players, I can't just switch off when I drive away from the training ground and, inevitably perhaps, the people I loved the most were the people I hurt the most. Sue and I argued, not because we were unhappy together but because I was unsettled at work. Time after time she would say, 'Look, don't take it out on us. Take it out on those so-and-sos at the club.' As the weeks went by, I missed our real home more and more, I missed Yorkshire and eventually, before the end of the season, I decided that the only way out of my problems was to move back north.

The writing was on the wall, anyway. Alan started taking me off during games and once or twice left me out of the starting line-up altogether. Let's face it, you don't do that to a million-pound player if you are totally happy with him, do you? I didn't make a song and dance about it, as I would have done in my younger days. Instead, I had a long chat with Curbs, telling him I hadn't really been able to settle and that I thought a move back north would be the best thing for everyone. He had every right to sound off at me. After all, he'd hung his hat on me after reaching the Premiership by paying big money and here I was, sitting down and saying things weren't working out for me, but he said he understood my problems and assured me that as long as I continued to give him 100 per cent, he would do the right thing by me. To be honest, I suspect Alan had realised that I wasn't the player he was looking for but, as ever, he was absolutely straight with me.

Towards the end of the season, Curbs called me in and said he'd had an approach from Huddersfield Town. Was I interested? Too right I was. They were a decent First Division side and I knew and liked their manager, Peter Jackson. In fact, Jacko had been on the Bradford City playing staff when I went for a trial after leaving Nottingham Forest and we had a laugh about it while we were discussing the move. I decided to wait until the summer before committing myself but felt sure that I would be playing at the McAlpine Stadium, just down the road from home in Holmfirth, the following season. Then Town's new owner, millionaire businessman Barry Rubery, sacked Jackson and brought in Steve Bruce as manager. I never heard from Huddersfield again. I was bitterly disappointed.

During the summer, rumours persisted in the media that I might be on the move but nothing happened. So I reported back for pre-season training in July and, before long, I was trotting out to warm up for the first of our pre-season friendlies against a local non-league club, with just a handful of Charlton fans there to cheer us on. By and large, I'd had a decent reception from the supporters during the relegation season, even though I hadn't scored the goals they expected. They saw that I was working my socks off for the club and, for the most part, they backed me. Clearly, though, there was at least one fan who hadn't been impressed and he was waiting for me as I began to go through the warm-up routine. It was only a small ground, we were close to the touchline, there were no stewards and I could sense he was looking for trouble.

'You're bloody rubbish, Redfearn,' he called. 'You're the reason we got relegated. Get back to bloody Yorkshire where you belong.' The players from both sides couldn't fail to hear him ranting on and so did the few fans who had already arrived and were taking their places on the terraces. 'Do you hear, Redfearn, you're bloody useless . . .' On and on and on he went. Mervyn Day came across and told me to take no notice and I did my best to ignore the non-stop barrage of abuse but my tormentor gave me a few more choice words as we left the field after the warm-up and, sure enough, he chimed in again as we emerged from the players' tunnel. He followed me around for the first 15 minutes, the first and only time I've been man-marked by a spectator. Eventually, when we won a corner on the right, he arrived on the scene as I was placing the ball by the corner flag. He was only an arm's length or so away so I thought to myself, 'Right, pal, this is where I come in.'

I turned to him, gave him a hard stare and said, 'Wait for me outside at the end of the game. We'll sort this out then. Just you and me, OK?'

He was a big, heavy chap and he looked up for it. In fact, for one moment I thought he was going to come on to the pitch and get stuck in there and then. I remember thinking I'd have to get the first punch in and make sure it put him down. It was ridiculous. A professional sportsman should never lose his cool with a fan and I was experienced enough to know better than to ask someone to step outside for the equivalent of a pub brawl, but we're only human. There's only so much abuse any one man can take and I'd had enough. I wasn't in the mood to back down and if he'd turned up, I would have taken him on. Fortunately, he thought better of it and was conspicuous by his absence when I came out of the players' entrance and made my way towards the team bus. It was an evening I could have done without, particularly as nothing seemed to be moving on the transfer front.

As the countdown to the new season continued, there was an enquiry from Sheffield United but nothing came of it. I was just beginning to think I was destined to stay in London when Bradford City came on the scene. They had been promoted to the Premiership at the end of the previous season and were wanting to strengthen the side with one or two experienced players. I spoke to Paul Jewell, their manager, and he impressed me. The lure of the Premiership was strong and after not really cutting it at Charlton, I needed to go out and prove the doubters wrong. There were no snags in the negotiations and I joined Bradford in time for their last pre-season friendly at Valley Parade – against, of all clubs, Barnsley.

I was relieved to be back on home soil but grateful, nevertheless, for having had the opportunity to spend a season working for Alan Curbishley, one of the best managers I have played for, if not the best. Throughout my stay, he backed me every inch of the way, both in public and behind the scenes. I learned quickly that one of his strengths was man-management. He realised what made his players tick on and off the field. Would-be managers can go on FA and PFA courses until they are blue in the face but man-management can't be manufactured; it comes naturally to the Alan Curbishleys of this world. He understood his players and seemed to have an uncanny way of knowing if we had any worries or problems that might be affecting our performance.

Curbishley is the perfect example for would-be managers of how important it is to be yourself and not try to imitate other people. There's no point trying to copy Alex Ferguson if that isn't your nature. Ferguson set out to rule the Manchester United players with a rod of iron and it worked, but he's a one-off. What works for him isn't necessarily going to work for others. Managers need to develop their style around their own personality. Alan is a gentler and more understanding man than many of his managerial contemporaries and that's what he brought to his style of management. Of course, he could be as hard as the next man if we stepped out of line or didn't come up to scratch in training or matches, but his strength was the humane side of his nature. That was what really made me want to go out and give everything for him. He's a top man.

His record at Charlton speaks for itself. After taking over in tandem with Steve Gritt in 1991, he took sole charge four years later and has won promotion twice and established what is basically a medium-sized club in the Premiership. It's a big surprise to me that he wasn't given an opportunity at one of the big clubs, either in London or elsewhere, some time ago. Maybe he hasn't quite been in the right place at the right time and the tendency for major clubs to appoint foreign coaches has undoubtedly worked against him. But he's one of the best English coaches around and his decision, at the end of the 2005–06 season, to leave The Valley after 15 years seemed certain to provide the chance for him to work on a bigger stage.

He gave Charlton so much and was rightly regarded as one of the leading candidates to succeed Sven-Goran Eriksson as the England coach. I'm so glad he didn't reach the stage of being taken for granted by the club and the fans. It can happen and there was a danger that some people might have started to forget where Charlton were when Alan took over, believing the club had a God-given right to be in the Premiership. That's nonsense and I'm sure that, now he's left, people will always appreciate just how important Alan Curbishley was for Charlton Athletic.

13 HOME SWEET HOME

BRADFORD CITY WAS A DREAM MOVE FOR ME. I WAS BACK IN Yorkshire, playing for my hometown club and still a Premiership player on decent money. What more could I ask? I have to admit, though, that my arrival at Valley Parade was not greeted with unbridled enthusiasm by everyone. In fact, as far as my dad's best pal, Derek Tordoff, was concerned, the move bordered on heresy. Derek is a lifelong supporter of Bradford Park Avenue, the other club in Bradford. Did I say the 'other' club? As far as Derek and a few hundred diehard fans are concerned, Avenue have always been *the* club in Bradford, with City very much the poor relation. Believe me, the rivalry between the two sets of fans has always been as intense as anything you'll find in Liverpool, Glasgow, Manchester, Birmingham or any of the other two-club soccer hotbeds.

Dad and Derek grew up together, loved their sport and were both good enough cricketers to play in the Bradford League. They also played football to a decent standard in their teens, before Dad turned professional, and from a very early age they used to go and watch Avenue play in their famous red, black and amber hoops. They grew up to be fanatical supporters, like the rest of their families, so when Dad signed for the club and went on to play first-team football for Park Avenue, it was a cause for major celebrations all round. However, when he came back to Bradford to play for City towards the end of his career in 1963, some of his relatives were not best pleased, and it was a very sore point as far as Derek was concerned, particularly as Avenue were still in the Football League at the time.

Avenue have a rich history. They number former England manager Ron Greenwood, Len Shackleton, nicknamed the 'Clown Prince of Soccer' during his heyday with Sunderland and England in the fifties, and ex-England striker Kevin Hector among their famous players. The club was founded in 1907 and actually started life in the Southern League, of all places, after failing to gain election to the Football League at the first time of asking. They were elected the following year. They had a couple of spells in the top flight but things began to fall apart in the 1960s when they had to apply for re-election three times in a row. They were finally voted out of the League in 1970. Derek and his pals will tell you until they're blue in the face that Bradford City were among the clubs who voted to boot Avenue out. I have no way of knowing whether that's correct or not but, either way, it isn't a theory that endears City to the Avenue faithful.

Derek and his fellow supporters have stayed loyal to Avenue through thick and very thin. The club declined quickly after losing league status and ended up playing local Sunday league football at one stage, but they gradually climbed back up the pyramid and, in 2004, reached the Conference North, two rungs away from their dream of a return to the Football League, although they have struggled a bit after dropping back into the Unibond League. John Helm, the television sports commentator, and former Yorkshire and England cricketer Geoff Cope are among the people who have worked long and hard to restore Avenue to something like their former glory. They actually approached me a couple of times to see if I wanted to end my playing career at my dad's old club, but I was keen to keep playing at a higher level.

I've always kept on eye on Avenue's affairs, though, and for me, the move to City was a chance to stay a bit closer in touch. That's not how Derek saw it. He was absolutely horrified when Dad told him what I'd done, and even though he'd come to watch me right through my career, particularly at Barnsley, he said he'd have to draw the line this time, insisting that no self-respecting Avenue fan would be seen dead at Valley Parade. Derek eventually decided to bite the bullet, however, and came to watch me three or four times – he denies wearing a disguise to avoid being spotted at a first-team match by any of his mates – and when I found myself out of favour towards the end of my stay, he was happy to come along to watch me in the reserves. There weren't many people around and he could sneak in without anyone taking much notice, find a secluded vantage point away from prying eyes and leave before the end, no doubt with his hat pulled down low over his eyes.

As far as I was concerned, it was a great feeling to sign for my home-town club, particularly as some fans could remember my dad playing at Valley Parade. That made it pretty special for us both. The move went through quickly – one call from City chairman Geoffrey Richmond to Mel Stein's office in north London and I was on my way north to sign. The family moved back almost straight away. We didn't have any of our own furniture at our rented house in Fyfield, so it was just a case of bunging all our clothes and personal belongings into a van, making sure we hadn't left the kids, the dog or the cat behind, and setting off.

Geoffrey Richmond had done a tremendous job in selling Bradford City to me. He went out of his way to say how pleased he was that I was thinking about Bradford and outlined his ambitious plans for the club now they had reached the Premiership for the first time. He wanted success on and off the field and saw me as part of his plans, a player who could help to give City a foothold in the Premiership. He sounded like a man who would have everything under control. Another big factor behind my decision to move was Paul Jewell, who was already being talked about within the game as a bright young manager who would go a long way. I'd played against Paul a few times and liked his attitude. He played the game hard but always shook your hand afterwards and usually found time for a word or two in the players' lounge. He was a football person, a pro's pro and a man I wanted to work for.

I passed the medical on the Friday and was named as one of the subs for the friendly against Barnsley at Valley Parade the following day. I hadn't met the rest of the players before the game, let alone trained with them, so the idea was that I would be given the last 15 minutes or so, just to play myself in. I suspect most of the Barnsley fans didn't even know I'd signed because the first thing I heard as I trotted out for the warm-up was a voice with a strong Barnsley accent, shouting, 'Bloody 'ell, what's Redders doing 'ere?' A few pithy comments came my way as I left the pitch to prepare for the kick-off with my new team-mates.

I wasn't sitting on my backside for long. Lee Sharpe was injured in the first few minutes and I came off the bench to make my Bradford debut against the club I had been so unhappy to leave 12 months earlier. The following week, it got serious – Middlesbrough at the Riverside Stadium, City's first game in the top division since 1922 and I was in the starting line-up. It was a new club, a new season and, basically, a new team that had not fared too well in the pre-season friendlies. None of us had any idea how it would go but we couldn't have had a better start. Boro shaded the first half but we ran them ragged in the second. Dean Saunders, signed from Benfica the previous day, came on and notched the winner in the last few minutes. We were on our way.

I stayed at City for around seven months and enjoyed it a lot, although I never really felt I was a major part of the set-up. At Barnsley, people had talked about Danny Wilson and Neil Redfearn as the two influential figures, the focal points for fans and the media. That isn't fair to all the other people who played a massive part in our success but, like it or not, that was the perception for a lot of people. At Charlton, I was the big summer signing and the focus of considerable media attention. At Bradford, I just slipped in through the back door on the eve of a new season. The club already had high-profile players, including Stuart McCall, Peter Beagrie, Dean Windass, David Wetherall, Lee Sharpe and, soon afterwards, Dean Saunders. I was content to knuckle down and really have a go at keeping City in the Premiership, although as soon as I signed, speculation started that I might become the first player to be relegated from the Premiership with three different clubs. To be honest, I never gave that a moment's thought. If Bradford had gone down, it would have been the responsibility of the whole squad, not one player.

Bradford City was a footballers' club and a great place to be. I soon came to appreciate what a clever manager Jewell was. He had won promotion with a good blend of youth and experience but decided that the way to survive in the Premiership was to lean heavily on older pros, players who'd been around the block a few times. It takes a good manager to put together a side like that – and a good judge of character. A hell of a lot of players with that amount of experience would expect to be in the starting line-up every week and would not take kindly to missing out, whatever the reason. That never happened in my time at Valley Parade.

Most of us had to endure the disappointment of being left out at one time or another and it always hurt. If a player doesn't hurt when he isn't in the squad every week, he shouldn't be a pro. Also, let's face it, there are times when players don't really mind their side playing badly because it means they have a better chance of being called up next week. I never sensed that kind of feeling in the dressing room at Valley Parade. Instead of moaning or back-biting, the players who weren't in the starting line-up got on with the job of backing up their team-mates on match day before working hard on the training ground to win back a place the following week. A lot of players had strong opinions, and they certainly weren't afraid to say what they thought, but there wasn't a single bad apple. A real feeling of togetherness ran through the dressing room. We all had a common cause – Bradford City. We were a close squad.

I was the fifth of six summer signings, following the arrival of Sharpe, Gunnar Halle and Wetherall, who had all moved in from Leeds, and Andy Myers from Chelsea. Saunders signed a week after me. We were all players who had proved ourselves in the Premiership and we linked up with the experienced pros McCall, Beagrie, John Dreyer, Wayne Jacobs, Lee Mills and Windass. There were some good young players around, too, in the shape of Robbie Blake, Andrew O'Brien, Jamie Lawrence, Isiah Rankin and Gareth Whalley. The only players who really missed out were home-grown kids such as Mark Bower and Scott Kerr, who had a lot of talent but, because Jewell had opted for experience, were never really given a chance. Five years later, I linked up with Kerr again at Scarborough.

McCall was club captain and very much the main man, a true legend at Bradford. He'd helped City win promotion to the old Second Division in 1985 only to endure the nightmare of the Valley Parade fire. He stayed to establish City in the division before moving on to Everton and Rangers, winning 40 Scotland caps. In June 1998, he returned to Valley Parade and less than a year later, captained City into the Premiership. Stuart led from the front, a bit like me in my Barnsley days, and was a major influence in the dressing room – a top man all round.

So, in a very different way, was Saunders. I used to make sure I arrived at the club in good time to tune in to Dean's banter. What a character! He'd played at the top level with Derby, Liverpool, Villa and Benfica and won 75 caps for Wales, but he was just one of the lads at Valley Parade and great with the kids. He was always first in the queue if there was an opportunity for a prank. For instance, one slot in the car park at Valley Parade was reserved for Geoffrey Richmond's Bentley, and we were left in no doubt that GR, as he was known to most of the staff, would be less than chuffed if anyone else parked there. That was like a red rag to a bull to Deano. If the chairman hadn't arrived before him, he'd go straight for that parking slot and amble into the dressing room to wait for the balloon to go up. Sure enough, a few minutes later, there would be a knock on the door and one of the reception staff would ask if the car parked in the chairman's space could be moved. Immediately. Deano would oblige, wearing an expression of complete innocence and proclaiming either that he'd forgotten the chairman parked there or thought he was away for the day.

Windass was a one-off, too. He'd come up the hard way after missing out at Hull City as a kid. Instead of buckling under, he went off to play non-league football with a local side, North Ferriby, and earned himself another chance with Hull. He didn't miss out second time around and he's gone on to have a good career that has featured two spells at Valley Parade, more Premiership action with Middlesbrough and stints with Aberdeen, Oxford and Sheffield United. He was equally at home in midfield or up front and scored goals from anywhere. Dean was full of aggression and power but he could play a bit, too, and he was as brave as a lion – mind you, with a face like that, you've got to be brave!

There was rarely a quiet moment with Windass around and the same could be said of Beagrie, who was always ready to join in with pranks and practical jokes. Beagrie was the dressing room's fashion guru and turned up in some incredible outfits. He was also a real professional and had tremendous talent. He'd been around for a long time, played for five other clubs, and you would have thought just about every full-back in the business would know his tricks, but no. He turned them inside out week after week and was still doing so with Scunthorpe when he was well into his late thirties as he passed the 700 appearance mark.

Andrew O'Brien was just a kid taking his first steps on the ladder that would lead to a big-money move to Newcastle and a place in the Republic of Ireland squad. O.B., as we called him, was quick, strong and brave but in those days, no one was quite sure whether his best position was midfield or central defence. In our first Premiership match at Middlesbrough, Andy was given the job of man-marking Paul Gascoigne. Word had leaked out to the media that he would be keeping an eye on Gazza and as we were lining up in the tunnel before the game, O.B. was standing about four places ahead of Gascoigne in the line.

Like everyone else, Gazza hadn't really heard of Andy but he'd seen his picture in the morning papers and spotted the size of his nose – O'Brien's hooter is even bigger than mine, which is saying something! The tension was starting to build in the tunnel when all of a sudden Gazza's unmistakable voice boomed out, 'So where is he, then? Where's this big-nosed pillock who's going to mark me out of the game?' I was standing just behind Andy and I could feel him cringing and trying to keep his head down, but I'll tell you what, Gazza hardly had a kick in the whole 90 minutes.

O'Brien's emergence as a top-class performer meant a hard luck story for Darren Moore, a central defender who had played a significant part in the promotion campaign. He was an absolute man mountain, a real gentle giant whose size belied a super touch on the ball. He was a lovely fella, too, but Jewell decided before a ball was kicked that he wasn't going to be able to hack it at Premiership level. He brought in Wetherall, a great signing, and Moore didn't play a single game. He subsequently proved with West Brom that he did, in fact, have something to offer in the top flight but the manager had made up his mind and Darren was sidelined.

It must have been a nightmare and no one would really have blamed him for being bitter towards Jewell or resenting Wetherall's arrival, but Darren was a born-again Christian, like Wayne Jacobs, and perhaps his faith and his closest friends carried him through. His beliefs were something I never discussed with him in any great depth, to be honest, but if finding religion marked a turning point for Darren, Wayne and the other born-again Christians on the circuit, that's fair enough by me. Their faith has probably helped them to cope with some of the pressures professional foot-ballers can face and neither Darren nor Wayne tried to impose their religion on anyone else. I didn't have any strong views one way or the other. As I tell the Jehovah's Witnesses who seem to make a bee-line for our doorstep on a Sunday afternoon, I don't know whether or not there's a God but I believe in Good. I try to bring up my family in the right way and to treat other people with respect.

It certainly wasn't any part of my business to discuss Darren's faith while he was having a bad time. I just tried to keep him going as best I could and include him in the life of the dressing room. We all knew the score because the same thing had happened to us all. A real professional's only public response has to be to buckle down, work hard and not undermine the rest of the squad, but it isn't always easy. Darren did things right, worked his socks off in training, gave 100 per cent in the reserves and, in the end, was rewarded with a good move to Portsmouth three months into the season.

Things never quite worked out for Lee Sharpe, either. He'd been signed from Leeds during the summer after playing for City on loan the previous season and after making his name with Manchester United and England. Lee was arguably the highest-profile player on the staff but he suffered a load of injury problems and started just 13 games. It was typical of that dressing room, however, that he never moaned about his luck. He worked at his fitness and his game and played a full part in keeping City in the Premiership.

Jewell also put together a strong coaching staff. He was still a young manager learning the trade and in Chris Hutchings he had a bright, enthusiastic young coach. Jewell was shrewd enough to appreciate that they needed some experience and know-how to fall back on, so he brought in Terry Yorath, whose last job had been as Peter Jackson's number two at Huddersfield. Yorath – Taff as he was known – later returned for a second spell at Town, again alongside Jackson. Taff had been one of my heroes when I supported Leeds as a kid, and he had a massive amount of experience on the coaching side. He'd coached City to promotion in 1985 and spent a couple of years as manager in the eighties. He'd also sampled the international scene as manager of Wales and been in charge at Cardiff and Swansea. I wouldn't describe him as technically one of the best coaches I've worked with but he knew the game inside out. On a match day, he could pinpoint problems and solve them in the dressing room at half-time. I had a lot of time for Taff and I like to think he felt the same about me.

We were treated like adults. We weren't over-coached because Jewell and his staff realised that would have been like teaching grandma to suck eggs. Instead, they kept things ticking over and encouraged a lot of input from the players. Even though I was one of the new boys, Paul encouraged me to say my bit. He made the decisions but he had brought in experienced players who were still hungry and he wanted some feedback. In some ways, the team managed itself out on the park because most of us knew the game backwards. If problems arose, we usually knew how to put things right. We were round pegs in round holes which, in my book, is good management. That sense of togetherness meant we were always going to be a tough proposition, particularly at Valley Parade. It was a tight little pitch, the fans were fanatical and we went at it from the first blow of the whistle. If the opposition weren't up for a fight, we'd roll them over.

We used to train at Apperley Bridge on the outskirts of town, just down the road from Leeds/Bradford airport. The training ground pitches were reasonable enough, although they were a bit heavy in winter and probably not up to Premier League standards. They certainly wouldn't be these days, anyway. The changing facilities were average, so in the mornings we used to report to the ground, have a cup of tea and a natter, get changed, pile into our cars and head off to Apperley Bridge, five or six miles down the road. I'm sure that daily journey through the morning traffic played a big part in team bonding because, instead of driving into training on our own, we all had to muck in together. There was always a fair amount of friendly argument about who hadn't been doing his share of the driving and if we suspected someone of not taking his car often enough, we'd leave him behind after training. We couldn't afford to be proud about the state of the carpets in the back of the car.

As the training ground was a bit windswept and decidedly inhospitable in winter, we didn't have many fans coming along to watch. There were one or two diehards but, by and large, the supporters waited for us at the ground. A few fans would always be there when we arrived in the morning and by the time we returned after training, quite a crowd had usually turned up, looking for autographs or wanting to have their pictures taken with the players. I've always believed that kind of thing comes with the territory. It's far better for players to have some kind of contact with supporters instead of being shut away in a private training complex behind locked gates. Fans should have a chance to talk to players and see what they are like close up, and if they go away saying what good guys we are, that's great. Most of the players at City had come up the hard way and weren't big-headed. They could relate to the fans easily.

One thing that always struck me about the people waiting around Valley Parade was the number of Asian kids. The City ground is at the centre of a big Asian community and I sometimes used to watch those youngsters kicking a ball around in the car park and see how skilful they were. They obviously loved playing the game and they were keen fans, too, wearing the team shirt and looking for an autograph or wanting a bit of a chat. Not many of them made it into Valley Parade on match days, though, and that was a shame.

If any Asians in Bradford want to support City, they should be welcomed with open arms by everyone at the club, especially the other supporters. I know City are very keen to increase support in the Asian community and Ian Ormondroyd, the former City, Villa and Leicester striker who is now their Football in the Community Officer, has worked hard at getting the message across to Asian kids. It probably won't be too long before some of them make the grade as players. There are still just a handful of Asians playing for Football League sides but quite a few are starting to filter through the system and I've no doubt at all that some of them will become top players.

Bradford's arrival in the big time was a roller-coaster season for everyone. Like virtually every other promoted side, we knew from day one that survival was the name of the game and, with our tremendous spirit, we had a strong belief that we would pull through. From a personal point of view, there were some memorable times. To play another Premiership game against Leeds at Elland Road was a great moment, and so was a fourth appearance at Old Trafford and a third at Anfield. A lot of players go through an entire career without playing at the big grounds but joining Bradford enabled me to live the dream for a while longer. I scored just one goal in 17 games, in a 3–1 win over Leicester at Valley Parade. That was probably my best performance in a City shirt. Leicester lined up with Muzzy Izzet, Robbie Savage and Neil Lennon in midfield against McCall, Windass and me. We knew everything would go through Lennon, who sat in front of the back four and dictated play from there – if you let him. We didn't. I played at the front of our midfield three and put him under pressure from the start. It worked a treat and we steam-rollered them. The goal came when I dispossessed Lennon in central midfield, found Blake on the right and got into the box to turn in the cross.

I thought it would be the first of many, even though I'd started slowly. My record doesn't lie. I've averaged around ten goals a season for nearly 20 years and while regular scorers will always have lean spells, they will come good in the end. I'm convinced that if City had kept faith in me, I would have scored goals. In fact, I did collect a perfectly good second goal with a diving header in the last five minutes of a 1–1 home draw with Chelsea in January. It would have given us a 2–1 win but instead it was disallowed for offside against Saunders, who was at least three yards onside.

In the end, the season went down to the wire and City had to beat Liverpool at Valley Parade on the final day to stay up. I was always confident they would survive. The combination of the back-room team and that bedrock of experienced pros gave Bradford the extra know-how that Barnsley and Charlton had not possessed in the two previous seasons. City won 1–0 and to celebrate Geoffrey Richmond organised a parade round the city in an open-topped bus, promising great things for the following season. By then, I was a Wigan player.

When City had taken over my Charlton contract, which had another two years to run, I fully expected to be at Valley Parade until the contract expired. I was 34 but I was fit and strong and I believed I could still do a job in the Premier League. In the event, I didn't nick the goals that I wanted but I think I played well. In fact, I would go so far as to say that in several of my 17 league appearances, I was outstanding. I started seven games at home and never finished on the losing side. That's a record I'm very proud of. I was in the squad on a regular basis at the start of the season before missing four games because of injury. From mid-October, I started 11 games out of a possible 14 and I was on the bench for two of the other three. Then after we had beaten Watford at Valley Parade on 22 January, I found myself out in the cold, with just one appearance on the bench in the next seven weeks. I found it hard to understand but these things happen in football and if a player is honest with himself, his own opinion is the most important. I knew that I could look anyone in the eye and say I had done a good job in the short time I had been at Bradford City.

I spoke to Jewell several times after I had been left out of the side and he emphasised that I still had a role to play, even though I wasn't going to be in the starting line-up on a regular basis, but I wasn't daft. I realised that Bradford would be prepared to offload me if the right offer came along and it wasn't long before clubs started to make enquiries. Wigan were the first to show an interest and a couple of chances came along to move on loan.

The first was from Walsall, who were struggling at the wrong end of Division One and eventually went down at the end of the season. Their manager, Ray Graydon, had been on the coaching staff at Watford during my time at Vicarage Road. I had a lot of time for Ray and fancied working with him but there was no chance of a permanent deal so I hung fire. Then I had a call from Bruce Rioch at Norwich. They were a mid-table First Division outfit and Rioch was looking for an experienced pro to bring along some promising young kids. Again, it would be on a temporary basis with no prospect of a permanent move. Norwich was a hell of a long way away and after the stay at Charlton, I wasn't too keen on uprooting again, particularly for a loan move. Rioch was articulate and convincing and wasn't a million miles away from making me change my mind, but in the end I said no.

Then just before the March transfer deadline, Wigan came in with an offer of £112,500, which Bradford accepted. I told Geoffrey Richmond I was prepared to stay and fight for a place but really I knew there was no mileage in digging my heels in. Reserve-team football would have been no use at all to me at that stage of my career. So I said farewell to my home-town club and I was on the outside looking in as Bradford City ran into trouble over the next couple of years. Jewell resigned and joined Sheffield Wednesday soon after securing Premiership survival, leaving Richmond to embark on what he later described as his 'six weeks of madness' by bringing in a string of high-profile players.

Dan Petrescu arrived from Chelsea, David Hopkin from Leeds and Peter Atherton and Ian Nolan from Sheffield Wednesday, and that was just for starters. With the new season only a few days away, Richmond signed Italian striker Benito Carbone, who had been released by Aston Villa, on a reported weekly wage of £40,000, higher than anything City had ever paid before. Then along came Ashley Ward from Blackburn Rovers and Stan Collymore from Leicester City. From the outside, I saw Petrescu, Collymore and Carbone as maverick players who had an abundance of ability but were never going to fit into the system that Jewell had put in place involving experienced, hard-working pros who would all pull together.

After relegation, City lurched deeper into crisis on and off the field, flirting with relegation once again while rumours of serious financial problems were beginning to surface. The collapse of the deal between the Football League and ITV Digital in March 2002 marked the beginning of the end. Early in May, shares in Bradford City Holdings plc were suspended, the club went into administration a week later and Richmond left the club before the start of the new season. An eight-year era that featured seven managers and in which City reach unimagined heights was over.

Harsh things have been said about Richmond but I couldn't really fault him, even though I was unhappy about leaving and said so at the time. He was a big man with a real physical presence and he seemed to have his finger on the pulse of the club. We all knew exactly who was in charge. When he took over in 1994, City were in the old Second Division, penniless and playing in front of sparse crowds in an ageing stadium. Five years later they were in the top flight and performing against Arsenal, Manchester United, Liverpool and Chelsea in a state-of-the-art stadium filled to a capacity of almost 20,000 that would soon increase to 25,000 plus – not bad going by any standards. It all ended in tears and recriminations but I suspect that, to this day, plenty of City fans would ride the dream all over again.

Leaving Valley Parade marked the end of a dream for me, too. To play at the top level had been a lifetime's ambition that Barnsley, Charlton and Bradford had enabled me to fulfil. I'd always wanted to pit myself against the best players and in 84 Premiership games, I'd done just that at some of the greatest venues in the world. When I was with Charlton, I even kicked Roy Keane up in the air – at Old Trafford, of all places. I arrived fractionally late in a tackle and Keane came off worse. The ref hardly had time to blow for the foul before Keane was up on his feet, snarling, 'Don't kick me on my pitch!' I had to laugh. I put on my most innocent expression and replied, 'Me kick you, Roy?' His response was a long, cold stare and I thought to myself, 'It won't be a problem if I do decide to have a dig. There's nowt to him.'

In my 25 years as a pro, I've mixed it with some tough characters, men like Graham Barrow when he was playing for Chester. At 6ft 2in and 13st 7lb, Barrow, who went into management after he retired in the mid-nineties, was a real giant and I speak from experience when I say no player in the world would want a munching from him. Physically, Keane wasn't in the same league; nor could he match Robbie Van der Laan, probably the toughest opponent I crossed swords with. Robbie, who played in central midfield for Port Vale, was a big strong lad who liked nothing more than a good old-fashioned physical battle. He wasn't a dirty player by any means but he was as hard as nails and never gave an inch. First tackle of the match he'd clatter me – or alternatively, I'd clatter him – and we'd take it from there, like a couple of kids scrapping in the playground.

It was like the OK Corral. He'd smack me, pick me up and amble over to the ref to collect his yellow card. Ten minutes later I'd whack him and the process would be repeated. There was never any malice and we always shook hands and had a bit of a laugh afterwards. He was a lovely lad, a good player, and I suspect he knew exactly what he was doing. If he suckered me into having a scrap with him in the middle of the park, I wouldn't be popping goals in at the business end. Ironically, he joined Barnsley soon after I left for Charlton but was forced to retire through injury in 2001. Before we played Port Vale I used to tell myself not to get involved, not to be sucked into a physical set-to with Van der Laan or maybe Robbie Earle, another man who wasn't averse to mixing it, vowing to concentrate on my own game and leave the two Robbies to get on with theirs. It never worked out like that.

Week after week in the old First Division, I would come up against players who knew my game and reckoned they had worked out how to stop me. I fancied I could scupper their plans and there was a lot of physical stuff. I've never seen myself as a particularly hard player but I've never backed down and I've always accepted that if I was going to dish it out, I'd have to be ready to take it, too. That's part and parcel of the game and I didn't come to any harm. During my three Premiership seasons, it was a tremendous experience to come face to face with world-class players whom I had only seen on TV before. Playing against men of that calibre taught me a lot ahead of my switch to the coaching side. Even in the middle of a Premiership game, I was able to admire the skills of the top players. In particular, it was eye-opening to see how the really top performers backed their ability in a tricky situation.

For instance, when Bradford played Chelsea at Valley Parade, I was part of a midfield three and the aim was to chase and harry the opposition into making mistakes. On one occasion, I closed in on Celestine Babayaro, the Nigerian defender who was playing left-back. Most players would have seen me coming and played a safe ball down the line or into central midfield but Babayaro looked up and, first time, hit a 35-yard cross-field pass right to the feet of Albert Ferrer, who was playing on the other flank. The slightest error would have exposed Ferrer and the rest of the defence but no, the ball flew like an arrow to the target and all of a sudden, we were on the back foot.

His Chelsea team-mate Gianfranco Zola was the best player I came up against in those three years and even after the millions

Roman Abramovich has invested, I still rate him as Chelsea's best ever Premiership player. Zola is a fantastic guy and a role model for young players because, although he had wonderful talent, he showed no conceit at all. The shirt he gave me after that 1–1 draw at Valley Parade is one of my most treasured possessions – mind you, I deserved it after the way he outwitted me during the game.

We were 1–0 down at the time and getting a bit of a chasing. When the ball was switched out wide to Zola, I moved in to close him down. I arrived at the perfect moment, just as he was about to take his first touch, and I was confident that I could go in really hard, take the ball and give him a bit of a clattering at the same time, just to let him know I was around. Instead, I was left tackling thin air. Zola flicked the ball behind him with his heel, completely wrong-footing me, and turned quick as a flash to avoid my charge. I was left facing a baying mob of Chelsea fans as Zola spun away to set up another attack.

It was the greatest piece of skill I have ever seen and something only a few players in the world could have done. I honestly felt like applauding. I sometimes wonder how the fans would have reacted if I had – but I had to chase back and couldn't afford to be messing about with the crowd. At the end of the match, I went across, asked for his shirt and offered to give him mine in exchange. He didn't seem bothered about that but later handed me his signed match shirt and gave me a couple more as souvenirs.

Apart from our infamous run-in during the game between Charlton and Arsenal, I always enjoyed playing against Patrick Vieira, again because I was trying to make some kind of impression against one of the really top players. I saw early signs of greatness in Thierry Henry, too, although the only time I played against him, he was out wide on the left. He was clearly going to be explosive.

David Ginola also impressed me a lot. He was a big man, much bigger than he looked on the telly, and powerfully built but he had a marvellous touch and was like a ballet dancer on his feet. When I played for Barnsley against Spurs at White Hart Lane, we seemed to be chasing him all afternoon. His skills were mesmeric. Unlike Ginola, Didier Deschamps, captain of France's World Cup winners in 1998, was always regarded as more of an artisan than an artist, a workmanlike player who kept the team ticking over, but he also had a lot of craft and guile that was perhaps overlooked because of his work ethic.

I first ran into Paul Gascoigne when I played for Crystal Palace against Newcastle in a Cup tie. He would have been around 20 at the time and nowhere near his peak but already a wonderful player. Steve Coppell, our manager, warned us beforehand how dangerous Gazza could be in the middle third of the pitch and said, 'Anything in that area, they look to give to Gascoigne. He's got marvellous feet and if you go charging in thirty or forty yards out, he'll go past you and cause all sorts of problems. So keep your shape and leave it to him to find options.'

So when Newcastle were awarded a free kick about 35 yards out and the ball was knocked short to Gazza, we did as we were told and kept our shape. He soon found an option. He looked up, took two strides forward and belted a 30-yard shot into the roof of the net. It was still rising when it hit the target and I'll always remember George Wood diving frantically as the ball hit the rigging. He looked just like the keeper in the Morecambe and Wise sketch, who launched his dive after the ball had gone in.

As Newcastle celebrated, we looked across to the bench as if to say to Coppell, 'OK boss, we kept our shape and look what happened. What about Plan B?' In that game Gazza was mercurial. He'd drop his shoulder and turn you one way and then back-heel the ball to a team-mate as you tried to recover. We couldn't live with him.

I never really rated David Beckham until Barnsley knocked Manchester United out of the FA Cup at Oakwell in 1998. I'd always thought he was a bit of a fancy dan, a good footballer who could cause a lot of problems from a wide right position but someone who might not want to know if you really got after him. I still think he sometimes makes a meal of it when he's been fouled, but he isn't the only one.

In that particular game, United had a few reserves in the line-up and Beckham played in central midfield. I was up against him in the engine room. Barnsley were two up in no time and we were really at them. They were trapped with nowhere to go and desperately needed someone to roll up his sleeves and fight back. Beckham did just that. While United were beaten in the end, they gave us a bit of a fright thanks mainly to Beckham's ability to dig in and inspire his team-mates. I can think of one or two so-called superstars who wouldn't have fancied that situation at all but Beckham seemed to relish it. His approach meant more than all his 30-yard cross-field passes and his spectacular free kicks because he was demonstrating that he really did have the stomach for a fight. He went up a lot in my estimation that night.

14 THE ROAD TO WIGAN FEAR

APPREHENSION WAS THE NAME OF THE GAME WHEN I ARRIVED at Wigan in March 2000. I sensed it straight away. From the outside, I saw a big club in what was a pretty average division. They had been out in front for most of the season and were still fourth in the table, well placed for automatic promotion. Turn the clock back three years to Barnsley and a new player would have walked into a dressing room buzzing with the conviction that promotion was just around the corner. At Wigan, behind the usual jokes about the new boy, the players seemed twitchy.

It was hard to understand. Even though they'd had a bit of a wobble since the turn of the year, confidence should still have been sky high with more than enough quality in the squad to finish the season strongly and win promotion. If it was so obvious to me, the players who had done all the hard work over the previous 34 matches must have known it, but instead the nerve ends were showing. Why? Probably because expectations were so high at the club which was owned, and being driven relentlessly forward, by Dave Whelan.

Whelan, owner of the JJB Sports empire, had the advantage of having played the game at a high level himself. Coincidentally, he had played in the same side as my dad at Blackburn. When I asked Dad about him, he replied, 'Dave Whelan? Good man – and a tough, aggressive player. Hard as nails. In our day we used to joke that players like him would have kicked their grandmother!' Dad left the club before Rovers reached the 1960 FA Cup final against Wolves, the day Whelan fell foul of the Wembley injury jinx. He broke his leg after 30 minutes. There were no subs in those days and ten-man Blackburn lost 3–0. I'm told he was never the same player again. He spent three years at Crewe before quitting in the mid-sixties and embarking on his successful business career. I bumped into him a few times during my time at Wigan but neither of us mentioned the family connection, although I can't think a man as shrewd as Whelan wouldn't have remembered.

He had transformed Wigan from a club that was performing in front of small crowds at ramshackle old Springfield Park into one of the most ambitious enterprises outside the Premier League. He had put everything in place for success and his big investment, combined with the switch to the futuristic, 25,000 capacity JJB Stadium, had raised the ante to the point where supporters assumed that promotion was just a matter of course. An unbeaten run of 24 games at the start of the season fuelled that belief and cranked up the pressure even more, particularly in home games.

Like Geoffrey Richmond at Bradford, Whelan was involved in everything. This was his football club and it was going to be run his way, but I soon formed the impression that, as a football man, he knew how important it was to leave the playing side of the operation to the manager and his staff. He saw the game from the professionals' point of view as well as the business angle and I didn't see any evidence of major interference from above during my 12 months at Wigan. Even though he kept a relatively low profile, everyone knew the score – success or bust. Perhaps that explained the apprehension among the players in those closing weeks of the season.

I'd known for a while that they were interested in signing me. Brendan O'Connell, a team-mate at Barnsley who was on the Wigan coaching staff, had come to watch me in a reserve game at Bradford, together with Colin Greenall, Wigan's reserve-team coach. Brendan and Colin talked to me after the game and asked if I fancied a move to Wigan. I said all the right things. I told them I was flattered that Wigan were interested but I wasn't going to leave a Premier League club to play in Division Two. At that stage I still thought I had a future at Valley Parade, even though I was no longer featuring in the first team. As the weeks went by, though, it became increasingly obvious that my first-team days were over at Bradford, so I agreed to have a look at what Wigan had to offer, driving over to meet O'Connell at the JJB Stadium.

What I found was no ordinary Division Two set-up – it was a Premier League club waiting to happen. Built on the same lines as Huddersfield Town's McAlpine Stadium, the JJB had opened at the start of the season and Wigan had moved out of Springfield Park to share the ground with the town's rugby league club, one of the most famous sides in the world. A second, smaller stadium, where the reserves used to play, had been built adjacent to the main arena, and two indoor artificial pitches had been laid in the JJB Soccerdome next to the ground. A new training complex was on the drawing board and opened a couple of years later. The facilities at the JJB Stadium were absolutely second to none and I couldn't fail to be impressed.

I was still reluctant to drop down two levels because I felt I was good enough to play two or three more years in a higher division. John Benson, the Wigan manager, accepted that view- point but he and his staff managed to convince me that the First Division was where Wigan would be at the end of the season. I never take anything for granted but all the signs pointed to promo- tion and I could sense that if they went up, Whelan would be ready to re-invest and they would do well at a higher level.

They took over my Bradford contract, which had a year-and- a-half left to run, and added another year on top. So it was a long- term arrangement and on the face of it, a good move for Wigan and a good move for Bradford. Perhaps I should have spent more time deciding if it was also a good move for me but I've always believed that if I'm not wanted, I might as well not stick around. It's an ingrained working-class philosophy, I suppose. If people treat me properly, I will give them everything. If they let me down,

I'll be off – and I was flattered to think that such an ambitious club as Wigan felt I could play a significant part in helping their dreams come true. So Wigan it was. With hindsight, perhaps I should have played a waiting game and maybe found myself a First Division club.

Another big factor in my decision was the opportunity to work with John Benson again. He'd been on the coaching staff under Mel Machin during my time at Barnsley and was a real football man. He'd enjoyed a good playing career, mainly in the lower divisions, before moving on to the coaching side. He'd managed Bournemouth, Manchester City and Burnley, worked overseas and spent a lot of his career working as assistant manager to John Bond, first at Norwich and later at Manchester City. I knew from my Barnsley days that he could be tough, particularly if he felt a player wasn't pulling his weight, but if you were really giving everything, he would back you all the way. He was an old-school coach with a deep knowledge of the game, but was shrewd enough to have a couple of young guys working alongside him in O'Connell and Greenall. He was also cute enough to realise that Bond would give him that little bit extra and had brought his former manager into the club in an advisory capacity.

Bond was just a few years short of 70 at the time but he was still a big name, even though his managerial days were behind him. He'd been a very high-profile manager, sharing champagne and cigars with Ron Atkinson when Big Ron was manager of Manchester United, but behind the flamboyant image, Bond was a professional who still had a lot to offer. He was the 'tips and hints' man on the training ground and came into his own on technical issues such as organising set-pieces. He would sometimes pull a player to one side to make a technical point and came across as a man who really knew what he was talking about. He seemed to take an immediate shine to me, telling me he'd always liked my approach to the game and that I was his type of player. Even though Wigan played a pretty straightforward 4-4-2 system, he and Benson encouraged me to adopt the same attacking role I had played at Oldham and Barnsley, which was a big plus.

So was the presence in the dressing room of so many familiar faces. Stuart Balmer, a team-mate at Charlton, had arrived 18 months earlier and three of the men who had won promotion with Barnsley, Andy Liddell, Arjan de Zeeuw and Darren Sheridan, were also major players at the club. Lidds, in particular, was a big crowd favourite. Andy had taken an unorthodox route into the pro game. He wasn't picked up as a junior and was playing for non-league Farsley Celtic in Leeds and studying for his A levels at sixth-form college when he decided to give it one last go. He wrote to every professional club in Yorkshire asking for a trial but only Barnsley bothered to offer him a chance. One look was enough and before long, Lidds had broken into the league side and won the first of his 12 Scotland Under-21 caps.

He was a first-choice striker at Barnsley in the three seasons leading up to the promotion year but after starting that campaign as a regular, he lost his place in the starting line-up when Danny Wilson signed John Hendrie in October 1996. From then on, Lidds spent more time on the bench than in the starting 11, although he was a key member of the squad. He never let Barnsley down in the Premiership and I will always believe he would have been a better bet than most of the front players who were at the club at the same time. He could play as an out-and-out front man, wide on the right or tucked in behind the front two and would give good value in any role.

When he couldn't hold down a regular slot at Barnsley after relegation, Lidds decided to move on and dropped down a division to join Wigan in October 1998. I wasn't convinced it was the right move because he was only 25 and I thought he was more than capable of winning a place in the starting line-up at most Division One clubs. Lidds threw in his lot with Wigan, though, stayed loyal and had seven tremendous seasons there before joining Sheffield United in 2004. In his first season, Wigan won the Auto Windscreens Shield and reached the Division Two play-offs. The following year they reached the play-offs again and finally won promotion as champions in 2003. By that time, Lidds had attained cult status at the club and he went on to become Wigan's record league scorer.

It was good to link up with him again and I played in the last 12 league games of the season, scoring six goals. At Charlton, and to a lesser extent at Bradford, a strict 4-4-2 system hadn't really suited the attacking side of my game but the extra freedom I was allowed at Wigan gave me licence to become more of a goal threat and I felt I was a dangerous attacking player once again. There were some good players in the Wigan dressing room, including Stuart Barlow, Simon Haworth, Carl Bradshaw, Pat McGibbon and Kevin Sharp, as well as Balmer and my ex-Barnsley team-mates. Most of the staff could easily have played at a higher level and they were a joy to work with on the training ground.

My first game was against Bury at the JJB. I'd been warned not to expect too much atmosphere and, sure enough, when we kicked off in front of around 7,000 fans, the stadium seemed empty and it almost felt like a reserve match. We won 1–0 and I picked up the Man of the Match award. The following week I scored twice against Notts County and we went on to win my first four games on the bounce. Then came the decisive match, against Preston at home. Like Wigan, Preston were very strong and this was a huge game between two of the big sides in the division. There was quite a contrast between the two clubs because Preston were steeped in tradition whereas Wigan were the new kids on the block. It was a midweek night match and one of those rare footballing occasions when the JJB Stadium played host to a 15,000 plus crowd. Attendances like that were normally the preserve of the rugby league team.

Preston were top of the league at the time and a win would put them farther ahead, as well as making life difficult for one of their main promotion rivals. On the other hand, it was absolutely vital that we won, not only to maintain the challenge for an auto-matic promotion place but also to convince the big crowd that we really did mean business. It was a strange sensation to come out of the tunnel and see the opposite side of the ground, the area reserved for away fans, more or less full. Usually, just a few hundred fans huddled together in one of the middle sections. The match was a cracker that could have gone either way. A draw would have been a fair result but Preston got the only goal and went on to win the championship with 95 points, seven more than Burnley. That result knocked us off course in a big way and was a huge downer for the fans – only 4,848 turned up for our next home match, a 2–0 win against Oxford. We won only two of our seven games after the Preston defeat and picked up just eight points in the process. Automatic promotion went out of the window and we eventually finished fourth, five points adrift of Burnley.

As we prepared to face Millwall in the play-off semi-finals, there was a lot of pressure on us all, particularly Benson, and those two games were as tense as any match I've been involved in, a million miles away from the FA Cup semi-finals with Oldham ten years earlier. In those matches against Manchester United, we were relaxed. We knew we'd done well just to reach the last four and while defeat was a disappointment, it didn't feel like the end of the world. Both the first match and the replay were great days out for the fans and overall a happy experience. Not this time. A whole season was on the line for two matches – three for the team that went through – and there was going to be no sense of achievement for the losers, who had already suffered the disappointment of missing out on the automatic places. I suppose that, on balance, the play-offs have been good for football because they prolong the interest in a season and increase the number of clubs with something to play for. For managers, coaches and players, though, they are no fun at all.

We kept to the script, edging home by a single goal in the home leg after a goalless draw at their place. Millwall's new ground, the New Den, didn't carry an X-rating for visiting players like the old place in Cold Blow Lane but it was still a hostile atmosphere. As we trotted out for the warm-up, I half expected to be confronted by the woman who had aimed a swipe at me with her brolly all those years back during my time at Palace, but if she was still around, she kept her distance this time. Millwall were a good side, with young players including Tim Cahill and Lucas Neill, who have gone on to play in the Premiership. We could sense that they were very tense, even more so than us, and we were much the better side for most of the match. We couldn't finish them off, though, so the boot was on the other foot at the JJB. Millwall knew they'd got out of jail in the first match. We were expected to win and so they were more relaxed than us. We managed to sneak in front after an hour with an own goal from David Livermore after Sheridan had curled in a free kick, and after that it was a case of hanging on.

We travelled down to London for the play-off final on the Friday afternoon, stayed at a north London hotel and trained on the Saturday morning, the day before the match. The attendance was over 50,000 and while our opponents, Gillingham, played in their yellow change strip to avoid a clash with our blue shirts, most of their supporters wore the club's first-choice blue. The place was awash with blue and white as we walked out. Our average home attendance that season was just over 7,000 but there were far more Wigan fans than that in the stadium.

We could and should have won. We went behind through a McGibbon own goal in the 35th minute but Haworth equalised soon after half-time and from then on, there was only going to be one winner. We should have killed them off before Sharp, our left-back, was sent off in the 86th minute for a second bookable offence. Even so, Barlow put us in front from the penalty spot nine minutes into extra time and after that it was a case of both teams slugging it out. On a heavy pitch, Gillingham's numerical advantage was always likely to prove decisive and they hit us with headed goals by Steve Butler and Andy Thomson in the last seven minutes. The previous year, Gillingham had lost out in the final after conceding two injury-time goals against Manchester City, so they must have felt this result was poetic justice. We felt we'd been mugged.

For me, there was the added disappointment of being replaced by Barlow six minutes from the end of normal time and two minutes before Sharp's dismissal. Benson never explained why he made the switch but presumably he wanted a fresh pair of legs on the field if the game went into extra time. Managers are paid to take decisions but I thought this was the wrong one. We were getting stronger all the time and I was full of running. I felt that we would still have been favourites in extra time if we'd stuck with the starting line-up and Benson should have gone with the flow of the game. As it happened, the dismissal of Sharp meant he had to take off Liddell in favour of Bradshaw, a defender for an attacker, halfway through extra time, when he also replaced Haworth with Jeff Peron. Gillingham manager Peter Taylor made his changes, too, but while we lost our edge after the switches, they went from strength to strength. Defeat was a bitter disappointment for the players who had dominated Division Two in the first half of the season and made promotion look certain for so long. It hurt me too, even though I had been at the club for just a few weeks.

What's more, another blow was waiting just around the corner. When we failed to win at Wembley, Benson felt he had little choice but to step aside and moved upstairs as general manager. John was well liked by the players and seemed to be popular with the chairman. Word was that Whelan would have been happy for him to continue, but it seemed Benson had more or less had enough. He'd had one or two health problems and decided it was time to let someone else have a go. That was a big disappointment for me personally. Benson had been one of the main reasons why I'd left a Premier League set-up for a Second Division club, so to some extent I felt let down. When I signed he'd given me the impression that he planned to see the job through, whether or not we were promoted at the end of that season. There had definitely been no suggestion on anyone's part that he might be tempted to step aside if we didn't go up. If there'd been even a whiff of doubt about his long-term future, I would have thought very long and very hard about signing for Wigan.

Any player at any club can be vulnerable when a new manager comes in. I suspect I'd been seen as very much a part of the Benson-Bond axis. Without them, there was a danger that I would be a bit exposed, depending on the identity of the new man. So when I heard our next manager would be Bruce Rioch, I thought, 'I've cracked it. He wanted me at Norwich, he's bound to want me at Wigan as well,' and I reported back for pre-season training confident that I would be an important part of his plans. It just shows how wrong you can be. I started six games in six months with Rioch in charge. It didn't make any sense to me at all and I couldn't help feeling that he was getting his own back for my refusal to join Norwich on loan a few months earlier.

I was in the side for the first game of the season at Swansea, a 0–0 draw, and I made a few more appearances over the next few weeks. Then, in the middle of September, I was transfer-listed and banished to the reserves. There was no unpleasantness on Rioch's part. He just made it plain that he didn't fancy me as a Wigan player any more – yet a few months earlier he'd been keen for me to sign for Norwich, who were playing at a higher level at the time. OK, Wigan did well without me in the starting line-up and I wouldn't have argued if he'd said he didn't regard me as a long-term proposition. All players have a sell-by date and, at 35, I appreciated that I was approaching mine. But I still believe that in the short term, he was wasting a good player. I was an experienced professional who knew about battling to win promotion, and I must have had something to offer, either on the pitch or in the dressing room, to a side that had blown it the previous season.

I trained hard and gave 100 per cent in the reserves, even though Rioch kept playing me out of position up front. Against Bolton at the Reebok Stadium, I had an absolute blinder and afterwards I joked, 'This is the start of a new era for Neil Redfearn – look what the game has been missing all these years!' There was an occasional appearance on the bench for the first team but I was clearly surplus to requirements. Rioch knew it, I knew it and so did everyone else at the club, although some of my team-mates seemed as baffled as I was about what was going on. I felt very low. The move to Wigan had been a bit of a gamble and when I was shunted into the reserves, I couldn't help wondering why things had gone so wrong and what would have happened if I'd joined Huddersfield when the chance came along towards the end of my time at Charlton. Instead, I'd hung on in case anything else cropped up and missed out on Huddersfield. That had looked a good decision when Bradford came in but now here I was, out in the cold at a Second Division club. It wasn't easy to keep putting on a brave face and stay upbeat, I can tell you.

In my younger days, I would have flown off the handle, demanded a showdown with Rioch and gone in with all guns blazing. Now I was older and wiser and I knew that my best chance of getting the move I needed was to keep calm and play it by the book. If I was going to move on with my reputation intact, the only option was to buckle down and retain my professionalism. If people came to watch me in the reserves, they had to see the real thing, not a disgruntled old hack who was just going through the motions.

It's fair to say that I had achieved most of my goals as a player by the time I joined Wigan. I genuinely wanted to help them achieve their own ambitions and it hurts that I wasn't given the chance, but I wasn't going to let those few months on the outside looking in sour me. By that stage of my career I was mature enough to see it as just another experience to put in the bank, and I had started talks with Halifax Town about moving to The Shay as player-coach when Rioch departed at the end of February 2001. Wigan were in fourth place at the time but had gone through a lean patch since the turn of the year and Whelan decided enough was enough. Colin Greenall took over as caretaker-manager before Steve Bruce moved in and guided them to the play-offs once more. They missed out for a second time.

I left Wigan more or less as I found them, high on ambition but short on achievement and support. Traditionally, Wigan is a rugby town, both league and union, and before the switch to the JJB Stadium, the football club were getting by on gates of around 4,000 at Springfield Park. The move upped the stakes in a big way and Whelan must have expected the fans to respond. Gates went up but only marginally and in my time at the club, when we were going for promotion in two successive seasons, home games were played in front of a small crowds in an almost empty stadium with little or no atmosphere. Even when they were chasing promotion to the Premiership, the average home attendance was around 10,000.

Whelan has persevered, however. With his money, he could have knocked on more or less any club's door and bought his way in but he stood by his club and finally achieved his dream of Premiership football when Wigan were promoted in 2005. The arrival of Paul Jewell as manager in the summer of 2001 was a masterstroke. Jewell has a happy knack of bringing in the right players at the right time. He's been around long enough to know the job inside out and his man-management is first class. Whether Whelan has the resources to invest even more heavily is another matter but you have to admire his achievement in driving the club into the top flight. With games against the two Liverpool clubs, Manchester City and Manchester United, Bolton, Blackburn, Middlesbrough, Newcastle and Sunderland, they were more or less guaranteed a full house of away fans at around half their home games – and with Premiership football on their doorstep, the locals finally got the message, too.

My year at Wigan was a roller-coaster ride and when I look back, the overriding feeling is a sense of frustration – first, the frustration of our failure to win promotion when we were clearly one of the best sides in the division. Then came the frustration of being dumped on the sidelines when I felt I could have been playing a significant role in a second promotion push. The one thing that no one can take away from those topsy-turvy 12 months was my second appearance at Wembley – something I feared had passed me by for good. Like any other soccer-mad kid, I'd dreamed of playing at Wembley for England or for my favourite club, Leeds United. Those dreams come true for a tiny number of people. For the rest of us, even professional footballers, Wembley was about watching Cup finals or international matches. Only the élite few were ever going to play there.

Then along came the promotion play-offs at the end of the

1986–87 season, and all of a sudden, the chance to play in a Wembley final moved a lot nearer for a journeyman pro. I'd missed out in the play-off semi-finals 11 years earlier at Watford and also failed at the final hurdle in the FA Cup with Oldham in 1990. By the time I signed for Wigan I had more or less accepted that my appearance for Crystal Palace against Sheffield Wednesday in the Mercantile Credit Football League Centenary Festival in 1987 would be my only game at Wembley.

I went to Wigan with one aim, automatic promotion, and the possibility of being involved in a play-off final didn't really enter my head. So to help them reach Wembley after they had gone through a long, hard season and endured the torment of missing out on automatic promotion was a big moment for me. The result was bitterly disappointing at the time and, as it turned out, a turning point in my career. Now, however, I can look back on the match and the whole occasion as a marvellous experience, particularly as I was involved in one of the last two club games to be played at the old Wembley stadium before the bulldozers moved in.

I suppose to some extent I'd taken my previous appearance at Wembley a bit for granted. The Mercantile Credit competition was a one-off, two-day competition to celebrate 100 years of league football, tucked in at the end of the 1986–87 season. The original plan was for all 92 clubs to take part but eventually entries were reduced to 16 teams in two groups of eight. The matches were 20 minutes each way and our game against Wednesday was one of many that finished goalless. We lost the penalty shoot-out 2–1 but at least I had the consolation of scoring our goal and becoming the first Palace player to score at Wembley. For the record, Nottingham Forest beat Wednesday 5–2 on penalties after a goalless final. The competition wasn't exactly a major event on the soccer calendar, I was still a young player and I probably thought my time would come again somewhere down the line. As the years passed and Wembley remained a distant dream, I started to wish I'd taken more notice.

So when, at the age of 34, Wigan gave me another chance to

savour Wembley's unique atmosphere, I was determined to soak up every moment, whatever the eventual outcome of the match – the coach ride down Wembley Way, the sight of the twin towers, the massive stands, the wait in the tunnel, the walk across the track on to the pitch, the roar of the crowd and the feel of the lush turf under foot. It was all a fabulous experience and something I will never forget. When I think about all the famous players who never made it to Wembley, I know how lucky I have been. Sue and the kids came along. Aimee and Lois wore Wigan shirts and scarves and Lois one of those great big tall hats – it was nearly as big as her. It was a wonderful day out for them.

About an hour after the final whistle, we were on our way north and heading for Scotland. We go to a log cabin near Dunoon for our summer holiday every year. It's quiet, peaceful and the chance of being collared by football fans is as remote as the place itself. Don't get me wrong – I'm not pretending I'm an instantly recognisable football celeb but we got caught out in Ibiza one year and wouldn't want it to happen again. We were staying at a quiet place round the far side of San Antonio bay and as soon as we unloaded the cases, the kids wanted to be on the beach. I was just starting to think in terms of a quick dip myself when a rousing chorus of 'One Neil Redfearn, there's only one Neil Redfearn!' started up behind us. I looked up and there, leaning against the guardrail above the beach, were four lads in Barnsley shirts. The second I made eye contact, they cheered and then turned up the volume. 'One Neil Redfearn, there's only one Neil Redfearn . . .' echoed around the beach. One of them turned round to display 'Redfearn 8' on the back of his shirt.

Not surprisingly, other people on the beach wanted to know what all the fuss was about and within seconds, we had become the centre of attention. I gave the quartet a friendly wave but when I turned back, Sue looked at me, I looked at Sue and we groaned in unison, 'Oh no . . .' We couldn't have put up with that for a whole week. Fortunately, we didn't have to. From then on, they seemed to spend most of their nights in the company of San Miguel and their days sleeping it off, so we hardly saw them again.

The Barnsley squad promoted to the Premiership in 1997. *Back row, left to right*: Malcolm Shotton, Eric Winstanley, Peter Shirtliff, Steve Davies, Adi Moses, Paul Wilkinson, Dave Watson, Adam Sollitt, Laurens Ten Heuvel, Arjan de Zeeuw, Neil Thompson, Andy Liddell, Colin Walker. *Front*: Mick Tarmey, Matty Appleby, Clint Marcelle, Darren Sheridan, Scott Jones, Martin Bullock, Danny Wilson (manager), me, Nicky Eaden, Jovo Bosancic, John Hendrie, Paul Smith

Goal! Turning away (second left) after scoring Barnsley's first Premiership goal against West Ham on the opening day of the 1997–98 season

Same game, same goal. Celebration time

My wife Sue has always been a tremendous support. Here we are on our wedding day at Birkenshaw Methodist Chapel on 22 June 1984

With my girls, Aimee and Lois, on holiday in Ibiza

A dog's life. With Dexter on one of our family breaks in Scotland

I bumped into one of them about halfway through the holiday and he was all over me, wanting to talk about football, Barnsley, Neil Redfearn. After about ten minutes, I managed to get across the message that I was on holiday, too, and we'd come away to have a bit of a break from football. I hate to upset fans and I've never consciously been rude when I've been approached while 'off duty', although sometimes it's hard. So when we need to switch off, Scotland is the perfect place.

We'd booked our holiday a while before I joined Wigan from Bradford and the prospect of appearing in a play-off final never entered the equation. By the time it became a possibility it was too late to change the starting date. After we beat Millwall, I explained the position to Benson and asked if it would be OK for me to set off straight after the final, win or lose. He said that wouldn't be a problem, so after half an hour or so in the players' lounge, I said my farewells and ambled out into the main car park, which by that time was more or less deserted. Sue had packed all our holiday gear into the car before driving down to Wembley. I climbed aboard and we set off, calling in at home to drop off some things we wouldn't need in Scotland and to collect the dogs.

I was pretty morose on the drive north. Defeat is never easy to take and to lose a Wembley final that we should have won was a big downer. We reached our destination in the early hours of Monday morning and went straight to bed. I was first up and took the dogs for a walk along Puck's Glenn, a lovely little track near the cabin. I was still preoccupied with the final but I'd set myself a deadline – High Noon. That's when I would stop replaying the game, forget all about being substituted, put the season to bed and get stuck in to a great family holiday. How was I to know that my Wigan career was about to unravel and less than a year later, I would be fighting to keep Halifax Town in the Football League?

15 HANGING IN THERE

'FROM HULL, HELL AND HALIFAX, THE GOOD LORD DELIVER US . . .'
It sounds like a lament from long-suffering football supporters,
doesn't it? Perhaps that's a bit hard on Hull City, now that they
have moved out of Boothferry Park and taken up residence in the
spectacular KC Stadium. However, The Shay, Halifax Town's
home since 1921, can still be a pretty inhospitable place for away
fans when an icy north wind comes blowing off the hills in the
middle of winter. Come to think of it, it's not all that welcoming
for home fans, either.

In fact, the old saying refers to the notorious gibbet, close to
Halifax town centre, where many a wrongdoer met a grizzly end
in the bad old days. The penal system had moved on by the time
I signed for the Shaymen as player-coach in the spring of 2001,
I'm pleased to say, but that didn't mean there wouldn't be some
pretty scary moments over the next 15 months. Character building?
You can say that again!

When I was transfer-listed by Bruce Rioch the previous
September, I expected to get fixed up pretty quickly, preferably
with a club in the same division as Wigan or higher. It didn't
work out that way and Halifax were only the second club to make
a formal approach. That was a blow to my pride but I consoled
myself with the thought that managers who might have wanted

me as a player might also have been a bit wary of my ambitions on the coaching side. Was I right? Only the managers involved can answer that, although I appreciate that some people will have looked at my age and decided that I wasn't a viable proposition any more.

I didn't see it that way. It's hard for a player to accept that time is catching up but when I was clearly surplus to requirements at Wigan, I tried to analyse my game as it had developed over the years and to work out how I might change to stay competitive. I saw an experienced player with good vision and good awareness who could strike the ball with either foot – that's always been a big advantage because defenders have never been able to work me in one direction to cut out a threat. I'd always been good in the air and while I was perhaps slowing up a bit, it wasn't hugely significant because I'd never had a lot of pace anyway. Stamina had never been a problem, I'd kept myself fit and, of course, I still had an instinct for goals.

While most of those qualities had stood the test of time, I knew that I would have to modify my game and use my head more than my legs. As a young player I just wanted to be involved all the time. I felt I had three lungs and could run all day. But in the later stages of my career, I would need to add subtlety – and to think more about how I could influence a game in other ways.

For example, after joining Halifax and on through my time at Boston, Rochdale and Scarborough, I was often man-marked – quite a compliment for a man approaching the age of 40. To counter this, I would sometimes drop off the pace a bit and not track all the way back when the other side were attacking. That allowed my marker to wonder if I might be tiring. The first couple of times I did it, he'd stick around. When it happened again, I could sense he was tempted to stray and join the attack and, in doing so, he handed me the opportunity to take up a more threatening position for when my side regained possession. So while I might have lost some of my mobility, I could influence a game in other ways.

Even so, as I grew older, I felt under increased pressure to perform well because, by and large, people think that players in their mid to late thirties are over the top, that their 'legs have gone', to coin a popular phrase. Legs? What about controlling the ball, passing, experience? Don't those qualities count for anything? I've lost count of the sides that have lost creativity in attack because the manager wanted 'legs' in midfield. If a player is in his mid-thirties and starting to slow up a bit, it's an easy excuse for moving him on. Why has he had a bad game? Because his legs have gone – not because he's simply played badly. If a 19-year-old has a bad day, have his legs gone, too? Of course they haven't. The older player is put in a pigeonhole because the manager needs 'legs' in midfield. I also feel that an element of resentment may exist among some managers and coaches. Most of them have hung up their boots in their early thirties, so perhaps they aren't happy about seeing a player who can still contribute at 37 or 38. If that's the case, it's a very short-sighted attitude.

As yet, there has certainly been no hint for me of the defining moment when a player thinks, 'That's it, time to go.' I'll know when it happens and in the meantime I'll continue to adjust my game to my fitness and strengths. I can't predict what turns my career will take over the next couple of years and moving into management will make a difference but, as things stand at the moment, I want to play for as long as I can. Provided I am clear in my own mind about what is expected of me and confident that I can meet those expectations, I believe I will have a role to play.

When I left Wigan, I tried to be honest with myself about the contribution I could make as a player at Halifax. I didn't try to pretend I could compete at the top any more but I was convinced that I still had plenty to offer, although the lack of interest from other clubs while I was out in the cold had made me realise that I should be thinking seriously about the long-term future. I'd played for 18 years under 17 different managers and gained a vast amount of experience in the process. I had also taken my preliminary coaching badges. It was time to start tapping into the knowledge I'd acquired and move towards a career in coaching and management.

The first offer of a move away from the JJB Stadium came from York City, who had been relegated into the Third Division the previous year and had brought in Terry Dolan as manager. Terry had been around a long time, knew exactly what lower-division football entailed and I liked his style. On the downside, York were prepared to take me on loan only, with a possible permanent deal in the summer, and there was no coaching role. I was tempted but my main concern was to make a complete break from Wigan, where I had been messed about since the opening weeks of the season. The last thing I wanted was to go out on loan and then find myself having to return to Wigan if something went wrong. I decided on a permanent transfer or nothing and, a few weeks later, Halifax came calling.

In October 2000, they had appointed Paul Bracewell as manager, a very ambitious move for a Third Division club. He had a good reputation as a coach and had managed Fulham for a year after Kevin Keegan left to become England coach in May 1999. He had big plans for Halifax, even though they were involved in a battle to stay in the League at the time. I met him at a Huddersfield hotel and he outlined his ideas. He was looking for a player who could add a bit of experience in midfield to help keep the club in the League, but he also wanted someone to bring some fresh ideas on to the training ground. He offered me an extra two years on the Wigan contract, which still had a full season to run, but above all he wanted me to join as player-coach. Obviously, Halifax couldn't match my wages at Wigan but, overall, it was a decent package.

I had to be realistic. Football people will tell you that anybody can play for nowt – but you've got to be a bit special to be a pro and you should be properly rewarded for the contribution you make. It doesn't always work out that way. I would go so far as to say that at most of my clubs I have been underpaid in terms of my value to the side. I've certainly never been overpaid, but money can never be the sole motivation. There comes a point when a player has to look at the bigger picture. I wanted a job involving coaching and if that meant taking a pay cut, fair enough.

It was a question of taking a few steps backwards to move forwards in the long term.

Bracewell knew the score. He appreciated that a coaching role made the offer a lot more appealing than a straightforward transfer to a struggling Third Division club. He also said that he'd discussed the position with Bob Walker, the Halifax chairman, and told him that if things went well and he was offered a chance to move to a higher level, he would expect to be allowed to take it. It would be important for the club to have a replacement in place to maintain a sense of continuity and he saw me as that manager-in-waiting. That was exactly what I wanted to hear and everything seemed to be slotting into place. Halifax was only a few miles down the road from home, so there was very little travelling involved, and once again, I was going to play for one of Dad's former clubs. I met Bracewell and Walker after playing for Wigan reserves at York and agreed a deal.

I'd slipped out of the media spotlight a bit since joining Wigan, particularly as I'd been messing about in the reserves for the best part of a season, but the news that Neil Redfearn was joining a club struggling against relegation from the Football League soon had the press boys on my trail once more. I'd led Barnsley to promotion four years earlier and was a Premiership player at Bradford just 12 months ago, so I could see the reason for their interest. To an outsider, it must have seemed a pretty sharp fall from grace when, in fact, the move to Halifax was an important staging post in my career. From that moment, I ceased to be a player pure and simple. I was taking my first steps on the road to full-time coaching and management. Bombarded with questions about my apparent decline, I think I succeeded in convincing most people that this was a fresh start, not another step along the road to oblivion.

After working for three Premiership clubs and Wigan, life in Division Three was inevitably a bit of a culture shock, but I've never lost sight of where I came from and I soon readjusted to how the other half live. I'd been lucky enough to work for clubs where the facilities were excellent but I'd also seen the other side of the coin on the municipal golf course in Lincoln and on Doncaster Racecourse. I wasn't proud and, when it came down to it, I still loved playing and training. Despite Halifax's lowly position, it was a professional set-up on the playing side. Bracewell had performed at a very high level, he'd coached and managed in the First Division and he wanted the job done properly. Even if money was tight, corners were not going to be cut in vital areas, such as the treatment and rehabilitation of injured players. Since the previous June, that had been the responsibility of Sarah Scott, one of two women physios working in the League at the time, and Tommy Gildert, the club's fitness coach. They were an excellent team.

I first encountered Sarah on the day I signed. I had to take a medical and after showing me around the ground, Bracewell told me to meet the physio in the car park. The only person about was a blonde girl in her twenties, so I hovered around the entrance for a couple of minutes until Sarah came across and asked if I was Neil Redfearn. Professional football is a very male-orientated environment and, apart from the office staff, you don't see many women around. For her to be part of the staff on the playing side in such a vital position was a big thing, particularly at a small club with a small playing staff. She could handle that. She knew her job backwards and was very professional. No one treated her any differently because she was a woman.

I don't think Bracewell had been totally convinced about having a woman physio when he'd joined the club but for the players, Sarah was just another member of staff. I thought at first that there might be a few problems with having a young lass around, particularly among the younger players, but there were no silly pranks and no suggestive remarks. She was regarded as a physio, not a woman physio, and that says a lot about Sarah and the respect she earned among the players. She rarely came into the dressing room. She had her own treatment room and if we needed treatment, some ice, a massage or a bandage, we went in there. That was her workplace. It's the same with male physios. The treatment room is very much their domain and not even the manager goes in there without making sure the timing is right. There's a special, confidential relationship between a physio and an injured player and, by and large, managers know better than to intrude.

A good physio knows what makes each player tick – which ones will try to get back playing before they are ready and which ones might be tempted to duck and dive in and out of the firing line. I've known people who have dropped out of a struggling side because of a minor strain and then suddenly find they can play through the pain barrier when results improve. Physios need to know who they can push and who they need to rein in. It's a fine line and a difficult job and in the end, the physio has to accept the player's word.

Inevitably, a few wolf whistles rang out when Sarah ran on to treat an injured player, and she got a bit of stick from the home fans when we were playing away. She was more than capable of coping with that but she did have a habit of falling foul of referees. She had previously worked part-time for Halifax Blue Sox, the rugby league club who were our co-tenants at The Shay, and in rugby league the physio can run on to the field to treat an injured player as soon as he goes down. There's no question of waiting for the nod from the referee. It works the other way round in football and early on in her time at Halifax, she had occasionally reacted with her heart and not her head. If she thought a player was badly hurt, she would run on to the pitch without permission. Some referees were not best pleased but she always contrived to get away with a mild ticking-off. She argued – and it's a fair point – that to a physio, the player's interests come first and if she thought someone might be badly injured, it was her duty to treat him immediately. Sarah returned to rugby after she left The Shay, working for Harlequins in rugby union's Premiership.

Bracewell ran a tight ship as far as players' diets and lifestyle were concerned, and discipline was firm. However, I soon discovered that even if everything was more or less in place behind the scenes, life on the training ground was going to have its problems. We would arrive in the morning not necessarily knowing where we would be training an hour later. The venue was a moveable feast and sometimes the coaching staff would have to ring round to find out where we could go. Once we received the go-ahead, we'd point the players in the right direction, chuck the gear into a van and set off. It wasn't a situation Alex Ferguson or David Beckham would have tolerated but this was Halifax Town – football on the breadline. During my first week, we trained at Elland Cricket Club. Elland are one of the big clubs in the Huddersfield League with a decent pavilion and first-class social facilities – the outfield wasn't bad, either. It was a beautiful surface to work on and even though we had to use temporary goalposts, we had some good sessions up there. We also used to train at the Lawrence Batley Sports Centre near Huddersfield, which was strictly speaking a rugby union facility. There was one soccer pitch that we were able to use.

Another venue was Spring Hall, just round the corner from The Shay. It was owned by the local council and featured a cricket field, hard tennis courts, a bowling green and a football pitch with a pretty alarming slope from right to left. We were allowed to mark out a running track on the cricket field, which was also a reasonable training area. During school holidays and half-term, the place would be awash with kids who'd come for a game themselves. At first they thought it was a bit special to watch the pros train but the novelty soon wore off and we got some pretty sullen looks when we asked them to move on and started putting the cones out.

Then there was the Moor, a bleak open space on the outskirts of town that housed about 20 pitches, owned and maintained by the council and used by amateurs at the weekend. The Moor was adjacent to Crossley Heath School and the pupils would use the pitches during games lessons. So did local kids who fancied a kick-about on the park after school or during the holidays. Halifax Town? No chance! We tried hard enough. The Moor was a few minutes' drive from The Shay, so the coaches would nip up there ahead of the players and put all the cones out ready for the session. Then, just as we were about to get started, some chap from the council, who must have been lurking behind a tree all along, would emerge from hiding and shout, 'You can't bloody play on there!' We'd try to reason with him but he wouldn't have it. 'No, we need to keep t'pitches reight for t'weekend. Go and laik behind t'goals if you have to laik anywhere.'

So we'd pick up the cones and start again. As it happened, one area where two pitches backed on to one another provided a pretty good surface with enough room to have a decent session. In fact, it was better than the real pitches – but we weren't going to let our pal from the council know that or he'd have turfed us off there, too.

He wasn't the only obstacle to a proper work-out. Time and again, we'd just be getting into a good tempo and feeling we were making some progress when the session would grind to a halt because some punter was walking his dog across our so-called pitch. When we stopped running around, it would dawn on him that there was a problem. I'd say, 'Come on pal, can't you see we're trying to have a proper training session here?' and he'd realise what was happening and hurry on his way.

Our friend from the council summed up the attitude of a lot of people within sections of the local community. We were the town's football club and I can think of a lot of places where organisations with the right facilities would have welcomed us with open arms, particularly as they knew we had no brass – but not in Halifax. The attitude always seemed to be, 'Don't do that lot any favours.' Maybe that was because it was a rugby league town and people saw us as the poor relation to the Blue Sox. Maybe some people wanting prompt payment knew they might not get their money for a while. In any case, it made life difficult and keeping the football side running on a professional basis was never easy. What we wouldn't have given for a little 'Xtra' help from The Halifax Plc, as the banking giant was known in those days. Their HQ was just a stone's throw from The Shay but, as far as I was aware, they'd never shown any real interest. During my time at the club, we were sponsored by the Nationwide.

When I signed, I was one of two transfer-deadline deals, along with Michael Proctor, who came on loan from Sunderland. Michael was just 20 at the time and has gone on to play for Sunderland in the top flight as well as Rotherham and Hartlepool and turning out on loan for York, Swindon and Bradford City. He was pacy, sparky and gave us a real edge up front alongside Steve Kerrigan, who finished the season with 19 league goals. There weren't many players around at that level with Proctor's pace and he was quite a handful. He didn't seem to notice the pressure of a fight against relegation. He was just a kid who wanted to play and score goals, enjoy himself and learn about league football.

When I looked round the rest of the squad, I couldn't work out quite why they had been struggling. I linked up once more with Steve Thompson, a team-mate at Bolton and a good pal. I assumed Bracewell would put us together in central midfield but for some reason he didn't fancy that and Steve spent a lot of time on the bench. Another senior pro was Chris Wilder, later to become the club's manager, who was on his way back from a bad injury. Lee Butler, a team-mate at Barnsley, was in goal and Graham Mitchell, previously with Huddersfield and Bradford City, played in central defence alongside Paul Stoneman, another experienced pro. Some good kids were coming along while Kerrigan had been scoring goals for fun. On the face of it, we should have been a mid-table outfit, not relegation material.

My first game was at Cheltenham. We lost 4–2 and slipped from 23rd in the table to 24th – rock bottom. Our rivals in distress were Darlington, Barnet, Exeter, Lincoln, Carlisle and Torquay, most of whom, like Halifax, knew all about fighting a survival battle. It was clearly going to be a dogfight but as we still had home games against Barnet, Carlisle and Darlington to come, not to mention away fixtures at Exeter and Lincoln, survival was very much in our own hands. So it proved. We picked up 13 points from our next nine games, including wins over Barnet and Darlington and draws against Exeter, Lincoln and Carlisle, and went into our penultimate match, against champions Brighton at home, knowing that a point would be enough. The two clubs below us, Barnet and Torquay, were just a single point worse off but had only one game left. Crucially, that game was between the two of them on the final day of the season. So if we could squeeze a draw against Brighton, one of them would be able to overhaul us if we lost our last match – but not both.

We fancied our chances, even though Brighton, managed by Micky Adams, had run away with the title and were the best side in the division by a country mile. They had been scheduled to visit The Shay in early April but the match was called off at the last minute, almost literally. When we arrived at the ground, the pitch was OK but an hour or so before kick-off a tremendous downpour left the place awash and the pitch unplayable. Brighton were absolutely gutted. They had travelled up the previous day and their fans had made the long journey in force. The game was rearranged for a Tuesday night at the beginning of May, by which time Brighton were already promoted as champions. They said all the right things about giving it 100 per cent but we suspected that if we got among them from the start, they might not really be up for a scrap.

It was a tense, nail-biting match in front of almost 4,000 fans. One or two factors worked in our favour. Bobby Zamora, who had scored 28 league goals for Brighton and was one of several players in the side more than capable of competing at a higher level, wasn't fit. Then Adams had to substitute his experienced goalkeeper Michels Kuipers with debutant Will Packham early in the second half. Even so, a Brighton side not firing on all cylinders was still capable of causing big problems and we did incredibly well to cling on for the point we needed. When the final whistle went, hundreds of fans swarmed on to the pitch and we only just made it into the dressing room. We wanted to give them a lap of honour but it was 20 minutes or so before the pitch was cleared and we could go back out. That night doesn't quite rank alongside the day Barnsley won promotion but Halifax had been right on the edge ever since I'd joined them and survival was a tremendous achievement. We'd stuck in there, battled hard and earned the right to stay in the League.

So, mission accomplished. We went away for the summer break, confident that we would do a lot better next time around. Bracewell called me in during the summer and asked if I wanted to stay on as player-coach or make the switch to full-time coaching. It was a tough call but I was happy with the way things had gone and saw no reason to change. He agreed and made sure I did a fair bit of coaching during the build-up. He'd invested the best part of a million pounds in assembling a new-look squad and there was a definite feeling that, on the playing side, Halifax were on the move – even though work on a new main stand had ground to a halt.

When hostilities began in earnest, a 2–1 win at Lincoln on the opening day was just what we were looking for, but it proved to be a false dawn. After drawing our first home match against Exeter, we lost the next three on the bounce and, at the end of August, found ourselves in familiar territory in the bottom six. That was enough for Bracewell. He left, saying that he felt he had taken the club as far as he could. Richie Barker, his number two, went as well. It was a bolt from the blue. Bracewell had worked hard during the summer to set things up and, even though we hadn't started particularly well, I didn't think that we were going to be relegation fodder once again. The following day, Bob Walker asked me to take over as caretaker-manager.

16 DOWN AND OUT

MY FIRST SPELL IN MANAGEMENT LASTED 40 DAYS. IN THAT TIME, Halifax Town played eight matches. We won two, drew three and lost three, scored three goals and conceded six. At one stage, after my first five games in charge, we had climbed to the dizzy heights of tenth place in the Third Division, but a couple of away defeats followed by a goalless home draw in my final match landed us in the lower half of the table once more.

It was nothing sensational but not bad progress for a club that had avoided relegation by the skin of its teeth four months earlier and made a disastrous start to the new season. Overall, I don't think I did a bad job. Who knows what might have happened if the Halifax board had given me the three-year deal I wanted as full-time manager. Instead, they brought in Alan Little and it was downhill all the way from there. At the end of the season, while I was in temporary charge for a second time, Halifax became the first club to be relegated from the Football League twice.

From day one, it was a daunting challenge but I didn't waste any time in accepting Bob Walker's offer to succeed Paul Bracewell in a caretaker capacity. It was the chance I had been waiting for and I appointed Tony Parks, who was the number two goalkeeper behind Lee Butler and later became part of the England coaching set-up, as my assistant. We'd been leaking a few goals so the first priority was to tighten things up at the back and we worked hard at that on the training ground. We lost our first game, 1–0 to a late goal at York, but then drew 0–0 with Macclesfield at home, beat Swansea 2–0 away and picked up a 1–0 home win over Mansfield, one of the strongest sides in the division. Then we drew 0–0 with Leyton Orient. Five games, eight points, one goal conceded – piece of cake, this management lark!

Tony and I weren't going to get carried away but we were well pleased with the story so far. So were the fans and, significantly, so were the board. As we prepared for a couple of tough away games, at Rochdale and Hull, both of whom were in the top six, I was offered the job full-time by Walker and his fellow directors, Ray Crabtree and Doug Tait. I told them I would accept – but on my terms. I said, 'Look, I know you won't be able to pay me big money and that's OK. I realise how tight finances are. But if you want me to make a fist of this job, I need time.' I pointed out that I'd inherited Bracewell's players and, on Halifax Town's budget, I wasn't going to be able to bring in my own people in a hurry.

I asked for three seasons. In the first, I would be aiming to keep the club away from trouble with the players I had inherited from Bracewell. As most of them were on short-term contracts, I would be able to change things round the following summer, bring in my own players who would, hopefully, establish the club in midtable with a chance of the play-offs. Then, in the third season, I would have a settled squad plus one or two more new arrivals. We would reap the benefits of the previous season and have a real pop at promotion. This was going to be my first management job and I was determined to do it properly. I had no intention of starting my managerial career on the wrong foot with a compromise that was no good for me or, in my eyes, for the club.

They seemed to agree and I went away thinking we could thrash out the nuts and bolts at our next meeting. Instead, I quickly realised they had gone cool on the idea. I couldn't understand it.

'What's the problem?' I asked Walker. 'You've agreed this is the way forward. Why can't we get on with it?'

'What happens if we give you a three-year deal and then have to sack you?' he replied. 'We won't be able to pay you off.'

Being sacked hadn't entered my head. I was interested in doing a good job for Halifax Town and getting them into a higher division. I was prepared to do the job on their terms financially but I wanted time to do things properly. For me, the glass was half full. For the directors, it was half empty. They were looking at the worst-case scenario. They had seen enough of me as a caretaker to offer me the job so surely it was worth giving me time to do it my way? But no, they were immovable and I certainly wasn't going to accept a short-term contract on the terms they were offering. It was deadlock and at the beginning of October, after we had lost the games at Rochdale and Hull and I'd been sent off for the first time in my career in a goalless draw against Scunthorpe, they appointed Little as manager until the end of the season. I reverted to my role as player-coach.

Little had started his coaching career at Hartlepool in the 1980s, moving on to York as assistant manager in 1988. He took over as manager after York won promotion via the play-offs from the old Third Division under John Ward in 1993. He left Bootham Crescent in March 1999 and had a spell at Southend before coming to The Shay. He took over just as Tony Parks and I were starting to bring the best out of the players and the atmosphere in the dressing room was really buzzing. We could sense the players were right behind us and they made it pretty obvious that they wanted us to be given the jobs full-time.

We had come in with a lot of enthusiasm and given everybody a chance. We all mucked in together and I like to think we made everybody feel a part of what we were trying to do. There was no segregation between the first and second team in training and once I was sure the players were fit enough, we made football the priority in every training session. We worked hard on organisation and set-pieces and tried to make them all feel part of their football club. I wanted the players to come in and enjoy training every day and believe there was light at the end of the tunnel for them and for Halifax Town. It was one for all and all for one and it worked. So when Little arrived, he found a dressing room of players who wanted Neil Redfearn in his job – and Redfearn was still around. If he'd produced a winning side, fine, but as long as the team was losing, people kept asking, 'Why did they get rid of Redfearn?'

I started in ten of his first 16 games in charge. Then I was left out for the match against Exeter in mid-January and never started another first-team game while he was at the club. He was cutting off his nose to spite his face. He didn't have so many good performers that he could afford to dump arguably his most influential player. He won two of his 23 league games and Halifax plummeted to the foot of the table once again. It was as clear as a bell that there would be no escape this time. Then, at the beginning of March, Little was rushed into hospital with a ruptured appendix.

With the club ten points adrift at the bottom and ten games to play, I was asked by the board to take over on a caretaker basis for a second time. I was entitled to say no after the way I'd been treated first time around but I didn't feel like leaving the players in the lurch and even though our chances of staying up were minimal, I was ready to give it another go. I suppose I still had a soft spot for the club because my dad had played there as well and quite a few people around the place had been family friends for a long time. I didn't feel I could just walk away.

The situation was stark. We would have to win at least four of our remaining matches and one of our rivals would have to lose four or more. That was an unlikely prospect and we got off on the wrong foot by losing my first three games back in charge, completing a sequence of eight defeats in nine games. We started to make inroads into the gap by beating Kidderminster and Cheltenham at home before heavy defeats at Luton and Darlington finished us off with three games still to play. Little had not been fit to return since his illness and left once relegation was confirmed. I'd experienced relegation from the Premiership with Barnsley and Charlton but this was a whole new ball game. At the time, it seemed like the end of the world, although now that I have worked in the Conference with Scarborough, I realise that there is a life outside the Football League and a good life it is, too. It didn't feel that way at Halifax in April 2002.

Statistically, I'd done OK in my two spells in charge. Halifax won eight league games all season and I was in charge for five of those victories. I think it's fair to claim we would probably have stayed up if I'd been given the job in October. I still wanted the job full-time and during that second spell, I started to put in place a set-up that would enable us to be in contention for a return to league football the following year. First, I brought in Dave Worthington as my number two. Dave was a member of the Worthington football family that also included his younger brothers, Bob and Frank. Dave and Bob had both started their careers at Halifax while Frank had played there as a kid before beginning his long and colourful career at Huddersfield. Dave had loads of experience after playing more than 400 games for the Shaymen, Barrow, Grimsby and Southend, and he was absolutely steeped in the club. So were the rest of the family. Frank said that if I got the job, he would come in and coach the strikers on a part-time basis. An ex-England player with 234 goals in 757 games for 11 clubs telling the players how to score goals? Not bad for starters!

I also made contact with Eric Harrison, my dad's former team-mate at The Shay and the man who, as Manchester United's youth coach, had nurtured the talents of Ryan Giggs, David Beckham, Paul Scholes, Nicky Butt and the Neville brothers. Eric was still involved with United on a part-time basis but he lived near Halifax and said if I needed any help, I could give him a call any time. Pat McGibbon, my former team-mate at Wigan, had just completed his physiotherapy course and I wanted him to come in as player-physio, creating one job in place of two and saving the club a salary. I also wanted Stuart Balmer, another ex-Wigan colleague, as player-coach on the same terms. Balmer and McGibbon would have played in central defence as well as bringing us their coaching and physio expertise.

The board appeared to go along with my ideas. They seemed

to recognise that they'd made a mistake six months earlier and that, if they gave me the chance, I would do my best to give the club some real foundations on the playing side. The financial problems were massive, though, which perhaps I didn't really appreciate at the time. The club was up for sale at £450,000, losing a reported £8,000 a month and operating on the tightest of budgets. We had to ask for money for boot polish or laces, something we'd normally be given out of petty cash, but there wasn't any petty cash. There was non-stop speculation that the club would go into administration at the end of the season and a constant stream of players knocking on my door wanting to know what was happening and whether they had a future. I didn't know the answer. I just had to go out and work with them on the training ground, and try to lift them for each match. They were a credit to themselves and their profession. They feared they had no future but they kept going.

The club went into administration on Friday, 12 April 2002, when we still had two games to play. The first was at Torquay the following day. We weren't allowed to stay over on the Friday night because of the administration order, so we ended up setting off at 5.30 on the Saturday morning, travelling there and back in the day. We won 4–2. Early the following week, Peter O'Hara, the administrator, announced that the players were likely to be sacked at the end of the season, irrespective of the amount of time left on their contracts. Mark Jules, our PFA (Professional Footballers' Association) representative, spoke to Mick McGuire, Deputy Chief Executive of the PFA, who was due to attend a meeting with O'Hara and the playing staff at The Shay soon after the final game against Rushden & Diamonds. He believed our contracts would be honoured but the administrator sounded ominously convincing.

To players who had expected the remaining year on their contracts to be honoured, married men with kids who suddenly found themselves facing life on the dole, it was an horrendous situation. It was just as distressing for the players who would be out of contract in the summer but believed they would be paid until their deals expired at the end of July. That was looking more and more unlikely and I couldn't blame the players for having serious doubts about whether to go ahead with the final fixture.

I told them, 'You owe it to yourselves and the supporters to go out and play this game, irrespective of what is going to happen next week. You have to show you are employable when you leave here. If you go on strike, people who might consider signing you in the summer will think again. They'll reckon you're a bad egg. See the season out and give yourselves a chance of finding another club. Halifax Town are going down but if the club is re-formed and I'm the manager, a lot of you will be offered new contracts here because I know what kind of people you are and what kind of players you are.' I said something very similar again in the dressing room before we went out to play that final match.

If I could have my time over again, I would say exactly the opposite. I would tell the players to strike because the only bargaining power we had was that one game. Rushden were challenging for a play-off place and if we had said in advance that we would not play unless our contract situation was sorted out, all hell would have broken loose. A strike would have brought matters to a head, created a mass of publicity and somebody, somewhere would have made sure something was done about honouring our contracts. Instead, we played the game, the season ended and football turned its back on us. 'Halifax Town in administration? So what?'

Five days after the Rushden game, we met the administrator and McGuire at The Shay. The meeting began at 10 a.m. and ended at 6.30 p.m. All the players except Matthew Clarke, a midfield man who was expected to move to Blackpool for around £30,000, lost their jobs. McGuire managed to secure some compensation through the PFA for those who had been dismissed. I was one of them and I had no qualms about picking up the money. In just about every other walk of life, an employee who is made redundant through no fault of his own is entitled to some form of compensation and I don't see why football should be any different. The money we were paid bore little relation to what we would have earned had our contracts been honoured and I didn't want to start dipping into my savings if it could be avoided.

When the dust finally settled, I was still locked in talks with the club about taking over as manager. I had agreed a deal with Bob Walker but the administrator wasn't happy with the terms. The wrangle rumbled on until mid-May when Walker decided he'd had enough of the whole business and quit as chairman. I went, too. I wanted to start putting things in place for the Conference but there was no longer a football club to manage and no guarantee that I would get the job if the club was re-formed. I had been up in the air for too long and felt I had no option but to walk away and start looking for another job. My first venture into management was over.

There's an old saying in football, and in life, that you have to sample the hard times to understand the good times. In those two brief stints in charge at Halifax, I was certainly given a harsh introduction to the facts of managerial life in the lower divisions. It was tough going but I enjoyed a measure of success on the field and gained first-hand experience of a club with huge problems behind the scenes. People talk about the pressure of winning and losing football matches but working at a club on the brink of collapse taught me about real pressure. From a managerial point of view, I like to think I handled it well but it can surely be no coincidence that the first two sendings-off of my career came during those two spells as caretaker-manager.

I received the first against Scunthorpe in the final match before Alan Little took over, although I didn't know at the time that he was about to replace me. It was for two yellow cards. The first came after a fifty-fifty midfield challenge on a young lad who just nicked the ball away before I caught him. He got up straight away and said to the referee, 'Don't book him for that.' Nice sentiment but it cut no ice with the official. The second booking came late in the game when we were pushing for a winning goal. We lost possession, Mark Jules, our left-back, was caught slightly out of position and we were exposed on that flank. I chased back like the clappers to cut off Scunthorpe's Lee Hodges as he raced away down the line. Neil Redfearn the player would have closed Hodges down, jostled him and waited for the defence to regroup. Neil Redfearn the manager, desperate not to lose to a late goal after guiding the side to a bit of success, didn't pause to think. I clattered into Hodges without a realistic chance of winning the ball and he went down like a sack of potatoes. The second yellow was followed by a red. I remember looking at that red card for a few seconds and thinking, 'What am I supposed to do? I've never been sent off before.' Then I turned away and trudged off.

The second dismissal was in Halifax's final game as a league club against Rushden & Diamonds and it was one of the lowest moments of my career. It was a straight red for retaliation. I was trying to shield the ball from Stuart Wardley, their midfield player, who was getting in tight and making life difficult for me. He niggled me a couple of times and I just turned round and kicked him. There was no real provocation and no malice on his part and to this day I can't understand what got into me. It was like an out-of-body experience, almost as if I was an onlooker, watching Neil Redfearn take a kick at an opponent and get sent off. We were 3–1 down at the time and I can only think that wild kick was the culmination of months of pressure as a sidelined player and the caretaker-manager of a relegated club. I was ashamed of myself but there's only so much a man can take.

To make matters worse, I had to find a seat in Halifax's half-built stand until the final whistle. Once a player has been sent off, he cannot sit on the bench or in the dug-out and that rule applies to managers, too. So I had to clamber into the stand and sit on one of the few seats that had been put in place before construction work stopped. From there I watched Halifax play out their last 36 minutes as a league club. I even had to wear a hard hat, which was about three sizes too big – if it had been passed round for a benefit collection, someone would have made a few bob. It soon fell off and rolled down the steps. I couldn't be bothered to fetch it and the stewards didn't insist that I put it back on. The away fans saw what had happened and chanted, 'Redfearn,

Redfearn, where's your hat?' I can look back on it now and have a laugh but it was a humiliating experience at the time.

Managing Halifax was, and always will be, a daunting challenge. Maybe they are destined to be what you might call a borderline club. Traditionally, they are a Football League outfit but somehow they are not quite big enough to make an impact, even though they are bigger than the average Conference club. The bottom line is lack of support. The fans will rally round in a crisis and gates will increase marginally if things are going really well, but it seems they are never going to attract crowds of much more than 2,000 and that simply isn't enough to give them the financial clout they need to make real progress.

That's life lower down the football scale and it isn't going to change. But when I eventually leave the game, I'll look back on my time at Halifax, Boston and Scarborough as fondly as Barnsley, Charlton, Bradford and the rest because I enjoyed myself just as much there as I did at the bigger clubs. Being a professional footballer is a fantastic way to earn a living and I've been very privileged to play for every one of my clubs. A lot of people don't see it that way. They only look at the big clubs and the good times but they don't know what they're missing and obviously they don't love the game as much as I do.

17 HARD TRAVELLING

WHEN I WALKED AWAY FROM HALIFAX IN THE EARLY SUMMER OF 2002, I was out of work for the first time in my adult life. It was a scary sensation. I was reasonably confident I would find another job but I knew it wasn't nailed on. I would be 37 at the start of the new season and no longer a long-term proposition for Football League managers. If I didn't find a job in football, what the hell would I do? Since leaving school at 15 to join Nottingham Forest as an apprentice, football had been my life and the only option as far as work was concerned. I had never seriously considered anything else. I was never going to spend my life sitting behind a desk or gazing at a computer screen.

At one stage, I'd toyed with the idea of setting up a business and looked at the possibility of opening a sports shop in Barnsley, where I would have been guaranteed a head start because of my popularity in the town. I wasn't convinced about investing so much capital in something I'd never done before, though, and worried that I might not have the time to run the business properly – or maybe I just wasn't brave enough to step outside my safety zone within the game. Either way, the idea went on the backburner, where it has stayed, and from the age of around 30, all the signposts have pointed me in the direction of coaching and management.

In the early part of my career I used to turn up at the club every day, work hard on the training ground, play hard on match days, think about the role I was given within the framework of the team and what would be expected of me in a match. I never tried to work out why coaches were doing specific things in training and what relevance any given session had as far as the next game was concerned. As time went by, I started to study what coaches such as Eric Winstanley were trying to do and began to look back at other coaches I had worked with and the way they operated. It snowballed from there and I took my first steps on the coaching ladder while I was still at Barnsley.

Since then I have acquired the UEFA Coaching Certificate and B Licence and started on the A Licence course. After attending a course run by the League Managers' Association (LMA), I have also gained a Diploma in Applied Management, recognised as the equivalent of the UEFA Pro Licence. But while I have an in-depth knowledge of football, I have to admit that my knowledge of life outside the game is quite narrow because football is all I have ever done. Apart from my coaching certificates and business management diploma, I don't have any formal qualifications, not even a few GCSEs.

Football is my chosen profession and I have attained, or will attain, all the qualifications I need to equip me for a career in coaching and management. In just about every other profession, I could reasonably claim to be set fair for the rest of my working life. When a banker, a lawyer or a doctor reaches the age of 40, having added around 20 years' experience to all his other qualifications, people don't ask him, 'What are you going to do next?' They know he is equipped to move on in his chosen career. That doesn't always apply in football because it is a volatile business and there's no way of telling what might be waiting round the corner.

Outside the game, the only formal training I've ever done was the groundsmanship and greenkeeping course during my apprenticeship at Forest. Once a week, I had to travel 15 miles to Loughborough University on public transport and it was a real drag. I didn't last long and was allowed to opt out after a few sessions because of my problems with homesickness, but Brian Clough wasn't going to let one of his apprentices off the hook while all the others had to go through the weekly grind. He soon came up with a scheme for me to continue my groundsman's training at Trent Bridge cricket ground under the watchful eye of his pal Ron Alsopp, the Nottinghamshire groundsman.

It was a big improvement on the trek to Loughborough and Ron was great. He knew I didn't have the slightest intention of becoming a groundsman but he put up with me and kept his side of the bargain to teach me a bit about the job. There were some harrowing moments for my tutor, though, notably the day I was put in charge of the mobile sprinkler that trundled up and down the square to keep the ground moist. The sprinkler stood on a platform with four wheels and if it was set up right, the rotating motion of the sprinkler would nudge the platform along. Ron showed me how to set it up and told me that the secret was to make sure the platform was perfectly balanced and absolutely level. If it was, the wheels would roll smoothly and the platform would stay parallel to the ground; if it wasn't, the platform would get a wobble on, tip to one side and start digging into the surface.

On this particular occasion, I reckoned I'd got it right and as the sprinkler set off on its journey across the square, I paused to take in the splendour of my surroundings. I was admiring the lovely old Trent Bridge pavilion when I heard a voice yell, 'What the bloody 'ell's going on?' It was Ron – and I saw to my horror that the sprinkler had ground to halt and was doing its best to plough up the Trent Bridge square. Ron did a passable impression of Linford Christie as he raced across the outfield in a state of high panic, fearing that his pitch preparation for the forthcoming one-day international against Pakistan was about to hit the buffers. Fortunately, the damage was minimal. He restored the sprinkler to its proper equilibrium and never let me near the machine again. For the record, England won the match by seven wickets so we must have prepared the pitch right.

I eventually took an exam, finished up with some kind of

diploma and was rewarded 15 years later when I was at Barnsley and we had a golf day during the run-in to promotion. I'm no great shakes as a golfer, so it didn't really bother me that one or two of the greens had little brown patches. The state of the putting surfaces did upset the low-handicap boys, though, and plenty of grumbling circulated in the locker room afterwards. I listened for a while and then informed the assembled throng, 'The problem's caused by leatherjackets, you know. They hatch their eggs in the grass and you end up with brown patches like they've got out there. They can be bloody hard to get rid of, too.' Hole in one to Ron Alsopp, I thought.

Funnily enough, I've had a thing about lawns ever since my time at Trent Bridge with Ron. We've got a decent-sized lawn at home and three lawnmowers, including a petrol mower. I like it rolled flat and cut nicely. I sometimes drive Sue mad with it and she'll say, 'It's only a lawn, you know, not a bowling green.' Sometimes, when I'm not looking, she'll try to claim some of my lawn to extend her flower beds – no chance!

However, my knowledge of leatherjackets wasn't a lot of use to me as I pondered the future after leaving Halifax. The offers weren't exactly rolling in and I was starting to worry when along came Boston. They had made an approach for me earlier in the year when they were going for promotion from the Conference and Halifax were clearly on their way out of the League. On the face of it, a move at that stage would have made sense. Neil Thompson, a team-mate at Barnsley, was Boston's number two at the time, assistant to Steve Evans, but I didn't really fancy going there just as a player. After my first managerial stint at Halifax, I felt it was important for me to have some involvement on the coaching side.

During the summer, after Boston had been promoted, Evans was suspended, first by the club and subsequently by the FA, after an inquiry into players' contract irregularities. The 20-month FA ban came into force in July 2002 and Tommo took over as caretaker-manager. He asked me to move in as his number two. I would be assistant manager and first-team coach but would still be registered as a player. He didn't have to ask twice.

The only downside was going to be the travelling. Take a look at the road map and you'll see that Boston is, to put it mildly, out on a limb on the south-east coast of Lincolnshire. It was certainly a hell of a long way from my home near Holmfirth, a few miles south of Huddersfield – an each-way journey of around 100 miles, picking up the M1 near Huddersfield before taking the M18, A1(M) and A1 and then heading east on the A17 just south of Newark. On a good day, I could make it from home to Boston in just over two hours. Hold-ups on the motorway or a lot of traffic on the A17 stretched that to anything up to two and three-quarter or even three hours. It was the same on the journey back – with the added complication that sometimes I would have to go to a game in the evening, usually on a Tuesday, to watch a player or forthcoming opposition.

An average day panned out something like this: up just after six, have a bite of breakfast – Sue took over the morning dog-walking duties – and then leave home at seven o'clock prompt. Arrive around 9.30, take a training session, have some dinner, a mug of tea and a natter at the ground, get back in the car and reach home at around 4.30. If I had a night match to watch, I'd grab something to eat, get changed and jump in the car again. Once or twice I had to go to Carlisle in the evening, which meant a ten-minute break at home before another two and a half hours up the M6. I used to leave just before the end of the game but, even so, I didn't stagger into bed until well after midnight, looking forward to my Wednesday off. I was sampling the muck and bullets of professional football, if you like, but as a coach or manager it's vital that you learn everything you possibly can about the teams and players who are out there, particularly those in your division.

Carlisle was the farthest outpost for my scouting trips but I often went to Macclesfield, Scunthorpe, Darlington or Hull, all fair drives after a day on the road to Boston and back. Every now and then, I'd hit the jackpot with Rochdale, Huddersfield or Bury, which were just down the road from home, and then sometimes Sue would come – it was the only way we could have any time together! At Rochdale, the steward used to see us coming and say,

'Look, there's a free hospitality box tonight, you might as well go in there,' and we'd sample the life of luxury, Spotland-style. I'm so thankful that Sue is genuinely interested and accepts that hard travelling is part of my job, although that doesn't stop her being a bit miffed sometimes when I have to head off yet again instead of sitting down for a quiet night in.

Soon after joining Boston, I became part of the Yorkshire shuttle service, which involved half a dozen of us sharing a car for some of the journey. The scheme involved Stuart Balmer and Tom Bennett, both of whom lived in east Lancashire but spent some of the week in a flat in Newark, and Peter Duffield, Graeme Jones and Lee Thompson, who were based in south Yorkshire. I'd link up with Peter, Graeme and Lee in the Morrisons supermarket car park near junction one of the M18, east of Rotherham, where a decision was made about whose car we would use for the next leg. This was supposed to be organised on a rota basis but sometimes involved delicate negotiations and disputes about whose turn it was.

Once that had been settled, we'd hit the road for our next halt, Blyth Services at the south end of the A1 (M), where Tom and/or Stuart would be waiting if they weren't staying in Newark. If all six were on parade, we'd have to make the final haul to Boston in two cars but sometimes we managed to squeeze five into one vehicle and off we'd go again in the direction of Newark. It was a fair hike even from there because after leaving the A1 we had to head east for another 40 miles, passing the turn-offs to Coddington, Beckingham, Leasingham, Cranwell, Sleaford, Kirkby la Thorpe and Wyberton before finally arriving at our destination.

I must admit, all the travelling caught up with me sometimes. If I'd been away scouting, or if the first team had a game, I might not be in bed until the early hours – but I still might have to get up and drive to Boston to coach the reserves or the kids, or to attend a meeting with the chairman. It was hard. In an ideal world, all professional players would be based near their club, say no more than 20 miles away. But at outposts such as Boston, Carlisle and Scarborough, it doesn't work that way because players are reluctant to dig up their roots and move their families out on a limb for a short-term contract on lower-division money. On the other hand, the clubs haven't got the finances to fund club houses. So there has to be a compromise and long-distance commuting tends to be the answer.

A couple of years ago, I heard about a group of four Carlisle players based in Yorkshire who used to get up before dawn on a Monday, drive to Carlisle for a 10 o'clock start, stay over Monday night, drive home Tuesday afternoon, have a day off with the family on Wednesday and then start all over again on Thursday morning. That kind of routine wipes some of the sheen off the so-called glamorous life of professional football but it's an existence that most lower-division and Conference players are prepared to endure. So are the clubs.

Apart from Lee, who was only 20 at the time, Boston's travelling army were all senior pros and keen to go into coaching. Graeme was a typical old-fashioned centre-forward who used to rough up the opposition and had split a few eyebrows in his time – his own and opposing defenders'. He had a decent touch, too, and had scored goals for Doncaster, Wigan, St Johnstone and Southend before joining Boston. He already had an A Licence and was combining his time at Boston with a part-time job at the Middlesbrough Academy. He later moved to Clyde, where he played part-time, worked full-time as football coach at Darlington Technical College and coached the Middlesbrough kids two nights a week. Stuart was already doing some coaching at Boston while Tom and Peter were working their way through the coaching exams.

So football, rather than last night's telly or the current number one hit, tended to be the main topic of conversation and the journey home was filled with non-stop discussions about coaching methods and in-depth inquests into the sessions I had been putting on that morning. That was great because when my sessions were put under the microscope by such experienced pros, I picked up a lot of feedback that I was able to take on board for next time. I sensed that, by and large, my fellow passengers respected what I was trying to do, which was reassuring.

After training and on match days, we'd all have to wait for the last person to be ready and, as the assistant manager, that would usually be me. There was always something to discuss with Tommo and I couldn't cut corners on that side. After games, one of the other lads would say, 'Come on, Redders, don't be messing about in the manager's office all night this time.' They'd go into the players' lounge and have a beer until I arrived and I did my best not to keep them waiting too long.

As the first season went by, being part of the shuttle became increasingly difficult because I was 'on the other side' as far as the players were concerned. If any of the lads had been left out or taken off in the previous game, they might be unhappy. It wasn't a case of giving me earache but maybe if I hadn't been around, they would have felt able to let off steam and have a bit of a go about the manager, the tactics or anything else. Sometimes they did start to talk about team selection or the way we'd played. I tried to be as diplomatic as I could if some of Tommo's decisions were brought into question, but there was always a danger that I would leave myself open or put Neil in a difficult position because of something I'd said. I realised eventually that I should put a bit more distance between myself and the players and, in the end, Neil and I sat down and talked it through. We decided it would be better all round if I travelled on my own.

That presented a whole new problem – how to pass the best part of six hours a day in solitary confinement. I've never been one for in-car entertainment, although I sometimes listen to Radio Five Live for the discussion programmes and the sport. If I do switch over to one of the music channels, it's usually Classic FM, although I don't pretend to know a great deal about classical music. I'm more of a Vivaldi man than the heavier stuff, but I've always found it relaxing and the best way to while away the time on a long journey – although you won't see me at the Proms!

Since I started to travel solo, however, the car has become more of a mobile office thanks to the hands-free phone. It's a chance to chat with other coaches and managers, out of earshot, and avoids having to make too many calls either at the ground or at home later on. I've discovered that there's no such thing as a short phone call between football people, so what I expect to be a five-minute chat on the road will turn into a 20-minute natter on how to put the football world to rights. It certainly helps to pass the time.

Apart from the endless travelling, Boston was a good place to be, particularly as it meant working with Tommo again. I'd known him from way back during our Forest days and we'd shared promotion to the Premiership at Barnsley. He's always been one of my best mates in football. We share the same drive and enthusiasm and the same ideas about how the game should be played. He'd put together a good blend of youth and experience but from the word go, survival was the name of the game. The club had been fined £100,000 and docked four points for the irregularities that led to Evans' suspension, so at first a bit of a cloud hung over the place, but we made a decent start and Tommo was given the job full-time in October. For my money, he did incredibly well to stabilise the club, make genuine progress at a new level and guide Boston into 15th position in the final table, six points above the relegation zone.

The first thing we did was get the side organised properly and in our first season we kept 14 clean sheets in 46 games and conceded 56 goals, not bad for a side finding its feet in the League. We were the new boys but we handled ourselves well. On a personal level, I played in 31 league games and scored six goals. After a decent season all round, we felt we had the basis of a side that could make a serious challenge for the play-offs the following year. Instead, we returned to find the club embroiled in speculation about a possible takeover by a consortium headed by Jon Sotnick, a Midlands businessman. Rumour had it that if the takeover went through, Evans would return as manager once he had completed his suspension. Neil and I weren't wet behind the ears and knew as well as the next man that a football club takeover is almost always followed by a change of manager, but the speculation was something we could have done without. It rumbled on for the first six months of the season and made Tommo's situation almost impossible.

Sotnick finally took over in early February and the axe fell two days later. I was walking round the Meadowhall shopping centre in Sheffield with Sue when my mobile rang. It was Tommo. 'I've been to see Sotnick. I'm out.' The following day, Friday, 13 February, the club issued a statement saying that Neil had left by mutual consent. I was shell-shocked. Just before the takeover was completed, Sotnick seemed to imply in a statement that Tommo would be given a chance and even though we knew Evans was waiting in the wings, we assumed Neil would at least be given until March when Evans would be available again. Instead, Tommo went and Jim Rodwell, a former Boston player, was brought in as caretaker-manager with Paul Raynor as his first-team coach. Evans returned on 20 March after completing his suspension.

I was left in limbo. As far as I was concerned, I had been sacked. I was under contract as Tommo's number two but on his depar-ture, a new number two had been brought in. Rodwell told me he wanted me to carry on as a player and said that the club would honour the playing side of my contract – but I didn't have a playing side to my contract. I had been employed as a first-team coach and assistant manager, who was also registered as a player. I decided not to take up that offer, claimed I had technically been sacked and asked for compensation. The club said no and clearly they weren't going to budge in a hurry. I talked to my lawyer and was advised that as my case was by no means rock solid, it might be best to cut my losses and walk away. I wasn't happy with the way things had been done and I still believe I was entitled to compensation, but it became increasingly obvious that Boston were going to dig their heels in. The last thing I wanted was a long, drawn-out legal battle. There are more important things in life and in football than money and the only sensible thing was to draw a line under Boston United and start all over again.

So, I was out of a job once more. I rang the PFA and asked them to put my name on the list of players available because the transfer deadline was approaching and I needed to get fixed up pretty quickly. I stayed in training and waited for the phone to ring. If I had received any compensation, I would have tried to fast track a few more coaching qualifications, but now there was a more pressing need – to earn some money. Rochdale, a few minutes' drive down the road, came up with the answer.

Soon after I left Boston, Steve Parkin, the Rochdale manager, had rung Tommo to ask about me. He was looking for an experienced pro to help dig his side out of a hole at the wrong end of the bottom division. Neil told him I was still fit and strong and would do a job for Rochdale. I spoke to Parkin and agreed to join on a non-contract basis until the middle of May with the implication, as far as I was concerned anyway, that we would talk about a contract if and when Rochdale retained their league status. I was given the number 38 shirt and, at first, I was amazed that a small club like Rochdale had used so many players already that season. When it was pointed out that I must be the only player in the League who wore his age on his shirt, I realised someone might just be having a joke at my expense. When a pressman asked me for a comment, I replied, 'It doesn't worry me – as long as I'm still around to be given number 39 next season!'

Parkin had already had one successful spell at the club before joining Barnsley in February 2001. It hadn't worked out at Oakwell and he'd returned to Rochdale in December 2003, following the departure of Alan Buckley after only seven months in the job. I was surprised that Buckley hadn't achieved more because I'd always rated him highly as a manager. He'd done a tremendous job in two spells at Grimsby, initially transforming what was then a Fourth Division outfit into a mid-table side, two levels higher. He had always believed in playing attractive, attacking football but while the formula had worked at Grimsby, it was less successful at Rochdale.

Parkin had been brought back to pick up the pieces and, frankly, when I arrived, Rochdale were in a mess. I'd been in the same situation twice at Halifax, where basically we'd needed snookers to get out of trouble, and managed to escape once. Parkin had invested in that experience when he'd offered me a job and it was a situation I relished. As I'd discovered at Halifax, you learn more from the hard times than the good times and my eight weeks at Rochdale were an important part of the learning process.

I wasn't frightened of the challenge and I was prepared to lead from the front, even though I wasn't the official team captain. I sensed straight away that the players were looking for strong leadership and, as a seasoned pro with over 900 games behind me, I felt I was the man they needed. That's not being big-headed, just honest and realistic. I have never feared any challenge in football. I believe in myself, I don't worry about the opposition or the crowd and I just get stuck into my own game. Danny Wilson was the same when he first arrived at Barnsley as player-coach and his influence rubbed off on me and on the rest of the players. I like to think I had the same effect on the players at Rochdale who, when I arrived, seemed frightened to death about fighting a relegation battle. They were a good bunch of lads and decent players but they had lost their way under pressure and needed leadership and direction out on the pitch. My approach took pressure off them and I think they felt better knowing that I was around.

With ten games still to play, there was time to clamber out of trouble or sink deeper into the mire. The first was against Carlisle, who had started the season disastrously with just one win and two draws in their first 21 league games. The arrival of a few new players around Christmas was the trigger for them to stage a tremendous recovery, and they came to Spotland with an outside chance of avoiding the drop, something that had seemed unthinkable earlier in the season. The match was a must-win for Rochdale and a must-not-lose for Carlisle. We won 2–0 and gave ourselves some breathing space, but we didn't win for another five games, losing three times and drawing twice. We were right back on the brink before a 3–0 win over Leyton Orient eased the pressure, and we travelled down to Kidderminster on 24 April knowing that three points would ensure survival with two games still to play. A goal from Leo Bertos was enough for the 1–0 win we needed. The next game, a 1–0 home win, was academic and I didn't play in the final game of the season, a 2–0 defeat at Oxford. We finished five points above the drop zone.

I wasn't offered another year. It was disappointing but, to be honest, I'd seen it coming. I suspect that, not for the first time, my ambitions in coaching and management were the problem. I'd gone in there, done well, the side had stayed in the League and the fans had taken to me. I would have looked like an obvious contender for the manager's job if things had gone badly at the start of the new season. I felt I was definitely worth a contract, Parkin thought otherwise. He was entitled to his opinion. It was his club and his team. He wanted to move things on for the next season and I suspect that, from day one, he'd seen me as a short-term measure. I like to think that when I face a similar situation, I'll handle it differently, but only time will tell. I've learned the hard way that, in football, people tend to say one thing and mean another and I suppose there's a danger I will fall into that trap myself, however hard I try not to do so.

My agreement with Rochdale ran until mid-May and they offered to pay me up until then. Once again, I was a free agent and looking for my 15th club, but first, I had a little business to attend to at the University of Warwick.

18 BESIDE THE SEASIDE

I NEVER THOUGHT THE DAY WOULD DAWN WHEN I'D SAMPLE LIFE on a university campus. After all, I was the kid who left school at 15 to be a footballer, without even bothering to take his GCSEs. What my secondary school teachers would have made of the sight of Neil Redfearn ambling around the University of Warwick in the summer of 2004 doesn't bear thinking about. At the very least, they would have been asking some serious questions about the quality of mature students these days.

With 17 other managers and would-be managers, I was attending a five-day course in business management organised by the League Managers' Association (LMA), the first of two residential weeks on campus. Between the two residential courses, I attended a one-day refresher each month in pursuit of the Diploma in Applied Management that I acquired in the summer of 2005.

I wouldn't argue with the view that the purpose of football management is to get the right results, but I also believe that a manager has a better chance of achieving those results if he prepares himself properly in advance. The more background education and training he acquires, the better equipped he will be to handle the pressures of the job. Management training has to be part of the package alongside coaching qualifications.

For the residential weeks, we stayed in Scarman House, student accommodation on the main campus but not quite at the heart of the student population. We were the corporate clientele, if you like. Our lectures took place in the Warwick Business Centre, based at the university, and the course covered a huge spectrum, not just football but all aspects of management. Professional people came in to give talks on subjects such as business psychology, professional strategy, man-management, marketing and media training. It was tough going for someone who hadn't given much thought to academic work since leaving school – and not a lot when he was at school, come to think of it. Days were nine to five with a short break for lunch and they kept us at it. One or two evening sessions were included. It was intense. At about three o'clock in the afternoon, we started to hit the mental brick wall and one or two eyes began to glaze over.

In the end, we made it over the line and the diploma means I am qualified for a management career outside the game, if the day ever dawns when football is no longer the top priority. After my school record, passing the various written exams on the road to gaining the diploma was a bit of a turn-up for the book, but I guess it proves that you're never too old to learn new tricks. I've always believed that I can succeed in football but now I feel I could hold my own in other walks of life if I had to put my mind to it.

Studying for the diploma was a great experience and the course provided an opportunity to meet other coaches and managers. Kevin Blackwell, Stuart Pearce, Kenny Jackett, Keith Curle, Glyn Hodges, Tony Adams, Paul Brush and Neil Thompson were second-year students when I started the course. Alongside me among the new recruits were Chris Hughton, Kevin Ball, Iffy Onuora, Kit Symons, Martin Allen, Steve Tilson, Mark Robins, Stuart Murdoch and John Taylor. The PFA was running a coaching course at the same time so loads more familiar faces were around, and at the end of the day, we'd sit down and talk football before and during the evening meal. One or two of the boys would stay around for a drink afterwards – although most of us were ready for an early night after all the brainstorming sessions.

Four officials from the LMA – John Barnwell, Frank Clark, Keith Burkinshaw and John Duncan – attended the course as mentors. Barnwell, chief executive and one of the founding fathers of the LMA, is a former manager of six clubs, including Wolves and AEK Athens, while Clark, my youth-team coach at Forest all those years ago, later managed Orient, Forest and Manchester City. Burkenshaw, who returned to front-line duty as assistant manager of Watford in 2005, twice won the FA Cup with Spurs in the eighties and Duncan, who guided Chesterfield to the semi-final of the Cup in 1997, also managed Scunthorpe and Ipswich.

They were all experienced men who had been through the mill and knew the job backwards and it was fascinating to hear their take on management. If, for example, we were having a lecture on business psychology, they were able to speak on the football aspect rather than just from a business point of view. Duncan was my personal mentor. He is a qualified teacher, who played for Dundee, Spurs and Derby before moving into management, and he offered to help me out on the coaching side, too.

As I started to immerse myself in the world of business management at Warwick, however, I also had to come to terms with the reality that after my short stay at Rochdale, I was out of work for the second year in a row. I believed I would find a club, just as I had when I left Halifax 12 month earlier, although once again I felt it was important to find a job that offered me a coaching as well as a playing opportunity. If I was only on the market as a player, there were going to be a lot of other people in the same situation and they would all be younger than me. I was aware that my preference for a player-coaching job pigeonholed me a bit, but I had enough self-belief to go for it.

After about six weeks in no-man's land, I heard on the grapevine that Scarborough of the Nationwide Conference might soon be advertising for an assistant manager. Russell Slade, who had guided Boro into the fourth round of the Cup and a glamour home tie with Chelsea the previous season, had joined Grimsby and the word was that Nick Henry, his right-hand man and my one-time Oldham team-mate, would be appointed head coach at

Scarborough. I managed to get hold of a phone number for Malcolm Reynolds, the Scarborough chairman, and gave him a call. I said I'd heard the club might be looking for an assistant manager and told him I was his man. I gave him my coaching background, said I could still cut the mustard as a player, certainly in the Conference, and that I'd played alongside Henry at Oldham and was confident we would be able to work together. 'Leave it with me,' he said.

The following day I had a call from Nick. We had a long chat in which he outlined his plans and he ended by asking, 'Do you fancy it, then?'

'Yes.'

'Right, come over to the McCain Stadium tomorrow and meet the chairman.'

I drove over and had a look around the set-up before meeting Reynolds. I liked the feel of the place straight away. He asked me what kind of money I would be looking for and I gave him a figure that I was fairly sure would not price me out of the market. Obviously it didn't because we agreed terms and I accepted a one-year deal there and then. I was back in the land of the living – and back on the road. Holmfirth to Scarborough isn't quite in the Holmfirth to Boston class when it comes to the loneliness of the long-distance traveller but it's a fair old hike and the A64 between York and the east coast can be a nightmare during the summer when holidaymakers and daytrippers are around. Usually, I allowed myself a couple of hours each way but on summer Saturdays or Bank Holidays, I made sure the players built an extra half hour or so into their travel time. As with Boston, the lads came from far and wide and many a tale of woe was heard about being stuck behind a tractor or legged up by a caravan all the way from Malton.

In late July and early September, cricket matches at Scarborough's North Marine Road ground caused extra traffic. For over 120 years, Yorkshire cricket lovers have flocked to Scarborough, particularly for the September Festival but aston-ishingly, my dad and his pal Derek Tordoff, both dyed-in-the-wool Yorkshire supporters, had never been to North Marine Road when I signed for Scarborough. We soon put that right. In late July, Yorkshire played Somerset and an expedition was planned for Dad and Derek to go to the third day's play. I dropped them off at the ground at around 9.30 in the morning and arranged to join them after training for the afternoon and evening sessions. So far, so good. It was a beautiful day and I was just about to set off for the cricket ground when I had a call on my mobile.

'We're not in the ground any more. We're sitting on a bench overlooking Marine Drive and the beach. The tide's out.'

'What's wrong? Why aren't you at the cricket?'

'What cricket? It's all over. You can pick us up outside the Cricketers pub instead. It's right opposite the ground.'

The morning session had been disastrous for the White Rose, not to mention the big crowd. Yorkshire had started 92 behind in their second innings with seven wickets in hand – not a brilliant position by any means but the consensus of opinion on the way over backed our boys to dig deep, show a bit of Yorkshire grit and give Somerset a decent target in the fourth innings. Instead, they lost their last seven wickets for 57 runs in just over an hour, which left Somerset needing six to collect their first win of the season. They obliged in the space of two balls and the match was over before Dad and Derek had even opened their packed lunches. So instead of enjoying the sound of willow on leather into the early evening, we were back on the A64 in the early afternoon and home ready for our tea at around 5.30. Some you win, some you lose, I suppose, and plans were soon laid for a return trip the following year.

Cricket apart, the early days went well. Nick gave me carte blanche to organise the pre-season programme and take the coaching sessions from day one, so I sat down and worked out a decent schedule. One of the problems was that I didn't know any of the players but I was confident I could handle that once they reported back.

For our first day's training, I organised the traditional long-distance run, this time up to the top of Oliver's Mount, a fairly serious hill on the outskirts of town. As we prepared for the off, I could see a fair few of the lads looking me up and down and wondering how long it would be before I packed it in and walked back to the ground. When we set off, I soon found myself tucked in near the back of the field but, just like in my old cross-country days at school, there was plenty of gas in the tank. By the time we started the climb up towards the monument at the summit of Oliver's Mount, I was nicely placed in the middle of the pack. On the way back down, I selected a higher gear and moved past some of the early pacemakers and to within sight of the front three or four. They were less than chuffed about being picked off by their 39-year-old player-coach on the run-in to the McCain Stadium. With a couple of hundred yards to go, only young Jimmy Beadle, approximately half my age, stood between me and the gold medal. I don't think he knew who was behind him and how close I was until he turned round to see who was in pursuit, did a visible double take and found enough to keep me at bay. I could sense him thinking, 'There's no way I'm going to get beaten by that old so-and-so,' and I headed off for a shower afterwards knowing that I'd proved a point.

From then on, whenever we went for a run during the season, I would always sneak up behind anyone who seemed to be struggling and whisper, 'Come on, I'll be forty next June. You shouldn't be finishing behind me.' It usually worked. Overall, they were a grand set of lads, and a pleasure to work with. We also had a few decent kids starting to come through and some of them were given a chance during the season. From now on, it will be down to them. If they're good enough and the attitude is right, they can make it. The jury is out but they are at a club where a good young player will be given opportunities.

From a playing point of view, I tried not to set myself individual targets at the start of my 23rd season as a pro because I was new to the club, new to the job and new to the Conference. As ever, I wanted to play in every game and I genuinely believed that I would be more than good enough to be worth my place, week in and week out. I accepted that I would have to take a back seat sometimes, though, if only to have a different perspective on the way we were playing. In the end, I missed just three games late in the season, all because of injury, and missing those three games was a real pain, proof that the old hunger was still there.

At first, I had a few worries about dropping down to the Conference but they soon disappeared. I found the overall standard was high, partly because the influx of foreign players higher up the scale has squeezed things in the lower divisions of the League and younger and better players are coming into the Conference. Most of the Conference clubs are full-time with a professional set-up behind the scenes and I approached the job exactly as I would have done if we were a Football League club. The style of football was a refreshing change, too. League sides tend to be a bit more cautious in their approach to away matches but I soon discovered that Conference teams are usually ready to give it a real go, looking for three points rather than one. Scarborough went through the whole of the 2004–05 season unbeaten at home, which made us a pretty daunting proposition on our own pitch, but only a couple of sides came with the sole intention of getting everybody behind the ball and stopping us. The rest seemed to see our record as an incentive to go for the win and we slugged it out for the 90 minutes.

To go through a whole season unbeaten at the McCain Stadium was a phenomenal achievement – the first time it had happened to me in my career. I struggled to recall many sides that had done the same thing anywhere, at any level. It wasn't as if we were a dour side, happy to settle for a point. We drew far too many games but they weren't bore draws, by any means – far from it. We were two down against Aldershot and fought back to 2–2, and we were leading Stevenage 3–1 at half-time before drawing 3–3. We gave the fans plenty to shout about and showed that even though we might not have been quite good enough overall, the attitude and spirit were spot on.

The players gave everything and the longer the unbeaten record survived, the deeper they were prepared to dig to defend it. It was a proud moment when we finished the final home match against Farnborough with the record intact. I sensed a definite feeling of 'Nobody beats Scarborough here' among the players and it's just a shame we couldn't take some of that mental toughness into away games. In the end, we drew too many at home, lost too many away and didn't get enough goals from the front players.

We tried to remedy that late in the season by bringing in David Reeves, who had scored a lot of goals in a long league career with Sheffield Wednesday, Scunthorpe (on loan), Burnley (on loan), Bolton, Notts County, Carlisle, Preston, Chesterfield and Oldham. He had loads of experience. We hoped he would make the difference and push us into the play-offs but he was injured soon after joining us, suffered a recurrence of the problem when he made a comeback and was never really the force we hoped. The fact is we were short of a front player all season, someone who could give us a cutting edge. On the kind of money clubs such as Scarborough can afford to pay, that is often going to be a problem. At any level, be it Premiership or Conference, proven goal-scorers are like gold dust. If a club finds one, they hang on to him and maybe pay him a little bit over the odds to make sure he stays around.

In fact, I was the leading scorer, with 14 goals from midfield. I was happy with that. The original plan was for me to sit in central midfield and use my experience to dictate things from there, covering any holes that might appear in defence and pushing forward if and when a chance arose. Chances did arise and I ended up scoring in each of the first four games. So it was back to the drawing board and from then on, I was encouraged to get forward as much as possible. Instead of hoping I might pinch a goal or two from a deeper role, Nick urged me to use that little bit of extra quality I still had in the final third and at set-pieces.

I could tell from the crowd's reaction that the fans knew where I was coming from. When you're out there in front of 15,000 or 20,000 fans, you only hear the roar. When there are only 1,300 or so, you can hear just about every individual shout. By and large, they were favourable to me. Since I started playing in the lower divisions there have always been one or two punters who seem to delight in taking a pop at me, probably because they've looked at my record and pedigree and expect me to reproduce Premiership form for their club. It could never work that way because I'm not as young as I was and, like any team game, football is a lot easier when you have quality players around you. As long as the fans pay their money at the gate, they can say what they like, of course, but I always give 110 per cent and I like to think people recognise that when things aren't going well. As I finished second in the *Scarborough Evening News* Player of the Year competition, I must have been doing something right.

Not for the first time, though, I discovered that the role of player-coach is a tough one. As always, I really enjoyed the coaching sessions and became totally wrapped up in my own work, demonstrating to the players what they should and should not be doing and why. But I had to keep reminding myself that I was not just a coach, I was also an integral part of the side, and instead of running the session from the outside, I needed to become involved as a player as well. It was important that Neil Redfearn the coach did not neglect Neil Redfearn the player, something I've been able to adapt to better as the years have gone by.

At Halifax, the job affected my whole game. I was trying to be all things to all people out on the pitch and found my own performance was suffering. I realised that in future I would have to free myself from all other responsibilities once the game started. There isn't a player in the world good enough to look after everybody else's game as well as his own, and at Boston and later at Scarborough, I learned how to take off the coach's head when I walked into the dressing room at 2.00 p.m. and become just another player. OK, I was involved in the game plan, but once we crossed the white line, I was a member of the cast, not the production team. That was an important part of the learning curve and another way in which my time as player-coach at Halifax, Boston and Scarborough has equipped me for what may lie ahead.

Being a player-coach will always be a balancing act. On the one hand, a player-coach is part of the management team; on the other, he's a regular member of the starting line-up. He needs to be a mate as well as one of the bosses. At Scarborough, I didn't change with the rest of the players at training – Nick and I used the referee's room – but I tried to spend time with the players in the dressing room afterwards, sharing a joke and joining in some of the banter. And from the start, I tried to have an open relation-ship with all the players. It was important not to show any favouritism and what I thought about each individual player's ability remained strictly between Nick and me.

I gave the players respect and expected them to respect me in return. I was available for extra work in the afternoon if any indi-vidual player or a group of players wanted to do some overtime. It was the same if they wanted to come for a one-to-one chat about their game or about what we were trying to do in training. At one of our first sessions together, I told them that I'd played the best part of a thousand senior games, which meant a lot of experience at all levels. 'If you want to tap into some of that experience, you only have to ask,' I said, and the response was good.

Of course, coaching will never be an exact science. In a way, it's a bit like driving. Basic skills have to be learned but it's only when a coach passes his test and goes out on the road on his own that he really begins to find out what the job is all about. When I took my first sessions at Halifax, a bit of all my previous coaches lurked behind everything I did, but just as you drive a car in your own way, so you develop your own style as a coach. Above all, you have to be honest and analyse your own performance. On some days, I've come in after a session and said to myself, 'That hasn't worked, the players didn't take enough out of that.' I've gone away and tried to figure out what went wrong so that I can make sure it doesn't happen again.

A coach organises a session for a purpose – there's no point playing five-a-side or possession football if specific areas need working on. Let's say, for example, that on a Saturday afternoon, the quality of the passing from back to front is below standard and there isn't enough movement from the front players. On the Monday, I'll put on a session that addresses those specific problems.

Maybe I'll sit the players down in advance and tell them what the session will involve and why, or maybe I'll just get started. I'll always explain afterwards why we did that particular session and what I expected them to take out of it.

I try to make the sessions interesting, to capture the players' imagination and hold their attention. I know from experience that coaching sometimes goes in one ear and out of the other so it's up to the coach to make it fun as well as relevant. From the outside, it's easy to say that running around on a training ground is always going to be fun, but that isn't necessarily the case. Like any other worker, a professional footballer arrives in the morning with other things on his mind and problems that he will need to sort out after work. The coach has to make sure that for the next couple of hours, his attention is focused on football and not how the hell he's going to find time to take the mother-in-law's cat to the vet before picking up the kids from primary school.

A coach is given a squad of players to work with and they are the tools of his trade. They all have different strengths and weaknesses and it's up to the coach to identify those and work on them to develop their individual game within the team. The best coach in the world will struggle to turn a group of average players into anything more than an average side, but those players can be organised so that they are efficient, work well as a unit and become difficult to play against.

For the most part, players like things to be simple – and I'm not being patronising when I say that. They are aware of their limitations and it's no good asking them to do something they know is beyond their capabilities. Only at the highest level can you expect players to work things out for themselves and know they will usually get it right. There you're working with exceptional players, whose technique, passing and movement are top class. Lower down, you have to concentrate on getting your own house in order rather than working on cultured attacking movements or sophisticated ways of stopping the opposition.

I have found that the more a coach works with a group of players, the more he warms to them. They are his for a season and he finds out about their strengths and weaknesses as players and as people and gives them as much of his own experience as he can. There aren't many situations that I haven't experienced over the last 25 years or so and my knowledge is something I can pass on to young players who are sampling things for the first time. I've been learning, too. I've always believed it's important to start at the bottom and find out about the job at that level. OK, if Alex Ferguson had called and asked me to take over as Manchester United's first-team coach, I wouldn't have said no. Long-term, though, I believe I will be a better coach and manager for having learned the rudiments and tasted the hard times at Halifax, Boston and Scarborough.

I've also discovered that nothing can ever be taken for granted in the lower divisions and the best-laid plans can unravel in the most unlikely ways. Take, for example, Scarborough's game at Woking in March 2005, towards the end of a season that was starting to fall apart a bit. We were still strong at home but after a reasonable start on our travels, we had hit a bad run after Christmas and desperately needed to avoid defeat at Woking to have an outside chance of the play-offs.

Scarborough to almost anywhere is a long trip but this was an evening game and the last thing we wanted was to be stuck on a motorway instead of preparing properly. The chairman dug into his own pocket so that we could have an afternoon break and a meal at a hotel near Aldershot, just a few miles down the road from Woking. What's more, we travelled down in style in the double-decker bus usually used by Middlesbrough, who organised their away travel through the same company as we did at Scarborough.

We arrived at the hotel in plenty of time, had a walk to loosen up and after the pre-match meal, we all climbed aboard for the short trip to Woking, or so we thought. To avoid the rush-hour traffic, our drivers had decided to use a side road and for the first few miles, all went according to plan. We were ten or 15 minutes ahead of schedule when the bus suddenly ground to a halt in front of a low bridge. If we'd been using our normal single-decker coach, the bridge wouldn't have presented a problem, but a double-decker? No. It was much too big to go under the bridge. That was the end of Plan A – and we didn't have a Plan B to fall back on. Road maps were produced and we soon discovered that the only option was to go back to the starting point and take our chances.

It was soon obvious that we wouldn't be anywhere near the ground at 6.30 p.m., our estimated time of arrival, an hour and a quarter before kick-off. In fact, for a while it looked as if we might struggle to make it at all. The traffic was horrendous. At seven o'clock, we rang Woking and told them what was happening. They agreed to delay the kick-off by 15 minutes and Nick phoned over the team and subs. Then the driver stopped the coach, we unloaded the skips, unpacked our kit and got changed on the bus, where Nick gave his team talk to 16 players in various stages of undress. It wasn't the easiest talk in the world either because, at that stage, we'd no idea what the Woking side would be. When we finally arrived 15 minutes before kick-off, to ironic cheers from the home fans, we hopped off the bus, put on our boots and ran on to the pitch for a few minutes' runaround until it was time to toss up – just like teams used to do before pre-match warm-ups were introduced in the eighties. We drew one apiece and might easily have taken all three points in what was one of our better away performances. So much for match preparation! But while it's funny to look back on that day now, it was an important game and could easily have been a disaster. Somewhere down the line, somebody should have known about the low bridge.

In the event, a draw was not good enough and the season fell away from there. We finished mid-table with a record of 14 wins, 14 draws and 14 defeats. You can't be much more average than that, can you? The final game of the season was at Aldershot on 23 April. We lost 2–0 and Aldershot made it to the play-offs. At times during the season we'd looked play-off material ourselves and our final position was disappointing for everyone – players, supporters, Nick, me, the chairman, the directors and all the people who had worked so hard behind the scenes.

From the start of the season, I'd sensed a real family atmosphere around the McCain Stadium, with everyone pulling in the same direction. When Sue came to matches, she picked up on that feeling, too. A lot of people at Scarborough, including John Birley, the president, and Tony Stockdale, one of the directors, have been around for years and the club has been a big part of their lives. They weren't in it to make money or gain personal glory. They just enjoyed working for the good of the club. The chairman Malcolm Reynolds was the same. He had stepped in and bailed Scarborough out when they were in desperate financial trouble a few years back, but again, I never felt that he was on any kind of ego trip. He and Ian Scobbie, an associate director, were massively enthusiastic about football and about Scarborough in particular and would go anywhere to watch a game. Yes, even Carlisle.

Carlisle had been relegated from the Football League in 2004 so Ian and I decided to take in a midweek match at Brunton Park shortly before we were due to play them in a league game. He picked me up at Ferrybridge Services on the A1 and we headed north to Scotch Corner before turning west over Shap Fell on the A66. It was a pretty bleak night but we were nattering on about football and making good progress until Ian put a damper on proceedings by announcing, 'I hope there's a petrol station on here, the tank's never been this low before.' Filling stations are few and far between in that part of the world and I was worried that we wouldn't make it. The warning light was on full time a good 20 miles before we re-entered civilisation at Penrith and if we'd run out, I don't know which one of us would have got out and hitched a lift. I might have 'remembered' a twinge from training earlier that day and opted not to risk aggravating the problem before Saturday's game.

I don't suppose too many assistant managers go to games with their chairman or associate director but it was never a problem. I enjoyed their company and if I saw a player who might be good for Scarborough, I could say why there and then without having to explain it at a meeting a few days later. For me, their keenness to be involved was part of the charm of Scarborough Football Club. There didn't appear to be a hidden agenda behind the scenes.

Straight after the final game at Aldershot, Nick took a couple of weeks' holiday so I had Sunday and Monday off and then, on the Tuesday, it was back to Scarborough and time to start planning ahead for the new season. I needed to begin work on a training programme and finalise our series of pre-season friendlies. I was on the phone from 10 a.m., putting in calls to, among others, Paul Jewell at Wigan, Peter Jackson at Huddersfield, Alan Curbishley at Charlton, Peter Taylor at Hull, Ian Evans at Sunderland and Chris Hughton at Spurs – yes, sometimes it pays to have played for a lot of clubs and met a lot of people.

The morning was rewarding in more ways than one. Talking to other coaches and managers brought home that we're all in the same boat – all that matters, whether you are in the Premiership or the Conference, is getting the right results. Over the last two or three years I've discovered that a strong bond exists among managers and coaches, and for the most part, we are happy to help one another. I was making calls about pre-season games but, without exception, the people I spoke to wanted to know how Nick and I were doing at Scarborough, what kind of players we might need and how much we could afford. A couple more names could usually be entered in our little black book at the end of each call. I also struck lucky as far as the pre-season programme was concerned. The new Premiership and Conference seasons were due to start a week later than the Football League, which presented a chance for Scarborough to fix up a game against one of the big boys. The outcome was a high-profile friendly against Sunderland at the McCain Stadium. We won 4–0!

Then it was time for a few days in Scotland with Sue, Aimee and Lois. The job never really ends, though. Throughout the close season, there were meetings to attend with Nick and the chairman, training venues to organise, pre-season to sort out, talks to arrange with local people about forging closer links with the club, and all the other things that tend to be squeezed out during the season. Everything had to be in place for the players when they reported back, with no loose ends still to tie up. Football was on holiday but behind the scenes at Scarborough, there was still a big job to be done.

19 MANAGEMENT MAN

BILL FOTHERBY BECAME A HOUSEHOLD NAME AMONG FOOTBALL supporters during his time as chairman and managing director of Leeds United. He was the driving force behind the appointment of Howard Wilkinson as manager in 1988, presided over Wilkinson's successful championship campaign four years later and contrived to keep the name of Leeds United in the headlines for the best part of his 30 years as a director at Elland Road. Once, when Leeds were still in the old Second Division, he managed to hit the back pages with a 'Leeds want Maradona' headline. The story ran for a few days and even though Diego stayed put at Napoli, Leeds were back on the map and Fotherby's reputation established·as a larger than life football personality.

His Leeds days were a fair way behind him, however, by the time he played an indirect role in my appointment as manager of Scarborough in November 2005. An FA Cup defeat at Harrogate Town, the club Fotherby adopted after leaving Leeds in 1999, ended Nick Henry's time as Scarborough's head coach. I was appointed manager ten days later. The game against Harrogate came just over two months into a season that began with the usual optimism but quickly drifted into disappointment. We won three and lost eight of our first 14 league matches and made the trip to Harrogate's Wetherby Road stadium for a fourth qualifying round

FA Cup tie struggling at the foot of the Nationwide Conference. We'd lost our previous four games and desperately needed a win to boost our confidence in the League and to make a bit of money from a Cup run.

Harrogate were doing well in Conference North, one level below us, so it was going to be tough. They had some solid pros in the side. Chris Brass had been York City's player-manager 12 months earlier, Lee Philpott had played in the Premiership for Leicester, Lee Nogan had scored 139 goals in 675 games for 11 league clubs, and Paul Stoneman had defensive qualities that I knew all about from our days at Halifax. Neil Aspin, their manager, had loads of experience as a player with Leeds and Port Vale and Fotherby was pulling the strings behind the scenes.

Fotherby had left Leeds claiming he was tired of football but, early in the new millennium, he was installed as chairman of Harrogate and from day one he set out his stall to take them into the Football League. After two promotions, they were in the upper reaches of Conference North when the draw for the fourth qualifying round paired them with Scarborough. The local media sensed an upset. So did Harrogate. In the build-up to the game, their fans wore tee-shirts bearing the legend: 'Rome wasn't built in a day – but then again, Bill Fotherby wasn't chairman'. They'd won six of their previous eight games and were looking for a fourth successive victory. Talk about a potential banana skin!

We knew we would have to be fully committed if we were going to win or, at worst, secure a draw and then finish the job at the McCain Stadium. Defeat was unthinkable, but the unthinkable happened. Without playing particularly well, we were the better side for an hour or so. Then their big striker Marc Smith nicked a goal when a free kick was floated in and they lifted their game by 15 per cent until the final whistle. I'd begun the game on the right side of midfield, my first start for a few weeks, and was substituted soon after the goal.

The following Monday seemed like just another working day, although inevitably everything felt a bit flat. I took the lads out training and while I expected Nick to come and join us, I wasn't too concerned when he failed to arrive, assuming he had other things to attend to. When I returned to the stadium, Nick told me he was leaving. Even though results had not been good, it was a shock. We had a brief chat, shook hands and I wished him all the best. It was a strange sensation to watch him walk away, knowing that he wouldn't be back in the morning.

Malcolm Reynolds asked me to take over on a caretaker basis for the home game against Aldershot on the Saturday and said we'd talk again the following Monday. It never crossed my mind to say no, even though Nick was a friend and former team-mate and we'd worked closely together for around 15 months. He wasn't going to be reinstated if I turned the job down. Scarborough would simply have looked elsewhere. While Nick was the manager, I was ready to work alongside him and help in any way I could, be it coaching or playing. Managing Scarborough was not on the agenda. As soon as he left, the goalposts were moved and I saw no reason not to accept the job.

I'd had an insight into what was involved during my two spells at Halifax and knew that the most important signing I would make would be my assistant. So even though I'd been appointed on a temporary basis, I asked Malcolm straight away if I could bring in Eric Winstanley, the former Barnsley coach whose last job had been technical director to the national side of St Kitts and Nevis, the Caribbean holiday islands. The North Yorkshire coast in the middle of winter would be a different kettle of fish but I knew Eric would hack it. He wasn't working, which meant there would be no contract problems with another club, and I'd already had a chat with him about the possibility of working together when I'd been linked with the manager's job at Barnsley a few months earlier. I'd played under Eric for a long time and our football philosophies had always been very similar. We'd worked well together before and I was sure we could do so again, even though the roles would be different. I would be the boss this time and he would be my right-hand man. I respected Eric immensely and I was confident that, above all, we would be a team.

I gave him a call, he said yes, and at 7.30 the following morning we met in the car park of the British Oak pub at Durkar, near Wakefield, for the first of our 150-mile round trips to the McCain Stadium. I saw Eric's arrival as a crucial part of the way forward. I believe he is one of the best coaches in the country. His knowledge of the game is second to none and he knows the 3-5-2 system I wanted to introduce inside out because that's how we played during the successful times at Barnsley. I knew I could have complete confidence in him and that if I had other things on my plate, I could leave the training to Eric and he would do the job properly.

My second major decision was what to do with Neil Redfearn, the player. Eric believed it was important for me to continue playing and pushed for me to be in the starting line-up. I resisted because I thought my first priority was to get my feet under the desk as manager. A million and one things had to be done and I wanted to look at the team from the sidelines. I felt I would be taking on too much too soon if I tried to play as well as manage, because from now on, the buck stopped with me. There would be plenty of opportunities for me to return as a player later on, although ironically when things began to go awry, I was out of action with a groin injury.

In that first game against Aldershot, we were two down after 50 minutes and the supporters must have feared the worst, but the players dug deep, pulled the two goals back and might easily have gone on to win. I was appointed manager on the Monday morning and we won my first game in charge, 1–0 at Tamworth. Earlier in the week I'd done an interview with *FourFourTwo* magazine, looking back at my playing career and my move into management. The reporter asked if they could take pictures at the game and I was photographed leaving the team bus, on the pitch during the warm-up and near the dug-out during the match. The Tamworth dug-out is set back among the fans and when they spotted the photographer, the home fans started to give me some stick. It was fairly playful stuff to start with. When a shot from one of the lads flew way over the bar, someone yelled, 'I see you've been coaching him, Redfearn!' I had a laugh back and took all the references to my Yorkshire background, my haircut, my love life and my waistline with a pinch of salt. Then when we went one up just before half-time, I turned round and said, 'There's something else for you to sing about!' That really got them going and I decided to keep my eyes in front from then on.

The following week, we drew 1–1 at home with Stevenage, one of the better sides in the Conference, before beating Halifax Town, another of the play-off contenders, 2–0, also at the McCain Stadium. I wasn't getting carried away, though, and sure enough, after losing our next game at Cambridge, we didn't win again until 14 January, a run of seven league games without a victory. I knew when I took over that it would be a difficult first few months. Let's face it, if the team had been in the top six, I wouldn't have been asked to replace Nick. Instead, we were threatened with relegation to the Conference North. Welcome to management!

So how was I going to approach the job? I've learned something from all the managers I've played for and I try to take on board some of their good qualities. I hope to have the mental toughness, self-belief and single-minded approach that Danny Wilson brought to the job at Barnsley. Danny didn't court popularity from his players but he earned their respect. He never hid as a player or as a manager.

I would like to develop the man-management skills of Alan Curbishley. He understood what made his players tick and, above all, he gave them leadership. Some players are mentally strong enough to cope on their own but others need guidance. People would be surprised at the number of times some players look across at the bench during a game, just seeking reassurance, a nod that says yes, you're doing OK. Curbishley was always there for his players.

He also took away the fear factor – a great quality, because if a player is frightened of conceding a goal, frightened of missing a chance, frightened of making a difficult pass, the team will suffer. He was able to divert pressure from his players by soaking it up himself. If results were going badly, he accepted responsibility and protected his players. Sir Alf Ramsey was before my time but I've read a fair bit about him and it strikes me that Curbs takes the pressure away from his squad in the same way that Ramsey shielded the England players of his day.

Don Revie was a contemporary of Ramsey's and I have also read about his style of management and the way he turned a struggling Leeds United side into one of the best English teams of the post-war era. He was renowned for his meticulous approach and attention to detail but equally important was the family atmosphere he created throughout the club, particularly in the dressing room. He was a father figure to a group of young players who grew up at Leeds and went on to become international stars, and he never criticised his players in public. Under Revie, Leeds were truly united and the strong team ethic was a major factor in their success and something I would hope to foster as a manager.

I try to learn from my contemporaries, too, and in that respect the time spent on the business course at Warwick University was beneficial, enabling me to watch how other would-be managers approach the job while picking up new skills. For example, Stuart Pearce has made such a big impression since taking over at Manchester City in May 2005 and I was so impressed with the way he knuckled down and worked really hard to take the full benefit from the course. I have seen players go into coaching who think they don't have a lot to learn. Their attitude is, 'I've played four or five hundred games, so why do I need an A or B Licence? What's the point of some fancy business qualification from a university course?' Not Pearce.

He had played at the very highest level but realised he was embarking on a new phase of his career and that the more he took on board from Warwick, the better equipped he would be when his time came. He looked at the record and experience of our mentors, John Duncan, Frank Clark and Keith Burkinshaw, and said to himself, 'These people can teach me something.' Stuart had been an electrician before becoming a professional footballer with Nottingham Forest and it had taken him two years to learn the job. He was prepared to take as long to learn about football management and accepted that his high-profile image as a player was irrelevant. When his chance came at City, one of the biggest and toughest jobs in football, he was ready.

However, while I can learn from Wilson, Curbishley, Pearce and Revie, in the end, I have to be Neil Redfearn. It's no good trying to copy other people because football is so unpredictable that it's impossible to have a prepared response to any given situation. Something new, something different is always lurking just round the corner and you have to be yourself in handling it, rather than wondering how another, more experienced manager might cope.

From a playing point of view, I don't intend ever to manage a side that just humps the ball forward. I know that's easy to say but I've always believed in getting the ball down and playing football. So that's how my teams will play and I'll stand or fall by that. When I took the Scarborough job, quite a few people told me Conference players wouldn't be able to handle that style of football but I believe they can. Hiccups and blips are bound to occur along the way but there's no reason why players at all levels shouldn't be capable of keeping the ball and playing a possession game.

I hope my players respect me. They don't have to think I'm the greatest guy in the world – in fact, they can dislike me if they want to – but I want them to feel that we are all pulling in the same direction and every decision I take is for the benefit of the club. I won't be the kind of manager who refers to his players as 'them' when things are going badly and 'us' when we're doing well. As far as I'm concerned, we'll all be in it together and anyone who buys into that will be on my side. I want them to know that when they cross the white line, I will have done everything I can for them and I will genuinely want them to do well for the club and for themselves. If it doesn't work out over the next 90 minutes, so be it. It won't be for lack of effort or preparation.

In management, honesty and fairness are everything. For any number of reasons, a manager will have confrontations with his players. I know from experience that no player is happy to be left out of the side and if it happens, he will want to know why. No one likes being substituted if he thinks he's playing well, but if players are given a fair and honest answer, they will usually accept it and the manager will keep hold of the dressing room. My confrontations with Steve Coppell at Crystal Palace eventually led to a transfer request but at no time did I think he wasn't being straight with me and I respected him for that. If, however, a player feels he is being patronised, fobbed off or, worst of all, lied to, word will go round and the manager will lose the players. That is the worst thing that can happen because if the players don't trust the manager, he has no chance.

Sometimes, however, a manager has to be a bit of an actor and hide his feelings. In one of my early games in charge, we played the opposition off the park for the first 45 minutes only to go in one down after conceding a silly goal in first-half injury time. I was absolutely seething about that goal and I've known managers who would let rip as soon as the players reached the dressing room. I knew I had to keep a lid on those emotions, though, because overall the side had played well. Players aren't daft. They know when they have performed well and when they haven't. On this occasion, the last thing they needed was a bollocking from me for one slipshod moment, even though we all knew it might cost us the game. So I stressed the positives, reminded them how well they'd played, told them to forget the goal and to go out and stage a repeat performance in the second half. They did and we won the match.

My number-one priority, of course, is to produce a winning team, and to do that I have to be prepared to stick my neck out and make difficult or controversial decisions. For instance, in one of my first games in charge of Scarborough, the home victory over Halifax, there was a bust-up in the tunnel after the final whistle. Two players were involved, our skipper Neil Bishop and the Halifax defender Denny Ingram, who had missed the match because of injury. The fracas received a fair bit of publicity and, rightly or not, talk of bad blood between the players circulated. Five weeks later, I made my first signing in the transfer window – Denny Ingram.

Inevitably, the deal caused a bit of a stir in the local press and among supporters, who were concerned that Ingram's arrival might cause problems in the dressing room. I didn't see it that way. It was an excellent piece of business for Scarborough Football Club. I regarded Ingram as the best defender in the Conference, and I wasn't alone in that view, he lived in Scarborough and wanted to play for the club. I believed the tunnel incident could be used to our advantage.

After all, it had blown up because Bishop and Ingram were passionate about their teams. Bishop was celebrating because Scarborough had won; Ingram was pig sick because Halifax had lost. There was a spark and, briefly, their emotions took over. That was the kind of passion I was looking for and the sort of commitment Scarborough would need to get away from trouble. After the signing, I didn't call in the two players for some kind of clear-the-air meeting because I believed that, as professional footballers and adults, they were capable of sorting it out between themselves. Sure enough, at training the following day, they were laughing and joking together. No one at Scarborough seemed concerned about Ingram's arrival but I suspect Halifax weren't too happy to see him go.

The signing may have upset some people but that was a chance I was prepared to take in the interests of the club. I have seen managers who will bend over backwards to please everybody from the chairman to the man who stands behind the goals every week. They try to be all things to all people and in the end they dilute the job they are there to do – produce a successful football team. In the end, that's all that matters. At times the manager has to stand apart and concentrate on managing his team to the exclusion of everything else – except his family, of course. A manager cannot cut corners but the family comes first because they need him more than the football club does. I could be a manager for 12 months or 12 years but the family will always take priority and I will never compromise my home life. Delegation is the answer, even though that isn't easy at Conference level or below where only a few people are around to take on extra responsibilities. I have to learn to say no to requests that I instinctively want to accept and understand when I need to get away from the pressure cooker. So the newspaper interview has to be postponed, the meeting with a player put back 24 hours.

I soon discovered that striking a balance between home and work wasn't going to be easy. I was never good at switching off as a player or coach and I found it even harder when I became a manager. Almost as soon as I took the job at Scarborough, I started waking up in the middle of the night, thinking about work. That never happened when I was just a player. Sometimes I struggled to go to sleep after a game because the adrenalin was still flowing but once I fell asleep, that was it. Now I sometimes find myself wide awake at 3 a.m., wondering which system to play on Saturday, trying to decide which pairing I should use up front, hoping I can close down the deal for a new player before the weekend. Management could easily become virtually a 24-hour job. Even though I use the car as an office on the way to work and on the long drive home, there always seems to be one last call to make when I land. Then, just when I think I've finally finished for the day, the mobile will ring and off we'll go again.

Another problem is that even when I do get away from the job for a while, everybody seems to want to talk football – friends, neighbours, shopkeepers, people out walking the dogs. They don't ask if we've seen the latest hit film, what we're doing for Christmas or where we're going on holiday. It's how did Scarborough get on at the weekend, what do I think about the FA Cup draw or the latest back-page sensation, will England win the World Cup? Conversations always seem to turn to football in the end and I'll find myself talking soccer clichés when five minutes earlier I was having a perfectly rational conversation about politics or the joys of a summer holiday in Scotland.

I'm not really complaining because all those people are showing a genuine interest in my job and the sport I love. It's just that sometimes I want to stop and climb off for a while because there's more to me than being a footballer or a football manager. If I meet a plumber on his day off, I don't start asking him about U bends and ball cocks or how many showers he's fitted recently. It wouldn't go down well at all. Football is another world and no one seems to imagine that football people might want to talk about something else sometimes, or that they might have interests outside the game.

For better or worse, that's the way it is, and it isn't going to change. I always said that when I finally became a manager, I would try first and foremost to enjoy it, and I'll stand by that approach. I see the job as a challenge to be won but I'm not going into it starry-eyed about my chances of landing a top job. As a player, I always believed in myself and in my ability to perform at the top level. I was ambitious and I had only one person to rely upon and that was myself. Once I had pulled on my shirt and laced up my boots, it was down to me and no one else. Even if the side played badly, I could still do well.

For a manager, there is no direct route to the top. However experienced or knowledgeable he may be, he remains at the mercy of 11 other people. On any given day, one or two may be below par, one or two may be mentally weak, one or two may make inexplicable errors. There's nothing a manager can do about that, however well he has prepared his team.

All he can do is learn his trade as he goes along and, above all, learn about himself. He needs to discover his own strengths and weaknesses and to use the strengths for the good of the team and not allow the weaknesses to affect his performance. He has to keep his feet on the ground. Why add to the pressure by saying, 'Yes, my ambition is to manage England' or 'I want to manage Manchester United'? If he is good enough, lucky enough and if he is in the right place at the right time, he might just make it but there's no point in setting targets. And every manager needs to remember that if the job becomes impossible, he can always walk away. There is life outside football.

So where will I be in five years' time? Who knows. I may even discover that management is not for me after all and return to coaching. Right now that seems unlikely but I wouldn't be the first to go down that route. We shall see, but one way or another, it's going to be an interesting ride.

20   THE PIED PIPER

FOR THE BEST PART OF 40 YEARS, FOOTBALL HAS BEEN LIKE A drug and I just can't kick the habit. I'll go anywhere to watch a game – it draws me like a magnet. Sometimes on a Sunday morning, I'll tell Sue and the kids that I'm just popping out with the dogs for an hour or so and they know exactly what that means – my local side, Hade Edge, are playing. I'll hurry down to their little ground and stand on the touchline, taking in every moment. It doesn't matter that the standard is a million miles away from the professional arena because I just enjoy watching a game, any game, and seeing the drama unfold. Something memorable always happens in a football match, whatever the level.

The other people watching seem to know who I am but usually leave me to my own devices. Sometimes there's a bit of banter. I remember one game where the visiting keeper was sent off for what looked from the sidelines like an horrendous foul, although the incident was literally a mountain made out of a molehill. He had come charging out of his box to clear a long through ball and it was a fifty-fifty race between him and the centre-forward. The keeper arrived a split second before the striker but as he took a massive kick, the ball hit a molehill, bobbled over his leg and he clattered the other lad instead. The striker went down like a bag of cement and the referee showed the keeper a straight red card.

Mayhem broke out in the middle and after a couple of minutes someone on the touchline called out, 'Come on, Neil, get it sorted. He should never have been sent off, should he?' I just smiled and replied, 'Nay, you're not getting me involved. I've enough trouble with referees on a Saturday afternoon!'

Lois, my younger daughter, has caught the bug, too. Often on a summer evening or on a Sunday afternoon, she'll say, 'Come on Dad, let's go and have a kick-around on the rec.' I'll get my togs on and we'll set off. As we're walking along, a few more kids will spot us and join in. I sometimes feel like the Pied Piper. Word soon gets round that there's a game going on the rec. Parents will drive by with the kids in the car, spot us on the field, drop the kids off and shout, 'Just popping into Holmfirth, Neil. We'll be back in an hour or so . . .' and off they'll go. If I'd charged them all a pound an hour, I'd be worth a fortune by now.

By the time we've finished, we'll have seven or eight-a-side and what was just going to be a kick-about with Lois turns into Holmfirth All Stars v. Man United, fifth round of the FA Cup. They love every minute. It's not a bad surface, either. It doesn't get too muddy, even in deepest winter, so the kids can turn it on a bit with their step-overs and drag-backs. They're learning, learning, learning all the time, like me all those years ago on the school playing field opposite our house in Birkenshaw. In some ways, the rec is as good as any professional club's academy because if any of those kids really have what it takes, they'll make it. Just like I did.

Lois has a natural talent for dribbling and has picked up Cruyff turns and step-overs by playing with the other kids, and she's got a right foot like a hammer. I've never actively coached her, although I've always encouraged her. When she was 11, she started playing for the Under-13s at Huddersfield Town Ladies. They train on a Wednesday evening on an Astroturf pitch in town and I like to go along as often as I can. One week, they were a bit short of players so they asked me if I'd go in goal. I let eight in – and yes, I was trying! The coaches are brilliant. They don't put any pressure on the kids. They show them what they expect and then leave them to it and let them find their own way. The kids are all absolutely full of it when the sessions finish.

Lois goes to school with some youngsters who are already training at Huddersfield Town's academy. It sounds as though it's a pretty strict regime run on professional lines. But as far as I'm concerned, professional football breeds pressure and that should not be part of the equation for kids of that age. The years between eight and 15 are some of the best days of their lives and they should be playing the game for fun, not as part of a professional structure. When I was playing on the school fields with the old ball that rattled, or turning out for Hunsworth Juniors and Stansfield Rangers in my early teens, a career in professional football was not the be all and end all. We were just kids having fun and, looking back, it was just about the happiest time of my footballing life.

Inevitably I suppose, today's academy intakes and their parents believe they're on the first rung of the ladder leading to the professional game. They don't appreciate that before they reach the next step, a lot of them will fall by the wayside. That's hard on the kids but a fact of life at a professional club, although I think some of the money they spend on their academies should be diverted to an old-fashioned network of scouts who would go out and watch local teams every week. They would see how youngsters perform in real matches and, in the end, that's what really counts.

In fact, I worry about academies. They are a good idea in principle but sometimes it seems that clubs set up an academy as a way of telling the world how much they are doing for the local community and how they are giving a lot of young kids an opportunity to play football in a professional environment. Who are they kidding? They know perfectly well that only a tiny fraction of the hundreds of starry-eyed eight, nine and ten-year-olds have the slightest chance of making the grade and becoming full-time students at 16. The rest go away disillusioned.

I also wonder whether full-time academy students are brought up with the right approach to the professional game. The emphasis seems to be on how the team and the individual perform and the result is secondary. Exactly the opposite applies at first-team level. Winning is all that matters and if you don't do the business, you're out. There's no arm round the shoulder from a coach telling you not to worry. Instead, the fans and the other players will be on your back. People's livelihoods are at stake. Sometimes the last instruction a young pro hears is, 'Don't let that lot take the bonus out of your back pocket.' That's the way footballers think and it can be a shock to the system but it's the harsh reality of professional sport and if you lose sight of it, you'll never make the grade.

That particular truth was rammed home to me in no uncertain terms when I was 17 and appearing in one of my first senior games for Bolton. We were playing Derby at home and drawing 0–0 when I made a sloppy back pass to our keeper, Jim McDonagh. Archie Gemmill nipped in, skipped round McDonagh and scored. We lost 1–0. I was distraught and in the dressing room afterwards, all I could do was say a feeble, 'Sorry, lads.' Mike Doyle, who had been a pro for the best part of 20 years, rounded on me.

'Sorry? Don't say sorry to me, son. Saying sorry won't help me and my wage packet.'

'Come on, Mick,' Tony Henry intervened. 'He's only seventeen. Give him a chance.'

'Give him a chance?' Doyle retorted. 'Why? I don't care how old he is, he's getting bloody paid like the rest of us, isn't he?'

I had two choices – go home and sulk about it or make sure it didn't happen again.

I learned the hard way and youngsters aged 17, 18 and 19 should be out there in the real world, too, playing against experienced pros. Young players from Premiership and Championship clubs, those who are probably not going to be first-team contenders because so many foreign players are blocking the way, should be loaned out to League Two and Conference clubs, say six kids per club per season, with three of them to be in the starting line-up every week. So instead of going in against lads of their own age, people they have probably played against several times over the previous two or three years, they would be up against senior professionals and would have to grow up fast – sink or swim in shark-infested waters.

I've managed to stay afloat for a quarter of a century since I signed for Nottingham Forest as an apprentice and I've been lucky enough to observe the ever-changing face of football from the inside. It hasn't all been a bed of roses. In the eighties, when I was starting to make my way as a professional, football went through a bad patch when gates were down and hooliganism was rampant. We went to play at places such as Millwall and Cardiff half-expecting trouble, but the hooligan element could erupt anywhere, anytime – Bath, for instance. Bath? The image is of the Roman baths, Georgian crescents and afternoon tea in the Pump Room, but believe me, the Bristol Rovers fans who moved into Twerton Park, Bath, when their team played there for a decade from 1986 could mix it with the best of them. I played there for Doncaster and I was happy to get out of the place in one piece.

For the players, hooliganism was a massive distraction. We were expected to get on with the match even though police were wading into the terraces to stop crowd trouble that sometimes threatened to spill on to the pitch. When you couldn't see what was going on, staying focused on the game was difficult, and if your own supporters were causing the problem, it was hard to work out why. They were supposed to be there to support the team not to undermine the players and the club by disrupting the match. It was a persistent problem in grounds at all levels but thankfully our stadiums are now, for the most part, free from hooligans. It's no good pretending that they've gone away altogether, though. The grounds may be safer places but the thugs are still out there, ready to use football as an excuse for street violence. And these days they are a lot more organised, which is a big worry.

Sometimes it's hard to believe some of the changes that have taken place – and I'm not just talking about the Premiership and the amount of money sloshing around at the highest level. For example, 25 years ago, could anyone have imagined that one day a female referee would be in charge of a professional match? I doubt it but it happened to me soon after I joined Scarborough

in 2004. Amy Rayner, who had already run the line in Football
League games, was certainly no worse than most of the men. In
fact, she was a damn sight better than some of them. I had to
watch my language, though.

Most referees accept swearing as part of the game and some
are prepared to have a bit of a go back, but it was different with
Amy. I queried her decisions on several occasions and each time
I consciously toned down my language. Quite a few of the lads
did the same thing, although she didn't turn a hair when others
turned the air blue. It's odd. Why do we swear with a male referee
in charge when we can discipline ourselves not to swear at a
woman? I suppose the simple answer is that we shouldn't swear
at an official, full stop, but that's easier said than done. Like people
in any other profession, we work hard all week to produce the
right end product on a Saturday afternoon and frustration creeps
in if things go wrong or decisions go against us. Swearing is as
natural a safety valve for footballers as it is for anyone else – but
for me anyway, not in front of a woman.

If that makes me sound old-fashioned to some people, so be it.
But I'm not so outdated that I pretend football in my early days
was better than the modern game. On the contrary, I'm convinced
that the standard of our football is higher than it has ever been
and standards will continue to improve. In another 25 years, the
professional game will be unrecognisable from the game we play
today. The dynamics are changing all the time. Training and
preparation have improved, players watch their diets, they know
about their anatomy and what makes their bodies work and they
take proper rest. Coaching is more sophisticated. In short, the
game is on a different planet from the one inhabited by Stanley
Matthews, Tom Finney and Nat Lofthouse after the Second World
War, and is very different from the one played by Denis Law,
Bobby Charlton and George Best in the sixties.

So just imagine how effective players of that calibre would be
in the modern era. I never saw any of them in action but I accept
that by any standards they were truly great performers. It's ridiculous to suggest that they would struggle to survive today. A great

player is a great player in any era and I believe that Matthews, Finney, Lofthouse, Law, Charlton, Best and all the other giants from the past would be even better players today because they would be fitter and stronger. Their skills were timeless and they would soon adapt to the greater physical demands of the modern game.

However, I would go along with the view that, for the most part, the so-called characters have faded from the scene during my time as a pro. For instance, they don't make 'em like Rick Holden any more. I first encountered Rick at Watford and then we were team-mates at Oldham before I left for Barnsley and he followed Joe Royle to Manchester City. He played wide on the left and was a tremendous crosser of a ball, but Rick wasn't a conventional pro footballer. He took his football seriously but never let the game take over his life. He was always up for a laugh and a joke and that approach enabled him to take pressure off himself.

In a way, he lived in a world of his own. He had no dress sense and would think nothing of arriving for training at Boundary Park wearing a cowboy hat and a pair of battered old brogue shoes that had been handed down from his grandfather. It never crossed his mind to throw them away. When the soles started to wear a bit thin, he'd take them to the cobblers and a few days later they'd be back, as good as new. While he was at Watford, the players went on an end-of-season trip to Majorca and apparently Holden arrived at the airport wearing his brown brogues, lycra running shorts, a white long-sleeved shirt and a brown suede waistcoat, topped off with his cowboy hat. His toothbrush was in his pocket and he was carrying his passport. That was it – no suitcase or hand luggage – and that's more or less how he spent a week in Magaluf.

Rick lived in Skipton, the gateway to the Yorkshire Dales, and sometimes he would turn up for training at Oldham in an old camper van that the family used for trips. Soon after the end of the 2004–05 season, a testimonial match was staged at Boundary Park for John Sheridan, the former Irish international who had played for Leeds and Sheffield Wednesday and finished his career at Oldham. The game was between Oldham and Wednesday and many of the players who'd been involved in the 1991 Division Two championship decider between the clubs were on show for the re-match. I certainly wasn't going to miss that one and when I arrived I couldn't believe my eyes when I saw Holden's old camper van in the car park. He was assistant manager to Andy Ritchie at Barnsley by that time but the camper was still on the road and he talked about going off in it for a few days the following week.

For a spell during his early days at Halifax, he was substituted virtually every week. This began to rankle after a while so before one home game, Rick decided it was time for a pre-emptive strike. In those days, there was no electronic signal to show which players were going on and off – the physio simply held up a tin plate showing the number of the player who was being withdrawn. On this occasion, as Rick went out for the warm-up, he spotted the bag containing all the number plates lying near the Halifax bench. It was too good an opportunity to miss and when no one was looking, he rummaged through the bag, whipped out the number 11 and sent it skimming like a Frisbee over the stand and into the trees between the ground and the main road out of Halifax. On he went with the warm-up and returned to the dressing room to don his match shirt – number 11.

The decision to replace him was duly taken early in the second half and, on the bench, confusion was followed by consternation when no number 11 could be found in the bag. Eventually, the Halifax physio had to persuade the opposition bench to lend him their number 11 plate – but by that time, Rick had enjoyed an extra ten minutes on the park. I bet that number 11 is still lying in the undergrowth outside The Shay.

While he was at Oldham, Rick began a degree course and eventually qualified as a chartered physiotherapist. Early on, he was learning about nutrition and body movement and one day after training he took our coach, Willie Donachie, to one side and, within earshot of the other players, started to tell him about the benefits of fish and chips. He explained in great detail about all the nutritional values involved and Willie fell for it hook, line and sinker. It wasn't until we were all digging into fish, chips and peas the following day that he realised he'd been set up.

I don't think for a minute that such an unconventional person as Holden would be tolerated as a player in the modern game and, in many ways, that's a pity. He'd be like a breath of fresh air at some of the highly regimented Premiership clubs where everyone is expected to conform. I can't imagine managers would risk having such a maverick figure in the dressing room, an eccentric character who might dent the professional image. That's almost certainly down to the pressures managers face from all sides. Results have always been paramount but there was a time when a manager would be given a few years to get things right. Now, if he has a couple of bad months, he's out, and if the next guy doesn't come in and turn it round quickly, he's on his bike, too. Nobody is given time. There's no such thing as patience. Instant success is what's required. I remember, when Graham Taylor resigned as England manager, he was asked what advice he had for his successor and he answered, 'Win matches.' He didn't say anything about playing good football. To a professional, to a club director and to a supporter, winning is all that matters. No wonder some of the fun has gone out of it.

The game isn't anything like as physical as it used to be, either. When I first started, players could get away with challenges that verged on actual bodily harm but now referees produce a yellow card for an offence that might not even have been considered a foul in the eighties. Some real tough guys were around then. Billy Whitehurst was one, a big striker with a fair amount of skill and even more muscle. Billy played for a lot of clubs and at all levels. I remember coming up against him when I was with Lincoln and we went to play Oxford United at the Manor Ground. I was warned in advance that Whitehurst was inclined to put himself about a bit and I discovered how true that was fairly early on. I was playing left-back and, while waiting for a high ball to drop, I was uncomfortably aware that Billy was closing in. Time seemed to stand still as I waited for the ball to land but when it did, I got a decent first touch and was going to move the ball upfield when Billy arrived. I went into orbit and by the time I hit solid ground again, Billy was face to face with the referee. The two of them were surrounded by jostling players as the ref reached into his pocket for his cards.

'That was a bad challenge, you're off,' he said to Whitehurst.

'Come on, you can't send me off for that,' Billy replied.

'I can. Off!'

'Well, I'm not bloody going.'

'All right then, you're booked,' and the official pulled out the yellow card instead. Billy would probably have been shown a straight red today.

And what would students of today's game make of the bottle of whisky on the dressing-room table at Bolton Wanderers? On cold days – and there were plenty of those at Burnden Park – it used to stand there among the liniment and bandages and the players would have a quick slug out of a little tot glass as they filed out into the tunnel. Unthinkable today, isn't it? Nowadays, alcohol is poison to a professional sportsman in the build-up to a match or a race because it is a diuretic and dehydrates the body. At Bolton, the tot of Scotch was all part of the camaraderie – team bonding as it would be called today – and nobody gave it a second thought. I wasn't even old enough to go into a pub but it didn't stop me having a nip before going out to play, although I never could stand the taste.

Afterwards in the players' lounge, no one turned a hair if we had a few pints of beer or lager before going home. Again, that's discouraged today because even though a drink helps a player to relax, its dehydrating effect can be harmful. The experts say the same thing about a mug of tea, although that used to be the staple drink at half-time and again after the match. Sports drinks are the fashion today and players are encouraged to have a swig when there is a stoppage during the game, something else that was unheard of 20 years ago.

Diet has been revolutionised. One of my first away games for

Bolton was at Crystal Palace, probably the first time I stayed overnight in a hotel before a game. After a gentle stroll on the Saturday morning, we trooped into the dining room for our pre-match meal at around midday. We sat down and when the waiter came round with a basket of white bread rolls, we all took one, piled on a knob butter and dug in while we were waiting for the main course – steak, potatoes and two veg. We would never dream of eating a huge chunk of red meat and all those veg before a game today. Instead, we have pasta, rice dishes, chicken. A few years ago, the Manchester United players even used to eat jam and bread after training and matches. That's what I sometimes had when I came home from school before going out for a kick-about. It was jam and bread or a banana sandwich, an ideal combination of fruit and carbohydrates and the perfect quick fix – I must have been way ahead of my time!

I don't go overboard about diet but I try to eat sensibly. The thinking now is that we should eat within half an hour of the final whistle or the end of a training session because that's when the body uses the food best. Of course, it's easy for the top clubs to make sure players eat the right food straight after a session because they have catering facilities at the training ground. It's a bit more difficult further down the leagues. In my first season at Scarborough, I got into the habit of stopping off at Morrisons supermarket on my way to work to buy a ready-made pasta salad. It cost £1.50, cheaper than a sandwich in some shops.

Pitches have been another part of the game's evolution. In the early days, I often used to play on real mudbaths and, in a funny way, I sometimes miss them. I had quite a reputation for my tackling and aggressive approach. A bit of mud and surface water slowed players down to my pace, giving me a chance to catch opponents in possession. If the rain was bouncing down on match-day mornings, I used to think, 'Great! I can really get stuck in today.'

We played on many a pitch that would have been declared unfit today, particularly in reserve games. Nowadays, if there's any doubt at all, a reserve match will be called off to prevent damage to the surface ahead of a first-team game. That didn't happen in the old days. As long as the ball rolled, it was game on and to hell with the first team on Saturday. After the match, the groundstaff would replace the divots and the groundsman would come on with the heavy roller to flatten everything out again. Soon the mud was compacted, there was nowhere for rainwater to go, the grass died off and by late autumn the pitch was as bald as a coot. Nowadays, most of them are like a bowling green for most of the season, particularly in the Premiership where they simply re-lay the whole surface if there are any serious signs of wear and tear.

In fact, on and off the field, football's élite have never had it so good. The Premier League is the number one competition in the country in any sport, and a lot of very cute business people have learned how to market the Premiership and make a lot of money on the back of it. Players' wages beggar belief to the average man in the street – but good luck to them. If the clubs are prepared to pay that kind of money, why should the players turn it down? I wish that just once in a while, though, the Premiership money machine would spare a thought for the rest of the football pyramid.

At the moment, just about all the money flows in one direction, towards the big boys, and stays there. A little bit filters down through the system in a trickle and small clubs in the Conference and League Two are left to pick up the scraps. How they all manage to survive I shall never know because some of them are living hand-to-mouth on a week-by-week basis with no guarantee that the players and staff will be paid on time. I've heard the lads in the dressing room at Scarborough having a real laugh when they read *Players' Club*, the PFA's monthly magazine. It's an upmarket, glossy production and features adverts offering such things as cabin cruisers in Barbados, villas in Florida and the best possible deals on a new Ferrari. That doesn't cut much ice with pros in the lower divisions.

Those players know their limitations and their worth and don't expect to be in the big league financially, but they are sound professionals and it's ludicrous that clubs are on the brink of extinction, struggling to meet a modest wage bill because they owe the taxman a quarter of a top player's weekly wage. Surely some kind of scheme could be set up to give smaller clubs a percentage of the Premier League millions. Unfortunately, most of the Premiership clubs don't give a damn about the lesser mortals. They are only interested in themselves, and if a few clubs go out of business or if the lower leagues are forced to go part-time, so what? But where will they turn for the next generation of players if the sponsorship money ever dries up and foreign players find pastures new?

I don't suppose that will happen, though. Football will continue to exist in a world of its own where the higher a player progresses, the more he is looked after. People fall over themselves to ease the path of superstar players who are already earning the kind of money most people can only dream about. They aren't expected to do anything for themselves because clubs, agents, hangers-on will do everything for them. When they walk down the street or drive around in their Ferraris, people stop and stare. If a top player goes into a shop or strolls into a bar or restaurant, people from all walks of life will go up to him and wish him well, say they saw him on the telly and how well he played. He is fawned upon virtually every moment of his life outside his work environment. That can't be right. And some of them can't handle celebrity status because they have forgotten how it feels to live in the real world. They accept the adulation at face value instead of seeing it for what it is – a brief phase in their life.

To a lesser extent, the same thing applies lower down the scale. A lot of players struggle when their careers are over and they come face to face with reality. It's not because their new life is hard – they can handle that because football is a hard job, too – but because they don't have the same down-to-earth approach as the average working man, who has been out there on the treadmill for most of his life. Too many ex-footballers seem to believe the rest of the world owes them something just because they have been high-profile sportsmen. It can be difficult to adjust when they discover the truth.

I don't think I suffer from delusions of grandeur just because I've been involved with professional football for so long. I've always tried to keep my feet on the ground and I certainly don't want people to look at me and think I'm a Big Time Charlie, because I'm not. I don't go in for Gucci shoes or Armani fashions. I buy my gear at Next and M&S and it looks all right to me, even if some of the younger players have begged to differ over the last few years. I wanted to be a footballer, not a caricature of the players we see on 'Footballers' Wives'.

And apart from my later days at Barnsley, I've never been conscious of people nudging one another in the street and pointing in my direction. In fact, it's a bit of a surprise when somebody recognises me. One day a while back, I was doing a few odds and ends in Huddersfield when I spotted Trevor Cherry, the former Huddersfield, Leeds and England player, walking towards me. Trevor was the Bradford City manager on the day of the Valley Parade fire and our paths had crossed once or twice since that dreadful day. While I instantly knew him – he was one of my boyhood idols – I didn't expect him to recognise me. I would have settled for a nod in my direction as our paths crossed. Instead, Trevor stopped, shook my hand, asked how I was getting on at Scarborough and joked about how good it was to see an old man like me managing to score so many goals from midfield. We ended up chewing the fat about football for a while before shaking hands again and going our separate ways. I was a bit taken aback, to be honest.

I like to think I've never forgotten my roots and the ethos that made me successful. Football has given me a fantastic life but I like to think I'm still more or less the same working-class lad who left home to join Nottingham Forest all that time ago. A few rough edges have been shaved off, perhaps, but not too many. What would have happened if I hadn't found another club when I walked way from Forest? There's no way of knowing but I would still have had a great time because I have my family. I've earned enough from the game to make sure they enjoy a good lifestyle but while Aimee and Lois haven't really lacked for anything, they're down to earth, they know what's right and what's wrong and they know the value of what they've been given.

And let's face it, you don't need fame and fortune to enjoy a day out at Bolton Abbey in the Yorkshire Dales – just ten quid's worth of petrol in the tank and enough in your pocket to get a bite to eat. The fresh air and the fun are free.

THE WARM-DOWN

I've been involved with professional football for a quarter of a century, played almost 1,000 senior games and sampled most of the highs and lows the game has to offer. I've played in the Premier League and savoured the good life by winning promotion with Oldham and Barnsley and reaching the play-offs with Watford and Wigan. I've appeared in an FA Cup semi-final with Oldham and a quarter-final with Barnsley and made a couple of appearances at Wembley. I've also seen the dark side of the moon in the shape of relegation with Barnsley, Charlton and Halifax. But I never thought the day would dawn when, more than a month after the end of a season, I wouldn't know which league my club would be playing in three months later. That's how it worked out for Scarborough at the end of the 2005–06 season.

We finished bottom of the table, which was bitterly disappointing. But I had no intention of walking away and, after the final game, a 1–1 draw at Exeter on 29 April, my initial reaction was to roll up my sleeves and say, 'Right, let's get this club straight back into the Conference.' But it wasn't as simple as that.

First, there was the possibility that Canvey Island, who finished in mid-table, would resign from the Conference because of financial problems. Decision expected on 11 May. Secondly, Altrincham, who finished three points above the relegation zone, were due to appeal to the FA Sanctions and Regulations Committee against an 18-point deduction, imposed by the Conference, for fielding an ineligible player. The appeal date? 23 May. If Canvey resigned, Tamworth, who finished one place above Scarborough, would be reprieved. If Altrincham's appeal was rejected as well, they would finish last and neither of the bottom two would be relegated – provided the Conference annual meeting on 2 June gave us the go-ahead to stay.

Surely decisions could have been made earlier? Instead, we were in limbo, not knowing whether to make plans for another Conference season or for a new life in Conference North as a part-time club. And, as the clocked ticked away, players who might have come to Scarborough opted to move elsewhere. It was one of the most frustrating spells of my career.

Finishing bottom of the table was even worse, of course, and in the immediate aftermath I was absolutely gutted. I could have taken the easy way out and looked for excuses, perhaps found someone else to blame. But as a professional and a manager, I had to be honest and face up to the reality of the situation: that the group of players I inherited weren't good enough.

I felt sorry for the players, who had given me 110 per cent as we battled against the drop in the closing weeks of the season, and for everyone behind the scenes who had devoted so much time to the club. But the people I really felt for were the supporters. Something like 150 Scarborough fans travelled all the way down to Exeter knowing that our destiny was not even in our own hands. And when our fate was sealed, I saw grown men crying.

Those people are the true football supporters. They didn't desert the club when relegation loomed, they came out in numbers. We had better than average attendances at each of our last four home games and the fans came because they cared. Scarborough is their home-town club and they were desperate to do their bit to keep us in the Conference. To me, their support is more powerful and carries more weight than the 60,000-plus who pack into Old Trafford to watch Manchester United. They aren't Johnny-come-lately supporters following a successful side. They have real passion, something I believe is worth fighting for.

As manager, did I let them down? No, I don't think so. I gave them everything I could. I worked my socks off to keep Scarborough in the Conference but in the final analysis, we came up short. I wasn't dealt a good hand when I took over in November but I played it as best I could. I managed to strengthen the squad with four decent players. But there was no money to play with and, at any level, money talks. The best players will always gravitate towards the best money and Scarborough start out on the back foot because they don't have much money and the town is way out on a limb.

A lot of supporters and quite a few people outside the club felt I should have played more, and with hindsight they were right. However, my gut reaction on taking over was to stay on the sidelines, although in the end, with 11 games left, I decided to dust off the boots and give it a go. I felt it was important to show people that I wasn't afraid to stick my head above the parapet and that I was ready to go out there and fight for the cause. I like to think the fans appreciated that. A few had a go at me and I could understand where they were coming from because their team was at the wrong end of the table and I was the man in charge. But I wasn't going to hide. And, without wanting to sound conceited, I gave the side some quality and made the opposition think a bit more. Maybe if I'd come back into the line-up earlier...

It was always going to be difficult, though. Last year we had a decent side that, for one reason or another, was broken up. Good players left and were not adequately replaced. Take the midfield. Tyrone Thompson went to Halifax and had an outstanding season, Scott Kerr played a season of league football for Lincoln and Keith Gilroy went to Burton and was part of their successful FA Cup run that ended with defeat by Manchester United. Add the 14 goals I scored from midfield and there was a big hole in the middle of the park.

And from day one, we had a major problem with our home form, even though we'd gone through the previous season unbeaten at the McCain Stadium. From the time I took over we averaged a point a game from 14 away matches and if we'd complemented that performance with some half-decent returns at home, we would have been in mid-table and perhaps looking at the play-offs, not threatened with relegation. Instead we won only four games at the McCain Stadium all season. Between 26 November, when we beat Halifax 2–0, and 15 April, when we defeated Burton 3–0, we picked up just three points from eight home games and didn't win once. It developed into a phobia for the players and, however hard we tried, there seemed to be nothing we could do to get the monkey off their backs. The problem was there all the time, festering in the players' minds.

Despite our precarious position, though, they gave me everything. But in the end we were a little bit low on ability and sometimes the attitude wasn't professional enough. During the last few weeks of the season, we gave away vital goals in stoppage time – against Woking in the 94th minute, Accrington in the 93rd minute and Canvey Island in the 92nd minute. You can say it's bad luck if it happens once, but if it happens three times in five matches, there's something missing. The four points that got away would have kept us out of the bottom two. Having to play six games in 15 days, the last four in an eight-day spell, near the end of the season didn't make life any easier, either. But in the end, we were bottom of the table when I took over and bottom of the table at the end of the season.

Soon after the end of the season, Canvey Island resigned from the Conference so it seemed our fate hinged on the FA hearing into Altrincham's appeal. Verdict? Appeal rejected. Provided we could give assurances about our financial position, Scarborough would be reprieved and I could start making plans for another season as a Conference club. It had been a difficult 24 days. Little did I know there was yet another twist in the tale.

For on 3 June, the day after the Conference AGM, it was announced that Scarborough had been relegated to Conference North and deducted 10 points from the start of the 2006–07 season. At the time, no specific reasons for the decision were provided but apparently the Conference board were not happy with the

Company Voluntary Agreement with the club's creditors which had been completed on the day of the annual meeting. Altrincham were reinstated.

All the signs were that this saga could run and run but as manager, I had to try and make something positive out of it. When I heard the decision, I was stunned. But my next reaction was to pick myself up and get on with the job of helping Scarborough start all over again. It wasn't the first kick in the teeth I've suffered in the last 25 years and it won't be the last. But let's face it, there have been some pretty good times, too.

CAREER STATISTICS

Neil David Redfearn, born Dewsbury 20 June 1965.
Career: Nottingham Forest apprentice August 1981, Bolton Wanderers June 1982. League debut 19 February 1983 v Rotherham United. Loan to Lincoln City March 1984, transferred July 1984 £8250. Doncaster Rovers August 1986 £17,500, Crystal Palace July 1987 £120,000. Watford November 1988 £175,000, Oldham Athletic January 1990 £150,000. Barnsley September 1991 £180,000. Charlton Athletic June 1998 £1,017,000. Bradford City July 1999 £250,000. Wigan Athletic March 2000 £112,500. Free to Halifax Town as player-coach March 2001 (two spells as caretaker-manager). Boston United July 2002. Non-contract to Rochdale March 2004. Scarborough player-coach June 2004, player-manager November 2005.
Honours: Football League Division Two champions 1990-91, Division One runners-up 1996-97.

Season	League		FA Cup		Lge Cup		Other Cups	
	Apps	Goals	Apps	Goals	Apps	Goals	Apps	Goals
BOLTON WANDERERS								
1982-83	10	-	-	-	-	-	-	-
1983-84	25	1	4	-	2	-	-	-
LINCOLN CITY (Loan)								
1983-84	10	1	-	-	-	-	-	-
LINCOLN CITY								
1984-85	45	4	2	1	2	-	5	-
1985-86	45	8	1	-	2	-	2	-
DONCASTER ROVERS								
1986-87	46	14	3	1	2	-	2	-
CRYSTAL PALACE								
1987-88	42	8	1	-	3	-	1	-
1988-89	15	2	-	-	3	-	-	-
WATFORD								
1988-89	12	2	6	3	-	-	5	1
1989-90	12	1	-	-	1	-	-	-
OLDHAM ATHLETIC								
1989-90	17	2	6	1	-	-	-	-
1990-91	45	14	2	2	3	1	1	-
BARNSLEY								
1991-92	36	4	1	-	3	-	1	-
1992-93	46	3	4	2	2	1	2	-
1993-94	46	12	4	-	2	-	2	-
1994-95	39	11	1	-	4	2	-	-
1995-96	45	14	2	1	3	-	-	-
1996-97	43	17	2	1	4	1	-	-
1997-98	37	10	6	2	3	2	-	-
CHARLTON ATHLETIC								
1998-99	30	3	1	-	2	1	-	-
BRADFORD CITY								
1999-2000	17	1	2	-	2	-	-	-
WIGAN ATHLETIC								
1999-2000	12	6	-	-	-	-	3	-
2000-01	10	1	1	-	-	-	2	-
HALIFAX TOWN								
2000-01	12	-	-	-	-	-	-	-
2001-02	30	6	3	-	1	-	1	-
BOSTON UNITED								
2002-03	31	6	-	-	1	-	-	-
2003-04	23	6	1	-	1	1	1	-
ROCHDALE								
2003-04	9	-	-	-	-	-	-	-
SCARBOROUGH								
2004-05*	39	14	2	-	-	-	1	-
2005-06*	21	3	1	-	-	-	-	-
Totals	850	174	56	14	46	9	29	1

* Conference

Other cups - Freight Rover Trophy 1984-87; Mercantile Credit 1988; 1988-89 Simod Cup (three games); Play-offs (two and one goal); 1990-91 Zenith Data Systems Cup; 1991-92 Full Members Cup; 1992-94 Anglo Italian Cup; 1999-2000 Play-offs; 2003-04 LDV Vans Trophy; 2004-05 Conference Cup.

INDEX